AF352403

Re-evaluating Irish national security policy

Manchester University Press

To my wife Fidelma Hawes and children Alexandra and Harry for whom the words 'husband' and 'father' have too often merged into one: 'work'.

Re-evaluating Irish national security policy

Affordable threats?

Michael Mulqueen

Manchester University Press
Manchester and New York
distributed in the United States exclusively
by Palgrave Macmillan

Published by Manchester University Press
Oxford Road, Manchester M13 9NR, UK
and Room 400, 175 Fifth Avenue, New York, NY 10010, USA
www.manchesteruniversitypress.co.uk

Distributed in the United States exclusively by
Palgrave Macmillan, 175 Fifth Avenue, New York,
NY 10010, USA

Distributed in Canada exclusively by
UBC Press, University of British Columbia, 2029 West Mall,
Vancouver, BC, Canada V6T 1Z2

British Library Cataloguing-in-Publication Data
A catalogue record for this book is available from the British Library

Library of Congress Cataloging-in-Publication Data applied for

ISBN 978 0 7190 8027 2 *hardback*

First published 2009

Edited and typeset
by Frances Hackeson Freelance Publishing Services, Brinscall, Lancs
Printed in Great Britain
by the MPG Books Group

Contents

Abbreviations

ACOUSINT	acoustic intelligence
ARW	Army Ranger Wing
ATCP	Aid to the Civil Power
C3	Forerunner to CSB
CSB	Crime and Security Branch
DDIS/FE	Danish Defence Intelligence Service/Forsvarets Efterretningstjeneste
DF	Defence Forces
EEZ	European Exclusive Economic Zone
ESDP	European Security and Defence Policy
FARC	Fuerzas Armadas Revolucionarias de Colombia
FCA	Fórsa Cosanta Áitiuil (forerunner to the Irish Army Reserve)
G2	Irish military intelligence service
HUMINT	human intelligence
MAR-INFO	Maritime Information Group
NSC	National Security Committee
ODCE	Office of the Director of Corporate Enforcement
OEP	Office of Emergency Planning
OSINT	open source intelligence
PDF	Permanent Defence Forces
PET	Politiets Efterretningstjeneste (Danish national security intelligence service)
PfP NATO's	Partnership for Peace
PRSTV	Proportional Representation by Single Transferable Vote
PULSE	Police Using Leading edge Systems Effectively
RTÉ	Radio Telefís Éireann
SÄPO	Säkerhetspolisen (Swedish domestic intelligence agency)

SDU	Special Detective Unit
SIGINT	Signals Intelligence
SIS/MI6	UK Secret Intelligence Service

Preface

This book examines how national security policy may prevent but also unwittingly facilitate terrorist attacks. September 11 2001 provides an obvious starting point. The immense public tragedy of that day confirmed the folly of assuming that state organisations – even those responsible for our security – could readily set aside their histories, bureaucracies and politics and prepare objectively against a shared threat. A striking conclusion to emerge from the investigations after the attack was the scale of the inter- and intra-organisational wrangling and the ensuing gaps in security.

Questions of policy and the organisational coherence it is meant to underpin are applied here in a theoretically informed analysis of the Irish national security response to transnational terrorism. The book closely examines Ireland's national security apparatus, about which little is known despite international interest in Irish political violence and the Northern Ireland Peace Process. Crime and Security Branch (CSB), the internal security agency operating within An Garda Síochána; G2, the military intelligence organisation; and the National Security Committee of senior officials and officers which advises the Irish Government on security matters, receive particular attention. The investigation begins with the Irish government's initial security policy response to the attack of 9/11 and ends with an assessment of where policy stands in mid-2008. Two sets of conclusions emerge. The first concerns theory and the second, policy.

Firstly on the theoretical foundations of security policy study, a historical approach is called for. Public policy-makers prefer to remain on reliable paths and so few junctures of fundamental change occur. In the Irish case political and public unity in the weeks after 9/11 combined into pressure for a complete reappraisal of the State's low-profile, low-cost national security policy. In a short time, however, the departments and agencies concerned managed matters such that they were able to revert to pre-defined patterns. What developments occurred carried with them a high degree of organisational familiarity, reflecting especially the structures, policies and traditions built up during almost forty years of violent conflict in Northern Ireland.

The Irish case also suggests that the period of confusion between the committal of an attack and the unveiling of a multi-faceted policy response can last but a matter of days owing, not least, to the pressure of public outcry for action. The scope for decision-making mistakes is obvious but the need to be seen to 'do something' is greater. Bureaucratic politics provides a means to underpin analysis of this period, during which the policy community is cut loose from its familiar traffic rules yet must take a decisive course. It may be one of the most established conceptual approaches in modern political enquiry but, as this study finds, it is well suited to the task of analysing the decisions of national security policy managers under severe political pressure.

Conceptual tools to identify the dynamics of policy decision-making must be accompanied by a model which helps assess the likely effectiveness of the policy itself. Key here, in the context of transnational terrorism in a new media age, is a model that can evaluate policy not only in terms of the traditional concerns of protecting the territory and institutional expression of the state, but also as it pertains to the idea that binds state and society. Such a model should – as is done here – consider the direct or indirect nature of the threat, the distance of threat and the probability and consequence of it manifesting into an attack.

On policy, this book argues that Irish national security reflects, among other problems, the complications to management and resistance to fresh thinking which intense political and financial pressures create. On policy, the scale and capabilities of Irish naval and airborne defensive arrangements suffer, unduly, the policy imperative to transform the Defence Forces, particularly the army, for more robust missions overseas. By consequence, Ireland's maritime and aviation security capabilities are sorely lacking; rules governing promotion to the most senior management ranks of the Defence Forces and army dominance of appointments at Defence Forces Headquarters have worked against attempts at building a more balanced force structure.

Anglo-Irish security cooperation, forged amid the Troubles, provides a policy strongpoint. To it can be attributed much of the Garda's considerable success in curtailing the activities of Irish republican extremists. However, measures taken since 2005 to reform the Garda leave open several routes by which political interference, or attempts within the force to pre-empt it, may lead to undesirable if not dangerous security outcomes. The cost may well be further erosion of the public's connection with and faith in the force.

This study finds significant shortcomings in the systems for the gathering and analysis of intelligence. Budget constraints, public distrust of the Garda and the country's changing demographic profile all pose challenges to the reliability of on-island intelligence. Off-island, the Irish agencies rely almost entirely on what foreign intelligence the organisations of other states choose to impart to them. In addition, evidence suggests that CSB has clustered information within its ranks, leaving other elements of the State's apparatus out of the loop. Little evidence emerged to suggest that the final outcomes of intelligence – the threat assessments – were challenged in rigorous debate at the most senior management levels; rather, the National Security Committee appeared vulnerable to the consensual dynamic known as groupthink.

Analysis of Ireland's emergency planning structures, which were overhauled within weeks of the 9/11 attack and amid the public fury that greeted an incompetent ministerial media interview on Ireland's nuclear incident preparations, reveals serious efforts to increase capabilities but also a management structure prone to create confused command and control. A policy revision undertaken in 2006 partially improved matters but left scope for incoherence in the event of a major catastrophe.

For at least two years after 9/11, the single greatest policy imperative for national security managers was to halt the flow of immigrants into the State; terrorists would hide within the 'non-national' community while planning their attacks elsewhere, according to official thinking. Instances of careless and cruel treatment of immigrants reflected the prevailing view. Subsequently the government created a junior ministry for integration amid evidence of extremism taking root within marginalised communities in the UK and elsewhere in the European Union. But comparatively tiny funding suggested a declaratory initiative, starved of substance in its critical early years. In this sense integration quickly came to resemble many other attempts at proactive security to prevent terrorism from emerging within the State.

Acknowledgements

I am grateful to the Irish Research Council for the Humanities and Social Sciences for awarding me a Government of Ireland Scholarship to carry out the first three years of my research, and to the staff of Manchester University Press for its publication.

I also wish to express gratitude to those within the Irish security community who agreed to be interviewed and to a number of others, who, although they were not formally interviewed, continuously supplied me with information and insights. I will not disclose their identities.

Ben Tonra's academic leadership ensured that a Ph.D. thesis proposal brim-full of disparate ideas and rough arguments developed into what is presented here. He showed immense patience and he criticised thoughtfully, supportively and with great humour. In addition Eunan O'Halpin, Andreas Dür and Tobias Theiler provided very helpful criticisms at the end. En route Nicholas Rees was ever ready to listen and advise.

Without Niall Ó Ciosáin's encouragement in late 2001 I would not have undertaken further study. When I did I was fortunate to have Eibhir Mulqueen for stimulating discussion, reassurance and a sharp copy-editor's eye. Camilla Fanning was indefatigable as a valuable source of assistance, support and ideas once our paths crossed at the Dublin European Institute, University College, Dublin. Lorcan Roche Kelly arrived later but in time to challenge the haze of my thinking in warm conversation and lively debate. Conor and Jack Kavanagh were ever ready to provide me with their insightful observations on matters of journalism and diplomacy; this is to say nothing of the unfailing kindness and generosity which the entire Kavanagh family have extended to me for many years. Branka Parlić was a constant companion in the long nights of writing; I am grateful both for her patient guidance through the repertoire of contemporary music and for our discussions on the governance and politics of Serbia, into which one day I hope to conduct further research.

My various editors at *The Clare People* and Jane's Information Group were always flexible in the face of my numerous research distractions. The Hawes family of Brickhill, Cratloe, Co. Clare never once refused the many requests I made for their practical help. Without them, quite honestly, I would never have finished this book. When, eventually, I did Liz Dore (née Hawes) of the Regional Medical Library, Limerick, agreed to compile the index. I am indebted to her for her patience, diligence and skill. Over a longer time span my parents, Mike Mulqueen and Regina Mulqueen, and my brother Billy and sister Elizabeth helped shape things such that I happily embraced academic pursuits. I wish, in addition, to express gratitude for the friendship of Mai Blaney, Mike Lavery, Bessy Murphy and her family and all at Flan's, Pat O' Brien, John J. O'Connor, Tony Rodgers and Michael Small.

Finally I wish to thank colleagues and students, past and present, at the Department of Languages and Cultural Studies at the University of Limerick, the School of Politics and International Relations at University College, Dublin, the Department of Government at University College Cork and in Journalism at NUI Galway for their support, inspiration and good humour.

For the shortcomings herein only I bear responsibility.

Michael Mulqueen
University of Limerick

1

Analysing Irish national security policy

Introduction

The attack of September 11 2001 demonstrated, to unprecedented effect, the vulnerability of states to transnational terrorist networks.[1] Within hours of the attack, the Irish government ordered the State's security and intelligence agencies to review the level of threat against Ireland (*Irish Times* 2001a). They began work that afternoon (Author's interviews). On September 25 the government, through its spokesman, confirmed that Ireland was not under threat of a direct attack but could suffer 'collateral damage' in the event of an attack close by (O' Connor and Minihan 2001). Days later, on October 3, the State's national security policy was significantly revised, with the introduction of new management structures for emergency planning (O' Connor 2001b). Since then, the agencies have kept government continuously informed of the level of transnational terrorism threat to Ireland (Brady 2002, 2004a, 2005a, 2005b; Reid 2005b). Some changes to national security policy have occurred in response, although there has been no fundamental departure from the positions adopted in the three weeks after 9/11.

What follows is an examination of Ireland's policy. It will focus especially on two phases of policy activity, a frenetic phase between September 11 and October 3 2001 and the period since then in which only minor revisions have occurred. The study will use models of historical institutionalism, threat evaluation and governmental politics decision-making as conceptual tools. Empirically, particular attention is paid to the 'frontline agencies' of the Irish security community, namely the Garda Síochána and the Defence Forces (consisting of the Irish Army, Naval Service and Air Corps). They have primary responsibility to uphold national security policy. The argument is the following: Irish national security policy against transnational terrorist attack was re-evaluated after 9/11 in an atmosphere of heightened financial and political pressures on Ireland's national security organisations. The re-evaluated policy contained serious weaknesses. Key policy problems persist.[2]

The opening section will explain why an analysis of Irish national security policy after 9/11 is both timely and worthwhile. It will also provide a brief summary of terminology that will crop up throughout the study. Two key tasks will be carried out in the remainder of the chapter. These are: 1) to outline and justify the chosen methodology, and 2) to set out the conceptual framework. But first, why is this book required?

Firstly, in all major respects, the policy revisions made within the three weeks after the attack still apply. The government ordered its security agencies to undertake a re-evaluation of Irish national security against transnational terrorism on September 11 2001 (Author's interviews; *Irish Times* 2001a). The fundamental shape of policy was agreed upon by early October, well before the attacks on Madrid (2004), London (2005, 2007) and Glasgow (2007). Only relatively mild adjustments were made after these attacks (Ahern 2005; Reid 2005b).

Secondly, since the late 1960s serious terrorist activity has been a feature of the island of Ireland, ensuring the State's national security agencies come with a particularly relevant history. They are regarded as being very experienced at combating terrorism. A study of the positions they have taken following 9/11, how they have arrived at these positions, and the consequences that have arisen for national security promises value to a wide audience.

Thirdly, Ireland presents significant strategic considerations to policy managers and academics in the national security field. The official threat assessment after 9/11 suggested that the risk of direct attack on Ireland was low but that the country might be used as a logistical base from which to launch attacks on other states, particularly EU member states (Author's interviews; Dáil Debates 2005b, p. 241). In this regard Ireland offers close access to Great Britain especially through the Common Travel Area. Plans which the Irish government unveiled in late 2007 to electronically gather passenger data on travellers arriving from outside of the area may help prevent undesirables entering Ireland and travelling onwards. But the effectiveness of this system is a factor of whether terrorists or criminals can overcome the technology underpinning it. At any rate the government decided against extending the system to incorporate travellers holding lawful residency within the Common Travel Area or to use it at the border with Northern Ireland (Author's contacts, Department of Justice; Collins, S. 2007; Collins and Keenan 2007). Hence avoided is the impracticality of policing the border but preserved is freedom of movement for terrorists holding rights of residency. Furthermore, Ireland rests on the European Union's westerly flank. The Irish sector of the maritime European Exclusive Economic Zone (EEZ) measures 165,200 sq. miles (427,900 sq. km). Some 70 per cent of civil air traffic between the United States and Europe transits Irish airspace (Air Corps 1998, p. 9). The United States military enjoys traditional landing and refuelling rights at Shannon Airport. Almost 900,000 US military personnel passed through there between early 2002 and June 2006, mostly en route to or from Iraq and Afghanistan (Deegan 2005, 2006). Between January and March 2008 some 67,000 troops passed through, representing a 144 per cent increase on the previous year (Deegan 2008). Numerous high-profile transnational corporations have located their EU bases in Ireland. Partly as a consequence of attracting so much international investment, Ireland has been transformed in less than twenty years into one of the world's most globalised places (Taylor 2003). The State has been held up as a model for other states to follow, not least because of its rapid accrual of wealth in the late 1990s (*Jamaica Observer* 2006). In this context, Ireland can be seen to be both profiting from and acting as a force for driving globalisation at a time when the benefits of globalisation are hotly – and sometimes violently – disputed.

Fourthly, Ireland is an active participant in the emerging security architecture of the European Union. Since the Madrid attack, in particular, this has provided a comprehensive framework of structures and procedures in an attempt to counter terrorism. The framework is designed in such a way that there is a heavy dependence on member states to secure themselves in order to protect the union as a whole (De Vries 2005; European Union, European Council 2001, 2004a, 2004c, 2004d). Conclusions concerning one of the participants in this framework may be of broader relevance to all member states.

Furthermore, with a number of notable exceptions, Irish national security has been largely overlooked as a subject for scholarly attention, although Ireland's international security policy has fared somewhat better. This investigation provides an opportunity to scrutinise contemporary Irish national security policy and Irish national security decision-making to a depth of review that has been lacking so far.

Before proceeding to explain the methodology and choice of concepts that will be used to support the study in what it seeks to investigate, some features of terminology need to be established. The Republic of Ireland is referred to throughout as 'Ireland' or as the 'State' (note capitalisation). The full titles of government departments are frequently shortened to their areas of responsibility (e.g. Finance for Department of Finance, or Defence, for Department of Defence). The term 'the Defence Organisation' is used to describe the Defence Forces and Department of Defence combined (Ireland, Department of Defence 2004). Transnational terrorism and transnational terrorist networks are also referred to. Sandler and Enders describe transnational terrorist incidents as 'transboundary externalities, insofar as actions conducted by terrorists or authorities in one country may impose uncompensated costs or benefits on people or property of another country' (Sandler and Enders 2004). Protagonists may not be of any one nationality. The conflicts in which they engage may or may not be conflicts between states and, as such, of an *inter*national nature. The term is also an apt one because the capacity for groups to organise effectively in loose, borderless terrorist networks has been demonstrated to a substantial degree (Sageman 2004, 2008). The term 'terrorist' is used, not to disregard the seemingly unquenchable debate to define what terrorism is but because the study is engaged in a critique of responses to a problem that decision-makers have continuously referred to as terrorism. Another feature of terminology to note is the book's distinguishing between proactive and reactive security. In the main, our concern will be with the management of measures to prevent an attack on the State (i.e. proactive). Nevertheless, the study will also examine aspects of reactive security (i.e. measures to cope with the aftermath of a major incident in Ireland). This is often termed 'emergency planning'.

Methodology

The author has drawn on various methodological studies in thinking about the research design and validity. Arksey and Knight (1999), DeVault (2002), Mason (2002), Maxwell (1998) and Smith (1995) helped inform decisions around the mechanics of method, sample size, codification, analysis, reliability and validation.

The research design employed here is intended, primarily, to facilitate the examination of policy from the perspectives of historical behaviour and crisis decision-making. This arises at root from the author's previous career as a jour-nalist specialising in Irish security.[3] The author assumed historical background was important when deciding the 'angle' of stories about Irish security policy in the past. This was on the basis of researching a large number of security stories. For example, it was common to find State security decisions were justified on the basis of past experience or that they reflected a 'culture' that appeared to have existed for a long time within the national security organisations.

In terms of evidence gathering, the semi-structured elite interview method was chosen because it offered a number of key advantages albeit also a number of serious risks (these are discussed further below). The chief advantage was the scope to ask respondents from individual agencies 'free association' questions to more thoroughly investigate historical and crisis perspectives. Interviews were conducted with a fairly large sample of twenty-two senior personnel of government departments, the Garda and the Defence Forces. Respondents were invited to characterise Ireland's preparedness against transnational ter-rorism attacks prior to 9/11, the measures taken and lessons learned from that attack, what areas of vulnerability still existed and how policy planning could be improved in the future. Mason recommends this 'before and after' style to get at emergent, historical phenomena (Mason 2002, p. 31). Free association helped garner evidence as to how policy actors behaved in what was perceived to be a time of crisis.

The author also engaged in informal verbal contacts with former and serving personnel of both agencies, as well as with former and serving senior politi-cians. The study makes substantial use of secondary source material, some of it State material classified as restricted, but mostly open sourced (e.g. media reports, annual reports). In relation to the restricted material, much of it is of a financial nature and its use here is, in the author's view, highly unlikely to pose any danger to anyone.

The performance of the chosen method of enquiry relates closely to the question of validity; how valid is the question under review? But validity can depend on how obstacles to enquiry are dealt with (e.g. compromises made, alterations to approach) (Arksey and Knight 1999, pp. 51–4). The starting point in deciding the method was to consider whether the study would utilise primary source material and, if so, who would the author target for it? The decision was taken that primary source material was indeed required, not least because there was insufficient academic literature available on the frontline agencies, especially the Garda (see Chapter 2). In terms of who should be targeted, the research question suggested individuals in the frontline agencies and their overseers in the various responsible government departments. There was a risk that respondents could deliberately provide misleading information, given that the study could stray into sensitive matters of national security policy. But with so little known about Irish policy against transnational terrorism the author sided with the argument that the risk of gathering some potentially flawed information was better than gathering none at all (Arksey and Knight 1999, pp. 51–3).

The following departments and agencies with responsibility for Irish national security policy were targeted for cooperation with the study: the Garda Síochána, the Defence Forces, the Departments of Justice and Defence, the Department of the Taoiseach (because of its role vis-à-vis the National Security Committee – see Chapter 2) and the Department of Foreign Affairs (because of the Department's traditional role in Ireland's international security policy). Officials of the Department of Finance were not targeted at this stage although the study sought to explore the issue of financial pressure. This was because significant scholarly work into Finance's role in national security had already been conducted (Farrell 1997, 2001; O' Halpin 1996, 1999; Regan 1999). The author was prepared to approach Department of Finance officials had the need become apparent later on (e.g. if there were any substantial indications of a departure between what was emerging in the fieldwork and what had been written of the department's role in national security policy-making in previous scholarly works). Ultimately, the author held with the original 'target list'. The only move beyond it was informal contacts held with senior politicians. These were conducted, in part, to assess whether political opinions should be sought in a more formal way. But again, it became apparent that no major advantage would be achieved by widening the list. Indeed, such a widening could jeopardise fieldwork manageability. To a certain degree the make-up of the representative sample was pre-determined by the subject matter. Ireland's national security community is a rigidly hierarchical one with the most important strategic and policy questions decided at the highest levels. Hence, the most senior ranking 'players' in the various organisations were the best qualified to comment on national security policy.

The next problems were which method would best yield information from these senior players, and how they should be approached for their cooperation. Alternatives to semi-structured interviews were considered, including questionnaires and structured interviews. Here, the author drew on his previous experience of the national security community as (naturally enough) a highly secretive one. Questionnaires offer benefits to respondents including anonymity (Arksey and Knight 1999, p. 34). Similarly, a fully structured interview, involving only pre-prepared questions, provides them with the opportunity to prepare, even script, all their answers. However, both methods deny the capacity to pursue respondents with follow-up questions especially in a discreet, 'off the record' way. On the other hand, semi-structured interviews promise this capacity but risk becoming, as Arksey and Knight put it, 'partly interviewer-led, partly informant-led' (p. 8). In this regard, the author, on the basis of some ten years spent as an interviewer for broadcast and print media was conscious of the danger that interviewees could attempt to control the interview (e.g. to 'lead' free association questions in certain ways). Similarly, the author could end up asking questions simply to appear knowledgeable or credible and so lead the interview down less relevant paths. Nevertheless, this had to be weighed against the opportunity to engage with respondents and, using past professional experience, draw them out through probing conversation.

The primary fieldwork methods and the range of respondents decided, there still remained the problem of securing the cooperation of senior figures within a normally secretive national security community. It seemed likely that respondents would decline interviews lest in sharing information they compromised secrecy. Moreover, someone who they would have known previously as a journalist was proposing to conduct the interviews.

The author was also concerned that if they did agree to be interviewed they would 'hold back' on what they said to an extent that could seriously jeopardise the validity of the method. A related problem concerned the principal means of conducting the interviews – tape-recording. A key objective was to compile a comprehensive set of verbatim transcripts in the interests of reliability (Smith 1995, p. 18; Maxwell 1998, p. 94). The author, having spent some years as a court reporter, could draw on shorthand but had a preference for tape-recording. Experience suggested that respondents committing themselves to audiotape would be less likely to deliberately utter misleading answers, although a written undertaking was to be given to all cooperating respondents that tapes and transcripts made for the study would never be made available to anyone else. With that said, tape-recording carried the obvious risks that respondents could feel that their conversation was taking place in an abnormal or pressurised environment and that their remarks about secret national security matters could be broadcast elsewhere (Smith 1995, p. 18). Through past experience as a broadcast journalist, the author felt confident that problems to do with respondents' nerves or their sense of artificiality could be overcome. But the confidentiality concerns were a different matter.

In essence, confidentiality raised three difficulties to be resolved: the first to do with manageability (would there be a sufficient interview cohort?) and the second and the third, to do with reliability (would they agree to be tape-recorded, and if so, would they hold back?) The following research tactics were employed to overcome these problems: The author drew up letters of approach aimed at the secretaries general of all relevant government departments, the Garda commissioner and the chief of staff of the Defence Forces. A research declaration, featuring an undertaking of confidentiality of sources, and a research schedule providing a detailed briefing of the research objectives and general points of interest for questions were also scripted. Each of these documents was submitted to trusted contacts – individuals serving as or recently retired from management roles in the Garda and Defence Forces. The contacts concerned were also chosen because of their experience in dealing with officials of the government departments relevant to the study (i.e. Taoiseach, Justice, Defence, Foreign Affairs). They were asked to assess the documents and consider whether the most senior officers of their respective organisations and officials of government departments would react favourably to the request for cooperation. The contacts' initial responses were not especially encouraging: They noted that their organisations had never before agreed to participate in a study of contemporary Irish national security policy. They expressed reservations to the effect that cooperation could be difficult to secure because of fears that the interviews would stray into 'live' operational issues. The essence of their advice was that the letter of approach needed to clearly emphasise that cooperation with the study was in the best interests of the organisations. Furthermore, they advised 'playing them off against each other' or listing out in each letter of approach, all of the organisations that had been approached. The idea was to build a momentum among all 'targets' not to be the one left out.

In cooperation with the contacts the documents were refined many times over several weeks before final versions were submitted. These went to the secretaries general of the Departments of the Taoiseach, Justice, Defence and Foreign Affairs, as well as to the Garda commissioner and the chief of staff of the Defence Forces. Among other things, each of the letters of approach acknowledged the author's previous career as a journalist specialising in security matters but stressed that the study was for academic purposes. The preference for tape-recording was clearly stated on the research schedule as was the method of interview (semi-structured) and topics for discussion. The option for respondents to speak 'on-record', 'off record' or on 'deep background' (i.e. only for the author's information but not for committal to the study) was set out in the research declaration. Positive responses were received from each of the government departments. The Garda commissioner was slow to reply. A senior official at the Department of Justice volunteered to encourage the commissioner to permit Garda cooperation which was confirmed some days later. The Defence Forces agreed to cooperate but conducted what one senior officer later described as a standard background security check of the author, via telephone, before interviews occurred. (This check involved a brief conversation between the author and an officer who said he was based at McKee Barracks, the headquarters of G2. The officer sought confirmation of name, date of birth and address.) In all, the various agencies and organisations permitted the author to conduct interviews with twenty-one serving individuals. Separately, the author secured the cooperation of one other recently retired senior Garda officer.

The initial data sort drew loosely on a model used by Smith (1995, pp. 21–2). Later, the codification was refined to correspond more closely with the conceptual framework. In sorting and evaluating the data the author strove, wherever possible, to find corroborations between primary sources or between primary and secondary sources. Unique claims by single sources were treated with caution although allowances were made where claims related to respondents' particular specialisations. Daily searches for Irish security-related stories on the web sites of prominent news media helped where such claims were made. Comparisons could be drawn between claims and reports.

This frequent use of news reports reflects the study's concern with policy after 2001. The major news sources are the web sites of *The Irish Times*, the *Irish Independent* and RTÉ (Ireland's public service broadcaster). Checks on these sites had the useful effect of helping to keep the author updated with current security developments after interviews had been completed. Downloaded scripts of Dáil debates dealing with national security matters were also used extensively as were official documents (e.g. strategy statements, financial reports). In the earlier stages of research the author engaged in continuous informal discussions with Defence Forces and Garda contacts. Comments arising from these informal contacts were used very sparingly in the analysis. They were more valuable as a means of corroborating primary and secondary source material and for keeping the author updated on issues. As the research wore on the author eased contacts with individuals in or connected to the frontline agencies to try to avoid ties of friendship or familiarity from influencing analysis (and to help prevent contacts getting blamed should their superiors react badly to the book's conclusions). Finally, a range of scholarly works relevant to national security was gathered through Irish university libraries and the Web. These helped, in particular, with the historical background for the analysis and are discussed in some detail in the literature review in Chapter 2.

The next task is to identify the conceptual framework to help analyse the evidence. The section will begin by profiling the first of the book's three conceptual approaches, historical institutionalism. This approach will be used to help provide a 'scene-set' of fundamental pressures bearing down on the security agencies. Next, the section will turn to a model of threat response evaluation which will be used to support a strategic and operational critique of Irish policy after 9/11. Finally, it will focus on how a governmental politics model can assist with the investigation of 'crisis' decision-making after 9/11.

Seeking familiar pathways

The study argues that the agencies worked under heightened financial and political pressures following 9/11. If so, it follows that these pressures were ongoing features of the agencies' work. But was it the pressures in themselves that weakened policy, the agencies' ways of dealing with them or did other issues matter more? A historical institutional approach can help illuminate these matters by identifying the pressures, the pressure-exerting mechanisms, the established ways of dealing with pressure and the policy effects arising. It is an approach that offers the capacity to analyse policy as a gradual development, to capture structures under which the agencies operate, the procedures they follow and the cultures that grow up within them that influence policy. So, what are the characteristics of historical institutionalism? According to one useful account, institutions can be broadly defined as:

> The formal or informal procedures, routines, norms and conventions embedded in the organizational structure of the polity … They can range from the rules of a constitutional order or the standard operating procedures of a bureaucracy to the conventions governing trade union behaviour or bank firm relations. (Hall and Taylor 1996, p. 938)

At its broadest, institutionalism represents an attempt to unravel how policy struggles are mediated by the institutional setting in which they take place (Hall and Taylor 1996). Historical institutionalism is associated with the identification of certain features of institutionalisation, most notably path dependencies and critical junctures. Path dependencies can be defined in terms of organisational reliance on familiar routines and practices of appropriate behaviour (e.g. how to deal with financial cutbacks). Self-reinforcing or positive feedback processes in the political system bolster path dependency. Established paths are shot through with power relationships that privilege some interests and ignore others. Institutions are, in the main, the results of gradual evolution as a consequence of path dependency (Pierson and Skockpol 2003, p. 709). But while historical institutionalism assumes incremental change as the norm, it can also account for occasional moments of significant transformation, known as critical junctures (Bulmer and Burch 1998, p. 605). Events external to existing institutions occur at a particular time and order of sequence to trigger a reaction which may ultimately result in moves to a new trajectory or pathway. So here it helps us to explore, for example, whether 9/11 represented a critical juncture in how the Irish national security organisations dealt with financial and/or political pressures. Tempering the likelihood of such fundamental behavioural changes are positive feedback mechanisms that support the recurrence of a predominant pattern. Hence, the policy process is frequently characterised by a powerful inertial 'stickiness' (Pierson and Skocpol 2003, pp. 701–2). Separating critical moments, which prompt only evolution, from critical junctures which activate organic change, is a notable feature of historical institutional investigations.

The study will draw on a model that has been used to investigate British governmental agency adaptation to participation in the European Economic Community (Bulmer and Burch 1998, pp. 601–28). In the British case, the model was used to examine a question of Europeanisation. The Irish security community operates in a EU context, especially since the attack on Madrid of 2004 galvanised member state cooperation. But the focus of this study is not specifically on EU affairs. This does not diminish the essential reason for employing the model: its utility as a means to assess institutions at play in governmental machinery.

The agencies are assessed along four gradations: formal institutional structure, processes and procedures, codes and guidelines and finally the cultural dimension. These, or variations of them, are common enough in historical institutional analysis (Hall and Taylor 1996; Thelen 2002). At the formal level are constitutional-legal rules, formal organisations and positions. Processes and procedures facilitate the day-to-day functioning of the institutions and govern the network of relations. At the level of codes and guidelines are found the conventions for handling business. Finally, there is the cultural dimension, which relates to norms, values and identities that are constructed around individual institutions and, on a micro level, within organisations.

Evaluating the response to threat

To provide a critique of Irish national security policy since 9/11, we need to know how agency managers responded to the perceived threat coming from transnational terrorism. Buzan's model of threat evaluation (1991) is used here because it can support a detailed description and critique of policy and its operational outcomes. The model identifies three components that each state must secure. It provides five criteria by which threats to those components can be evaluated. It is designed, in the first instance, to gauge threat intensity but that is no barrier to its use here, where the State's judgement of intensity is accepted. The three components it provides can be readily applied to the Irish case. The five criteria can simply be switched from providing the means to consider a response to providing orientation points for investigating the response already made.

What are the three components that Buzan says each state must secure? States must protect their physical base of population and territory. They must protect the institutions used to govern the physical base. They must protect the idea of the state, which establishes its legitimacy in the minds of its people and binds them to it. The binding idea 'is the most abstract component of the model, but also the most central' (Buzan 1991, p. 80). It 'can be penetrated, distorted, corrupted and eventually undermined by contact by other ideas'. In this regard, British Prime Minister Tony Blair warned of the need to combat the terrorists' 'poisonous propaganda', after repeated MI5 claims of British citizens being radicalised to commit attacks (Blair 2006). Buzan cautions against an over-zealous approach to securing the binding idea. This 'can give rise to a dangerous streak of absolutism in national security policy' (Buzan 1991, p. 81). The five criteria for evaluating threat/considering response are as follows:

1   the specificity of its identity;
2   its nearness in space and time;
3   the probability of it occurring;

4   the weight of its consequences;
5   whether or not perceptions of the threat are amplified by historical
    circumstance.

The model is broad enough to explore an entire gamut of possibilities, from the spread of disaffection about the State to threats of physical attack. For example, the implementation of rigorous immigration controls was Ireland's primary response to 9/11 in terms of attack prevention. This approach was taken because Ireland was particularly vulnerable to abuse of its immigration system for terrorist ends, according to senior figures in the security agencies (Author's interviews). Specifically, the security agencies warned government of foreign 'sleeper cells' coming to reside in Ireland, especially for the purposes of mounting an attack on targets in the UK in the medium to long term. The model supports at least three lines of relevant enquiry. Firstly, there is the question of how the State's response measures up to the perceived threat to the territory of Ireland and the EU from terrorists who intend operating there. Secondly, there is the question of how the response protects the State's institutions from infiltration by terrorists wishing to pass themselves off as legitimate immigrants. Thirdly, there is the question of tensions between robust immigration controls and the key objective of securing a healthy, binding idea of the state.

The study suffers one significant limitation in its attempts to examine operational matters. It does not have access to all secret information in possession of the State's security and intelligence agencies. That does not preclude taking what the agencies say is the level of threat to the State and assessing whether anomalies in the response suggest the influence of financial, political or other evident pressures. Even the official assessment of threat can be evaluated, albeit up to a point. Ostensibly, it is the product of intelligence analyses from experienced organisations, but here we can consider whether the intelligence process is sufficiently rigorous.

High stakes decision-making

At this point, the framework is equipped with models to help analyse historical and operational evidence. But a third issue remains. The review of policy has had two discernible phases; the first and most active which occurred between September 11 and October 3 2001 and the other which has been ongoing since. Some fundamental decisions were made during the initial phase, including the decision that Ireland faced a low risk of direct attack and that emergency planning was the principal concern. Is it accurate to say these decisions were taken in an atmosphere of heightened political pressure when national security policy-making worldwide was considered to be in crisis? At such a time, is it not possible that financial and political pressures exerted on the agencies lessened or disappeared? Or did they, as the study suggests, increase? What of other forces at play? In these contexts what can be concluded in respect of the structures in which the Garda and Defence Forces continue to operate? Allison and Zelikow's model of governmental politics is used to support the investigation of these issues (1999, pp. 255–324).

Technically, the governmental politics model assumes that national security decisions are the outcome of a game which can be analysed in four parts. In the first part are players. These are individuals occupying roles in the major channels for producing action on national security issues. In adopting a position, these players may have obligations to their superiors, to colleagues in other organisations, to international organisations, to parliament or to the public. In the latter regard when faced with a sudden gap in security preparedness such players must decide the opportunity cost of filling that gap relative to other demands (e.g. education, healthcare and so forth). In the second of the four parts are the factors that shape players' perceptions, preferences, and stands on the issue at hand. Representatives of the organisation in a group decision-making process will be sensitive to the organisation's orientation. Officials are prone to believe that the decision should not harm their organisations – including their budgets. Politicians and their political appointees rarely fail to consider domestic political consequences of their choices. Depending on their responsibilities, decision-makers will see differing aspects to the same problem. Deadlines and moments of crisis will force decision-makers to take positions. The third part contains the factors that determine each player's impact on results. These include the formal authority and responsibility of the player and that player's actual control over resources, expertise and control over relevant information. Finally, there is the nature of the game. The game is highly structured by action channels which pre-select the major players, determine their usual points of entrance into the game and distribute particular advantages and disadvantages for each game. The rules of the game are the institutional setting. The pace of the game is furious as players deal with an overcrowded agenda of issues. The law of the game is competition as players compete with one another to advance their point and get the others to see the issue from a less parochial perspective.

Applied to the Irish case the model will be used firstly to shed further light on those decision-makers who played key roles in the review of national security policy after 9/11. It will also help to investigate what factors influenced the findings they arrived at. Thirdly, it will support enquiry into which players impacted most on the review of security policy after 9/11 and why. To what degree, if any, did their dominance have to do with financial and/or political pressures on the agencies and what other factors were at work? Finally, it will be used to find out if the 'rules' governing the scope, extent, style and pace of the review affected the influence of such pressures.

Conclusion

Several reasons, strategic and otherwise, justify why Irish national security policy shaped after 9/11 should come under close review. In summary, these relate to the continuing relevance of policy made after that attack, the unique experience of the Irish security community in combating terrorism, the collective nature of EU counter-terrorist efforts, the Anglo-Irish Common Travel Area, Ireland's location as a centre of globalised commerce and its geo-political positioning, especially in relation to transatlantic aviation and maritime affairs. Furthermore, the Irish national security community has attracted only marginal academic interest.

Methodologically, the study relies upon semi-structured interviews with leading decision-makers within the security community for primary source material. It uses a range of secondary sources. A fundamental point here is that any method involving external evaluation of a state's national security network is going to throw up resistance and other difficulties relating to reliability. In these circumstances trade-offs are inevitable. The preparation that went into the letters of approach provides a good example. This involved the author seeking the assistance of 'insiders' within Ireland's national security organisations. Following their advice put the reliability and validity at risk; would they seek to steer the enquiry in certain ways and if so, how valid would its investigations be? Despite this and other potential difficulties, twenty-two interviews with senior officials and officers and full transcripts of each interview to aid data codification, was the end result.

Conceptually, a model of historical institutionalism will be used here to help show how the Irish security agencies have dealt with financial and political pressures in the past and whether these established ways have had, or could have, detrimental effects on Irish security policy after 9/11. The investigation will encompass matters including the legislative frameworks within which the agencies work, their top command structures, the intelligence processes they use, organisational problems within the Garda and relations between the Defence Forces and their civilian overseers.

Buzan's model of threat/response, with its three vulnerabilities of states and five factors of threat evaluation, can support a wide-ranging critique of operational policy and strategy. But this phase of enquiry carries one significant limitation, the absence of perfect (e.g. State secret) information. The way out is to accept what the Irish security community say are the threats since they fixed policy after 9/11 and to evaluate how their responses have measured up, paying close attention to any evidence of acute financial and/or political pressures, especially where they indicate problems in the structures of the intelligence process.

The initial re-evaluation of Irish national security policy was conducted under pressure and at a furious pace in the weeks after 9/11. An onus rested on the security agencies to come up with clear answers fast. The bureaucratic politics model is applied to help establish whether, or to what degree, heightened financial and political pressures bearing down on them influenced the agencies in their decisions at this time. Bureaucratic politics is a well established means of analysing decision-making at crisis times, prompting the question of whether its application here will throw up any unusual or unexpected dynamics.

The only remaining task for this chapter is to set out the order of things to come. Chapter 2 will, to aid clarity, provide a summary profile of the frontline agencies of Irish national security and their government overseers and how they coped during two previous security crises. It will also examine security and intelligence agencies in other European states.

The study is located in the context of existing scholarship, in Chapter 3. The literature is grouped into three categories, reflecting the key empirical concerns of the authors. They are firstly, political pressure on the Garda Síochána; secondly, financial pressure on the Defence Forces; and finally, Anglo-Irish considerations in Irish national security. This chapter sets out the main arguments associated with each category and identifies where they depart from and/or provide a context for what the study claims.

Chapter 4, drawing on historical institutionalism, considers the established ways that the agencies have made policy. Do the institutions – political, financial or otherwise – in which they work make for effective policy after 9/11? Specifically, Chapter 4 investigates how the legislative frameworks within which the agencies work affect policy. It will also assess agencies' senior management structures for their impacts on security policy and the agencies' intelligence relationships with other agencies. Finally, it will examine the effects on policy of organisational problems within the Garda and of the traditionally difficult relations between the Defence Forces and their civilian overseers.

Chapter 5 will use Buzan's model of threat intensity to evaluate Irish security policy against threats that the frontline agencies have identified. Among other issues, it will provide a critique of policy in respect of emergency planning, immigration and maritime and aviation threats. It will also further consider intelligence gathering/analysis. This chapter will investigate from the perspectives of specificity of threat, range of threat, probability and consequences and the historical dimension of threat.

In Chapter 6 the focus will narrow to the time frame between September 11 and October 3 2001, when Irish security policy underwent significant revision and all the main aspects of current policy were put in place including the decision to emphasise emergency planning as the primary concern. Taking a governmental politics perspective, this chapter will consider the responsibilities of and stakes for the agencies during this period. Consequently, it will conceptualise the 2001 policy review as a kind of game. The analysis will establish who played, what influenced their positions, why some players were more influential than others and finally the rules (or constraints) of playing the game.

The concluding chapter, Chapter 7, is divided into two parts. The first draws conclusions about the research design including underpinning theory. The second deals with the empirical evidence and the issues that arise from it.

Notes

1   The term 'transnational terrorist networks' is discussed in more detail later in this chapter.

2   It is not argued that political and financial pressures on national security are unique to Ireland, but that after 9/11, significant Irish policy problems can be linked with them. The weaknesses in security claimed here are defined in terms of threats to the State identified by the agencies themselves.

3   For a concise discussion on how the researcher's background 'experiential knowledge' can act as 'a major source of insights, hypotheses and validity checks', and a strategy to facilitate/validate these, see Maxwell 1998, p. 78.

2
The Irish national security apparatus

Introduction

To engage with the investigation presented in this study knowledge of the principal organisations at the frontline of proactive security is necessary. So here, general characteristics of these organisations are set out together with a brief analysis of how the State coped with two previous crises, the Emergency of 1939–45 and the Northern Ireland Troubles since 1969. Doing so will also help contextualise subsequent analysis. For example, the discussion on Northern Ireland will consider, among other issues, the use of law against subversion, what on-island terrorism meant for the Defence Forces' operational posture and the challenges which border security posed for the frontline agencies. Finally, and by way of placing contemporary Irish national security arrangements in a broader setting, also included is an overview of the arrangements operating in other European states, especially Sweden and Denmark.

The network of departments and agencies

The Irish security community is organised hierarchically and the format of the discussion will reflect this, beginning with the top tier (cabinet) and then focusing on the National Security Committee and the frontline agencies. In accordance with Irish law and governmental procedure the Taoiseach and the ministers for defence and justice, equality and law reform hold the main responsibility for Irish national security (Author's interviews; Dunne and Kerrigan 1984; O' Halpin 1999).[1] The Taoiseach, as head of government, holds ultimate responsibility. Not least because of this the government's high-level group on national security, the National Security Committee, falls under the

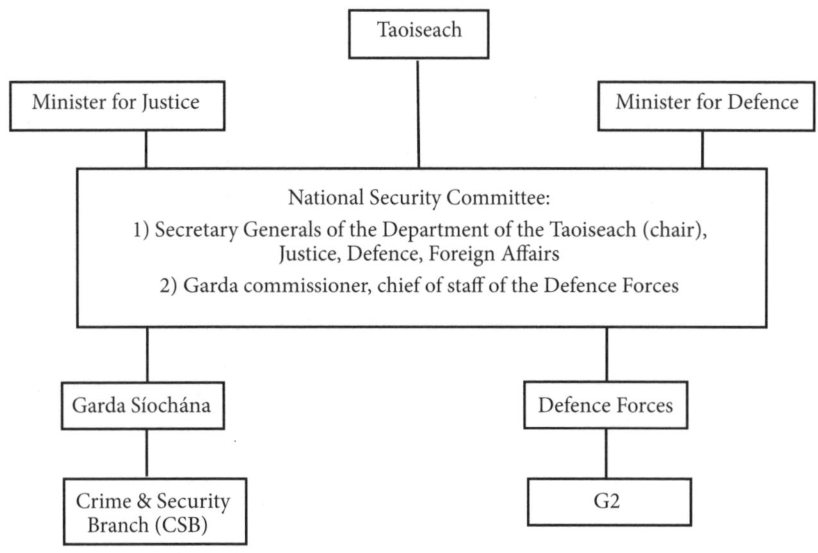

Figure 2.1: Key actors responsible for proactive Irish national security policy

remit of the Department of the Taoiseach (Dáil Debates, 2006, p. 379; Author's interviews). The secretary general of the Department of the Taoiseach, who is secretary general to the cabinet, chairs the committee and reports directly to the Taoiseach on its deliberations (Dáil Debates 2006, 2005b, 2005c, 2004; Author's interviews). In terms of the Department of the Taoiseach's broader role in national security policy management, its secretary general, Dermot McCarthy, provided the following summary to the Commission of Investigation into the Dublin and Monaghan bombings of 1974:

> The Department of the Taoiseach is frequently called upon to discharge a co-ordinating role in relation to major or sensitive issues, particularly where there is a cross-cutting dimension. Also, the department usually services cabinet committees and, of course, the department is involved where issues arise that are of particular concern to the Taoiseach, as head of government …
>
> The role is not a formal one, unlike the Garda Síochána and the Department of Justice, Equality and Law Reform. The Department of the Taoiseach does become involved from time to time in a co-ordinating capacity where particular circumstances require it. (Commission of Investigation 2007, p. 238)

Subordinate to the Taoiseach, the minister for justice is head of the Department of Justice, where a 'high-level goal' is to help ensure the security of the State (Ireland, Department of Justice, Equality and Law Reform 2003). The department has a remit over the Garda Síochána, which is host to the State's main national security agency, Crime and Security Branch (CSB). The Department of Justice aims 'to further develop policies and implement measures to underpin the security of the State and to pursue such policies and measures in the wider international context of security' (2003, p. 34). Officials work to keep the minister and the government advised of whatever legislative, administrative or operational measures are required to combat threats (2003, p. 35). UN and EU responses to transnational terrorist networks since 9/11 have 'impacted significantly' on the department's work programme (2003, p. 54). The most significant activity appears to centre on the areas of immigration, counter-terrorism legislation and emergency planning (Author's interviews).

In parallel to Justice, the minister and Department of Defence aim to 'contribute to the security of the State principally against the threat of armed aggression' (Ireland, Department of Defence 2001a, p. 5). This they do under the terms of the Ministers and Secretaries Act 1924, which assigns to the Department of Defence various administrative and business management responsibilities over the Defence Forces (2001a, p. 1). Defence is not a policy-making department comparable to, say, the UK's Ministry of Defence (O' Halpin 1999, p. 344). The role of the Irish Department of Defence is 'essentially a supportive one' to the Departments of Foreign Affairs and Justice (Ireland, Department of Defence 2001a, p. 6). But interviewees claimed that the policy role of the Department of Defence, especially in relation to international security, is gradually increasing.

Coordination at the highest levels of these departments and between the Garda and Defence Forces takes place at the National Security Committee. The committee was formed by cabinet order after a confidential review of national security by a senior judge, Mr Justice Finlay, in 1974 (Dunne and Kerrigan 1984, pp. 83–4; Commission of Investigation 2007, pp. 67–73). It fell into dormancy – no interviewee including those who sat on it were able to remember for how long this was so – but was reactivated to improve high-level coordination within days of 9/11 (Author's interviews). It is not that high-level cross-departmental and cross-agency exchanges did not continue apace prior to its return. But they took place in the absence of such a dedicated senior management forum.

The National Security Committee (NSC) consists of the secretaries general of the Departments of the Taoiseach (chair), Justice, Defence, and Foreign Affairs, the Garda commissioner and the chief of staff of the Defence Forces. Other senior officials and officers can be called in to advise the NSC from time to time as required (Author's interviews).[2] Members expressed differing views regarding the committee's influence. One described it as 'the very top strategic level'. Another described it as 'grandly-called, over-stated' (Author's interviews).

The exact role of the National Security Committee has been the subject of some political debate since 9/11 (Cudmore 2003, p. 63; Ireland, Dáil Debates 2004, 2005a, 2005b, 2005c, 2006a). The stock response of government to the opposition parties' probing has been that the committee is concerned with ensuring that the Taoiseach and the government 'are advised of high level security issues and responses to them …' (Ahern cited in Cudmore 2003, p. 63; Dáil Debates 2005b, p. 238; 2005c, p. 492; 2006a, p. 378). However, the government qualifies this by adding that the committee's advice does not involve 'operational security issues', a phrase which appears to refer to actual operations against suspects (e.g. Dáil Debates 2005c, p.492). Taoiseach Bertie Ahern, in a statement to the Dáil in November 2005, said the committee examined intelligence and then formed 'a judgment and opinion on how to deal with that' (2005c, p. 496). This seems to suggest that the NSC is some kind of intelligence analysis group. But that is not in line with the evidence of interviewees including committee members (Author's interviews). These officials agreed that the National Security Committee considered threat analyses that the frontline agencies supplied to it (Author's interviews). These analyses reach the committee via the Garda commissioner and the chief of staff of the Defence Forces. The committee is exclusively reliant on these officers or, occasionally, high-ranking subordinate officers. As one member of the committee said:

> All of that, of course, is entirely a matter that we rely on the security professionals to do. In a sense, we are consumers of their net outcome of that analysis. (Author's interview)

Generally, raw intelligence detail provided to them is kept to a minimum, according to civilian members of the committee (Author's interviews). As for specific analysis, the description of one NSC member is instructive:

> Coming into the National Security Committee would be very short, terse reports. 'No threats from this group. No threats from that group. These fellas have taken a bad hit. We're a bit concerned that these are active, some of their activists have been seen.' So it's very broad-brush stuff that comes up. (Author's interview)

Having received their 'broad-brush' briefing, it is for the committee to draw up for the Taoiseach and government whatever national security recommendations that the members agree are necessary. To further clarify this process in the wake of the 2007 attacks on London and Glasgow, the committee requested the agencies to draw up criteria to inform threat evaluations, akin to those already operating in the UK (Brady 2007). Such a move reflects Anglo-Irish security cooperation more than an identified domestic need; consistently since the Emergency threat briefings to government have been to the effect that the risk to Ireland of external attack is low (Author's interviews). One National Security Committee member summed up what was a quite common view among respondents when he said that benign briefings were 'invariably' the case. He said this was because of Ireland's geostrategic position as a small state on the periphery of Europe and its good international reputation (Author's interview).

Below the 'security departments' of government (i.e. Department of the Taoiseach, Justice and Defence) and the National Security Committee are Ireland's frontline security and intelligence agencies. The State has never maintained a dedicated national security agency (Author's interviews). The Garda Síochána is both Ireland's police force and the home of the State's principal security agency which is known as Crime and Security Branch (CSB) and formerly known simply as C3 (Author's interviews).[3] This incorporates the following units: Security and Intelligence, Crime Policy and Administration, Liaison and

Protection, International Coordination Unit and the Special Detective Unit, colloquially known as the 'Special Branch'. CSB 'has primary responsibility for … the protection of the State' (Ireland, Dáil Debates 2005a, p. 142). Its personnel comprise Garda detectives transferred from policing duties (Author's interviews) and some civilian administrative staff. The agency acts mainly as an internal security service. It is headquartered at Garda Headquarters in Dublin under the command of an officer known as the assistant commissioner for crime and security. This officer provides intelligence briefings to the Garda commissioner, deputy commissioner (operations) and the minister for justice, as well as to the National Security Committee when required (Author's interviews).

The statutory basis for the Garda's security function is set out in Section 7 (1) of the Garda Síochána Act 2005: The function of the Garda Síochána is to provide policing and security services for the State with the objective of

(a) preserving people and public order;
(b) protecting life and property;
(c) vindicating the human rights of each individual;
(d) protecting the security of the state;
(e) preventing crime;
(f) bringing criminals to justice, including by detecting and investigating crime;
(g) regulating and controlling road traffic and improving road safety.

Operationally CSB relies heavily upon human intelligence, known as HUMINT, gathered by detective and uniformed members around the country, and signals intelligence, or SIGINT, such as telephone tapping pursuant to the Interception of Postal Packets and Telecommunications Messages (Regulation) Act 1993 (Author's interviews; Commission of Investigation 2007, pp. 64, 69–70). During the Cold War the sources of intelligence information to security and intelligence agencies were typically classified as human intelligence (HUMINT), signals intelligence (SIGINT) or a sub-field of SIGINT known as imagery (Herman 1996, 2001). But the development and social penetration of the Internet has raised the importance of open source intelligence, or OSINT, which is gathered from published organisational data and online media reports, chat rooms, discussion forums and 'blogs' (Author's interview). HUMINT can involve operative infiltration into an organisation/state or the recruitment of informers, a tactic used successfully against the Provisional IRA in Northern Ireland during the Troubles (Herman 2001; Moloney 2002). Stand-alone agencies such as Britain's Government Communications Headquarters (GCHQ) gather SIGINT using sophisticated equipment to intercept and monitor electronic communications (Herman 2001, pp. 66–72). SIGINT was used extensively by the British security forces in Northern Ireland during the Troubles but they considered imagery, involving the use of satellite and other forms of aerial photo-reconnaissance and a major feature of Cold War espionage, to be of marginal value (Herman 1996, p. 76). Below HUMINT, SIGINT and imagery, multiple sub-classifications emerged or developed as a consequence of bipolar international tensions. One such category is ACOUSINT or the use of unattended devices to detect sound or vibration (1996, p. 71).

Garda management expect all members, regardless of rank, to submit to CSB any HUMINT they have which relates to subversive activity or serious crime (Author's sources; Commission of Investigation 2007). This reporting is conducted using a standard paper form known as a C.77 which is forwarded to the assistant commissioner for crime and security. Information other than that to do with subversive/serious crime or likely to reveal the identity of an informant is recorded on the Garda's computerised collating and intelligence system, PULSE. However, information on C.77 forms is uploaded, in summary form, by CSB detectives to a separate dedicated system for the exclusive use of CSB. This is known as the National Intelligence Database. Also placed on it is intelligence received from other sources, including the Departments of Justice and Foreign Affairs. The database is indexed and searchable using a text retrieval tool within its software.

CSB personnel archive all paper material received that is considered relevant to intelligence work. In evidence to the MacEntee inquiry the Garda commissioner, Noel Conroy, explained this process:

> Files on persons or incidents are opened by desk officers as the need arises. The title of the file is entered into a sequential file register in the registry in Security and Intelligence. Items of correspondence are added to the file on an ongoing basis and the information is also entered on the National Intelligence Database. (Commission of Investigation 2007, p. 205)

Electronic records of all correspondence received identify the source of the correspondence and also set out how it is to be further processed. Reflecting a clear need to effectively manage these records, Garda management favours the introduction of an electronic file tracking system within CSB. It is worth noting, in this regard, the observation contained in the final report of the MacEntee inquiry that the computer system dated from the early 1980s while space required for paper storage was 'plainly inadequate' (Commission of Investigation 2007, p. 206).

The intelligence arm of the Defence Forces (DF) is known as G2. Its staffing and financial resources are much smaller than those of CSB. Instead, it provides 'complementary' intelligence gathering and analytical capabilities (Dáil Debates 2005a, p. 153; Author's interviews). By early 2009, the government was taking steps to redraw the boundaries of military involvement in domestic intelligence; the Criminal Justice (Surveillance) Bill 2009, published in April, sought to provide to personnel of the Garda, Defence Forces and Revenue Commissioners powers to covertly appropriate intelligence admissible as evidence in the Irish courts. In the Dáil the government sought to portray its inclusion of the Defence Forces as reflecting G2's 'parallel responsibility in protecting the security of the State, mainly against threats posed by subversives and international terrorism' (Dáil Debates 2009, p. 31). But the potential for terrorists to engage with criminals and in criminal activity to fundraise and procure weaponry made unlikely a clear separation of the military from the gathering by the Garda and Revenue of evidential intelligence concerning criminal matters. G2 is tasked with tracking threats to the State emanating both off-island (including threats to DF personnel serving overseas) and on-island (i.e. internal subversion). Responsibility for the latter sphere falls to personnel of G2's National Security Intelligence Section (*An Cosantóir* 2005). CSB and G2 have worked closely together since 9/11 (Author's interviews). According to the minister for defence in January 2005,

> There is ongoing and close liaison between the Garda Síochána and the Defence Forces regarding internal security matters including in the intelligence field. Both agencies gather and share information and assessments in relation to perceived and/or emerging security threats. (Dáil Debates 2005a, p. 153)

G2 is based at McKee Barracks, Dublin, under the command of a colonel known as the Director of Intelligence. This officer provides intelligence briefings to the minister for defence, the chief of staff and the deputy chief of staff for operations as well as the National Security Committee when required (Dáil Debates 2005a, p. 153).

Intelligence personnel in the Army's three brigades, the Air Corps, and the Naval Service report to G2 but combine intelligence with other roles, such as press and public relations officers (Author's interviews). The MacEntee inquiry's report of its investigation into G2's intelligence management system provides useful insights (Commission of Investigation 2007, pp. 212–13): The use of 'cardex' (card index) was phased out in early 2000 and in its place new file covers were instituted for clearer reference of documents. G2 maintains a secured information technology network and a registry of classified documentation. Staff of the registry control access to it. It is worth adding that for at least two years after 9/11 the CSB and G2 computer systems were not interlinked for the purposes of information share and cross-analysis (Author's interviews).

No dedicated Irish foreign intelligence agency exists. CSB and G2 provide what amounts to a shoestring foreign intelligence service to the State with CSB taking the lead role (Author's interviews). In interviews for this study, senior figures from both agencies said the system worked as follows: instead of running foreign intelligence agents or relying on electronic intelligence-gathering methods overseas, CSB personnel rely on networking with their counterparts in the agencies of other states. These include the UK Security Service (MI5) and Secret Intelligence Service (MI6), the Federal Bureau of Investigation (FBI) and the Central Intelligence Agency (CIA) (Author's interviews). They receive information through groups and agencies including the Club of Berne (an international 'club' where heads of national security agencies meet to discuss matters of mutual interest), Europol, Eurojust and Interpol (Author's interviews). Taoiseach Bertie Ahern acknowledged to the Dáil on at least two occasions in the two-year period following the 2004 attack on Madrid, Ireland's 'extensive' intelligence reliance on Europol and Eurojust (Dáil Debates 2004,

p. 555; 2006a, p. 379). CSB also receives reports from Irish diplomats abroad and liaises with embassies on Irish territory (Author's interviews).

Defence Forces personnel serving overseas report to G2 but their focus is, in the main, on possible threats to existing or likely Irish areas of operation. At a formal level, the organisation receives and provides intelligence assessments internationally via the EU's recently developed military intelligence structures (O' Halpin 2002, p. 35; Author's interviews). All intelligence electronically transmitted to G2 from abroad comes via secured data links to the Army's Intelligence Comcen (communications centre) where messages are decrypted and electronically logged before being passed on for analysis. Like their Garda counterparts Defence Forces management are interested in installing an electronic system of intelligence file management (Commission of Investigation 2007, p. 213).

The Departments of Foreign Affairs and Justice operate information gathering and analytical functions that more broadly inform security policy debate and action. The information gathering role of the Department of Foreign Affairs, done in the course of diplomatic duty, is quite separate from the function of an overseas intelligence agency as one of its officials explained:

> Our embassies abroad would be involved in a lot of different sorts of work and I think it would be fair to say that they don't see the gathering of intelligence on terrorism as a key area of their work. Nor have we sought to make it one. We're not intelligence agents. One has to be realistic. We're never going to get the type of information that MI6 or other external agencies are going to be able to get through their sources. I am not aware of the full extent of the sharing of information between other EU member states external intelligence agencies and our own security forces, whether it's the guards or the army. We don't see it, certainly, that sort of raw intelligence and I don't think that's unusual. (Author's interview)

In comments to the MacEntee commission in 2005 the secretary general of the Department of Foreign Affairs, Dermot Gallagher, described the role of the department in security matters and Northern Ireland:

> The scope of our contact and information includes, but is by no means limited to, security matters in Northern Ireland ... Contact and information reports are compiled, generally on a weekly basis, in a digest which is copied, *inter alia*, to the Taoiseach, Tánaiste [deputy prime minister], minister for justice, equality and law reform, and the attorney general ... Some material which is too sensitive for inclusion in even this confidential circulation is sent directly to a very restricted readership ... It would be rare for contact and information work to yield information relating to a security threat against the State. If this were to occur it would immediately be passed to the Department of Justice, Equality and Law Reform for appropriate follow-up by the Garda Síochána. (Commission of Investigation 2007, p. 232)

While never operating an intelligence agency per se either during the Emergency or the Troubles, the Department of Justice actively maintained intelligence files within designated divisions of the department. These files drew extensively on Garda reporting (Commission of Investigation 2007, pp. 215–30; O' Halpin 1999, p. 204). It was and remains standard practice that files of the Security and Northern Ireland Division are maintained in a special registry in storage areas separate and distinct from all others (Commission of Investigation 2007, p. 225). In 2005 these files were transferred onto a secured section of the department's electronic word-searchable file record system (2007, p. 226). The department's intelligence 'personality' was largely the creation of its former secretary, Peter Berry. During the Second World War, or what was in Ireland termed 'the Emergency', he was appointed by government to a special position within the department to oversee security and intelligence affairs and, until his retirement in 1971, received security briefings directly from the Garda commissioner and the head of C3 (then a chief superintendent) (Browne 1980, p. 33).[4]

It should be noted, finally, that apart from CSB and G2 other State organisations with intelligence capabilities operate, albeit focused primarily on interrupting criminal rather than terrorist activities. Among these, the Office of the Director of Corporate Enforcement (ODCE) has sought to counter breaches of company law, since its inception in 2001. The Customs Service collates intelligence while targeting drug smuggling and other illegal freight movements. In terms of foreign intelligence, the Customs Service is represented in Europol. Through membership of the Maritime Information Group (MAR-INFO), comprising over twenty European countries, the service has access to transferred information between states on the movements of suspect containers, ships and yachts.

Placing the Irish apparatus in an international context

The discussion now turns, for the purposes of locating Irish arrangements in a broader setting, to security and intelligence agencies operating in other European states and, in particular, in Sweden and Denmark. This is not to attempt a full comparative study but should provide a more helpful perspective to the reader. The section will conclude with a brief consideration of how the Irish agencies coped during previous security crises before moving on to the review of Irish security policy literature.

The Swedish domestic intelligence agency is the Säkerhetspolisen or SÄPO. Throughout the Cold War the service was an integral part of the national police force. But in 1989 it was restructured to become a more freestanding body. Now it is a part of the Swedish National Police Board albeit an independent entity within it. SÄPO reports to the Swedish government, is funded directly by it and has its own director general. It is charged with five areas of responsibility: counter-terrorism, protection of the Swedish Constitution, protective security and dignitary protection. The service also works to prevent the proliferation of weapons of mass destruction and acts in support of the functions of other state agencies. As a law-enforcement agency with security responsibilities (its agents hold policing powers) and with the remit it holds SÄPO is not dissimilar to CSB although its independence within the Swedish national policing framework is more apparent. One key structural difference is in SÄPO's regionalised establishment. CSB detectives are based in Dublin and do not gather intelligence, relying instead on what is imparted to them by members around the country. Whereas most of its staff members are based in Stockholm, SÄPO maintains personnel at five regional units across Sweden.[5]

Another difference concerns the civilian component in the respective services. Overwhelmingly but not exclusively CSB is made up of Garda detectives. Just over half of SÄPO's members are detectives, the remainder being civilian analysts, technicians, translators, interpreters, economists and administrative staff.

Swedish military intelligence is conducted by the Militära Underrättelsetjänsten (MUST) or Military Intelligence and Security Agency. The Försvarets radioanstalt (FRA) or the National Defence Radio Institute provides SIGINT.

Like their Irish counterparts the Swedish authorities encourage intelligence cooperation between friendly states. However military intelligence cooperation has been a source of some controversy. In 1992, Swedish Prime Minister Carl Bildt established the Commission on Neutrality Policy to investigate accusations of secret cooperation, despite Sweden's professed neutrality policy, on defence and intelligence matters with NATO, the United States, Norway, Denmark and Britain (Weller 2000, pp. 177–8). Such cooperation was found to be close and frequent even to the point of having plans in place for an exchange of liaison officers to each foreign sister agency in the event of the crisis. Especially close contacts were noted as regards signals intelligence with Norway and Denmark. But, significantly, the commission arrived at the benign conclusion that cooperation meant that Sweden was privy to information that it might not otherwise have the resources to gain.

It is worth noting a parallel in the Swedish and Irish rationales for cooperation with neighbouring military intelligence agencies. Until the mid-1990s secrecy hung over G2–MI5 collaboration throughout the Emergency. The extent of liaison, which included MI5's training of Irish officers, and de Valera's abiding imprimatur of it, points to an official view that isolating neutrality from regionalised strategic concerns was impractical if not unacceptably dangerous. Civilian primacy in Anglo-Irish intelligence exchanges throughout the Troubles immunised Irish officials and officers from a controversy like that which gripped Sweden. But the convention whereby C3/CSB, rather than G2, provided the operational link with British agencies owed little to the delicacies of Irish neutrality. Rather, G2's embroilment in a plot to smuggle arms into Northern Ireland in 1970 fatally undermined the agency's prospects of once more playing a first order role in security relations with the British (Author's sources).[6] Since 2000, with a settlement in Northern Ireland in place and with questions of neutrality sidestepped under the framework of the Petersberg Tasks, Irish military personnel are formally engaged in processes of international intelligence assessments through participation in the EU's military structures.

The Danish national security intelligence service is the Politiets Efterretningstjeneste (PET). Denmark's Forsvarets Efterretningstjeneste (FE) (also commonly referred to in English as the Danish Defence Intelligence Service or DDIS) is both the country's foreign intelligence and military intelligence service. PET is part of the Danish police and, in terms of organisation, is a department of the National Police (Department G). However, due to the special nature of its assignments PET reports directly to the Danish minister of justice.

PET's range of responsibilities is set out in the Danish Penal Code Chapter 12 (Offences against the Independence and Safety of the State) and Chapter 13 (Offences against the Constitution and the Supreme Authorities of the State) but, in summary, the service's objectives are defined similarly to those of CSB. In terms of regionalisation it is headquartered in Copenhagen but has personnel based in Aarhus. It has contact persons in all police districts. Its range of personnel is broader than that of CSB, being made up of police officers, legal, academic, communications and administrative staff, translators and technicians.

Like CSB, PET efforts to counter terrorism are based on a criminal justice approach. PET regards intelligence cooperation with the services of other states to be of high importance. One noteworthy difference between CSB on the one hand and PET and SÄPO on the other is in their styles of interaction with the public. The Danish and Swedish agencies maintain web sites detailing such information as mission, responsibilities, personnel duties, chain of command, control and oversight and so forth. In the UK, MI5 and MI6 do likewise. The Cabinet Office regularly updates the *National Intelligence Machinery Booklet* which sets out, at length, UK security and intelligence institutional architecture, background information on senior managers and so on. It also maintains a web site, which is dedicated to explaining online the UK intelligence machinery.[7] The Garda web site, when devised some time between 1999 and 2001, was an altogether tamer affair detailing little or nothing about CSB responsibilities, strategies or tactics. In part this may reflect the absence of clearly defined institutional boundaries between CSB and the rest of the force, boundaries which are quite well established in respect of the Danish and Swedish security services.[8]

Denmark's FE is based at Kastellet in Copenhagen. Its remit extends to the collection, analysis and dissemination of intelligence of political, financial, scientific and military interest. It includes among its concerns international terrorism and extremism, international arms trafficking and the proliferation of weapons of mass destruction.[9] Like G2, the FE provides to government military intelligence about deployments overseas. But when referring to closed-source foreign intelligence FE distinguishes between its collection of HUMINT and intelligence collected through cooperation with other intelligence services. Clearly this suggests the capability to gather intelligence independently of what other states are willing to share, something which the Irish services do not have the capacity to do.[10]

To summarise, cooperation is a key priority for Irish, Swedish and Danish agencies but there are important differences between Irish arrangements and those operating within the Scandinavian states. These include (1) the clearly developed regionalisation of the Swedish internal security service, SÄPO (2) the availability to Swedish policy makers of SIGINT from FRA, and (3) the capacity of the Danish FE to collect as well as process foreign intelligence concerning homeland threats.

Security responses to previous crises

The next task is to briefly outline Irish security and intelligence responses to two previous crises, the Emergency of 1939–45 and the Northern Ireland crisis since 1969. The value of doing so is to ascertain whether experience and performance in these crises has had any bearing on the State's response post-9/11. This should make for a more informed context for the study as a whole. The analysis of the Emergency considers issues of Anglo-Irish intelligence cooperation, legislative measures to counter subversion and public support for the security authorities. Five issues are considered in the context of the Troubles. These are: the use of law against subversion; secondly, what the Troubles meant for the Defence Forces' on-island operational posture; thirdly, consequences of C3/CSB centralisation in Dublin; fourthly, attempts to secure the border; and finally, the extent to which espionage troubled the State's authorities.

At a policy level perhaps the most crucial determinant of the Irish security response to the arrival of war in Europe in 1939 was de Valera's pledge that the Irish government would not permit its territory to be used as a base of attack against Britain, but that Ireland would remain neutral so long as partition remained. British analysts rightly saw this as the Irish government setting the ground for benign cooperation between the two states while denying die-hard republicans fuel to ignite a civil war with potential strategic benefits for Germany (Fisk 1983; O' Halpin 1999, p. 151). In terms of intelligence the Irish priorities were twofold: disrupt the IRA and thwart, in particular, any German–IRA alliance aimed at harming either the State or British interests to a point that could endanger the State. In delivering on these priorities G2 personnel engaged in cooperation with their British counterparts which was remarkably close (O' Halpin 1999, 2000a, 2000b, 2003, 2008).

In 1939 C3, as the State's lead security agency, was reorganised and an eight-man squad ordered to conduct counter-espionage operations in coordination with Army intelligence (Brady 2000, pp. 233–4). However, the government, and more particularly de Valera, determined that a new defence security intelligence section should be established within G2, which would be part-answerable to de Valera's Department of External Affairs. This represented, according to one scholar, 'a dramatic shift in the balance of power' between C3 and G2.

> This expansion of the counter-espionage brief it had been given in 1938 turned G2 into a ubiquitous security organisation. While the Special Branch retained its primacy as the State's front line against the republican movement

– it was Garda officers who made the arrests, and it was Garda officers who died at the hands of IRA gunmen – a combination of government decisions and incidental developments ensured that through G2 the Army became the dominant influence on every aspect of security policy with any bearing on external relations. (O' Halpin 1999, pp. 203–4)

The new counter-espionage service had to be built up from scratch, a task which in its execution reflected the interest calculations of officials in Dublin and London: MI5 staff briefed the G2 officer in charge of the new service in methods of enquiry and investigation and the British supplied (and thus, were probably able to intercept the information from) Ireland's postal interception and telephone-tapping equipment (Meehan 2000; O' Halpin 1995, p. 104; 2003, pp. 22, 27).

The service was indefatigable when conducting surveillance on figures of interest, including leading members of the Dáil. Its officers confronted and readily dispensed with US clandestine activities (O' Halpin 1999, p. 239). Axis covert operations proved more difficult to disrupt but most Nazi or Nazi-inspired agents were rapidly picked up (pp. 239–45). A notable G2 innovation was the establishment by one of its officers of a secret unit, the Supplementary Intelligence Service (SIS), made up of hardened republicans who would not take an oath to the Free State but were willing to surreptitiously work with it. SIS information would subsequently lead to the uncovering of an IRA agent working as a detective for Garda intelligence (p. 166).

By the quality of their cooperation G2 kept MI5 convinced throughout the war that, on balance, Irish neutrality was of strategic benefit to the Allied cause. This realisation, which ran counter to the stubborn and truculently expressed suspicions of Churchill and US diplomatic figures in Dublin, was achieved despite G2 personnel adhering at all times to 'strict political control' and thus, as MI5 chiefs would later acknowledge, cooperating only to the extent that it suited Irish policy (O' Halpin 2003, p. 23; 2008, pp. 247–99).

While espionage and joint Anglo-Irish efforts to counter it were paramount in Irish security policy during the Emergency, they were not the only features of the State's response worth noting for the purposes of this study. C3 prosecuted a vigorous and bloody campaign against the IRA. In no small part the agency benefited from the Garda's productive relationship with the RUC and the Irish government's introduction of tough anti-subversion laws (O' Halpin 2003, pp. 24, 201–3). This twin track of cross-border cooperation and draconian legislation has a contemporary feel to it. But by present standards the legal provisions introduced during the Emergency were harsh. The State assumed the power to intern suspects and to dispense justice through military tribunals in which those sentenced to death were denied recourse to the regular courts. 'The lives of those brought before this court were thus placed entirely in the hands of military men unfamiliar with the law and quite untrained in judicial process' (O' Halpin 1999, p. 202). It was under this regime that six IRA men were executed between 1940 and 1943. One of the men, George Plant, when brought before a civilian court was acquitted of murdering an informer but convicted when brought before the military tribunal.

Largely in reprisal for what was befalling their volunteers under the new regime, IRA commanders stepped up a campaign of targeting gardaí and twelve died although, ultimately, C3's intelligence network coupled with the grim determination of its members and officers won out (Brady 2000, p. 234). An indication of the network's effectiveness came relatively early in the Emergency, in December 1939, with the IRA's spectacular robbery from the magazine fort at the Phoenix Park, Dublin, of almost all of the Army's small arms ammunition. Although it appears that Garda officers ignored a fairly obscure G2 warning of IRA activity prior to the theft, within a year the force recovered more ammunition than was stolen during it (Brady 2000, pp. 234–5; O' Halpin 1999, p. 205).

A final feature of policy to note is that relations between the broader community and uniformed members of the force stayed generally warm (Brady 2000, p. 237). Moreover, Irish society, in the main, appeared to tolerate if not approve of the various laws introduced in response to IRA violence despite the constraints these measures placed on fundamental civil rights (O' Halpin 1999, p. 203). In response to the magazine fort raid, the government charged Garda management with the establishment of a Local Security Force (LSF) to act as a police auxiliary force in each division of the country. The new organisation attracted some 25,000 volunteers (Brady 2000, pp. 232–3). Public forbearance lasted the duration of the Emergency by which time the combined efforts of C3 and G2 had extinguished the IRA threat for another decade.

The discussion now turns to how the State handled the crisis that began in 1969. Five issues are considered: firstly, the use of law against subversion; secondly, what the Troubles meant for the Defence Forces' on-island operational posture; thirdly, the implications of C3/CSB centralisation in Dublin; fourthly, the success or otherwise of attempts to secure the border; and finally, the extent with which the authorities were concerned by espionage within the State.

Apart, perhaps, from a brief period prior to the 1970 Arms Crisis, during which five people, including two government ministers – Charles J. Haughey and Neil Blaney – faced charges, later dropped, relating to the importation of weapons for the IRA, the Irish government broadly maintained the policy towards IRA activities which de Valera had adopted from 1936 onwards (O' Halpin 1999, p. 324). As before, tough legislation was to the forefront of the response at government level. For example in 1972 the Fianna Fáil government passed the Offences Against the State (Amendment Act) which provided for the conviction of anyone considered by a Garda chief superintendent to be a member of a proscribed organisation. The Special Criminal Court was reintroduced the same year, albeit with civilian judges. A proposal for internment, briefly considered, was quietly dropped (Dunne and Kerrigan 1984, pp. 74–5).

Operationally, because the conflict was mostly played out within the borders of Northern Ireland, the primary task of policy implementation for the Irish security forces was to close off republican supply lines (Author's interviews). Operationally this translated into duties such as the uncovering of arms dumps, watching safe houses, suspects and sympathisers and preventing easy access to cash through bank raids and extortion. A continuous watch was kept on the border for terrorists about to launch or escaping from an attack (Author's sources).

The part that G2 officers played in the importation of weaponry at the beginning of the Troubles, whether sanctioned by government or otherwise, was a source of lingering embarrassment to the Defence Forces (Author's interviews). It was a cause of distrust between G2 and C3 and ensured no repeat of the favour which government, and especially de Valera, had shown to military intelligence during the Emergency (Author's sources; O' Halpin 1999). Army officers were sent across the border into Northern Ireland on intelligence-gathering missions in 1969 (1999, p. 306). But from 1970 to the end of the Troubles the military authorities played down whatever role G2 played in domestic intelligence gathering. The usual response of Defence Forces spokesmen to media queries consisted of an insistence that within the State the job of tackling terrorism was first and foremost that of the Garda. Irish military intelligence was overwhelmingly about assessing the risk to Defence Forces personnel prior to or during deployment overseas. In contrast the Defence Organisation appeared to have little difficulty after 9/11 admitting that G2 was engaged in surveillance of Islamic radicals within the State (Brady 2004b, 2005b).

The violence of the Troubles particularised the aid to the civil power roles to which the Defence Forces strictly adhered in its domestic operations in the wake of the arms trial. Border deployment in support of the police was a significant drain on military resources, prompting the government to sanction an expansion in the size of the Defence Forces in the mid-1970s (O' Halpin 1999, pp. 339–40). When not at the border soldiers endured the boredom of cash escort duty, driving in jeeps from bank to bank to protect money deliveries and the gardaí watching over them. Air Corps pilots flew reconnaissance missions in support of Garda operations against subversives and major criminals. This continued to be one of the Air Corps' main tasks until the Garda established its own air support unit in 1997.[11]

Considerable inefficiencies were apparent in how the Defence Forces played out its aid to the civil power role. But successive governments, while content to have the Defence Forces operating as an armed police force in reserve, showed little interest in the detail of how they did it. For example, if the captain of a Naval Service ship suspected a vessel in his area of operations was smuggling arms or other illegal material he had to firstly await Garda permission to interdict. Lacking the power of arrest, he then had to sail his ship to shore to collect a garda, charge back out again, locate where the suspect craft had gone and, on finding it, launch a boarding party including the arresting garda who might have no experience of traversing Ireland's stormy waters in a small rigid inflatable boat (Author's interview). Only when the government passed the Criminal Justice Act 1996, some eighteen years after the Troubles began, were Naval Service officers empowered to act independently of the Garda in operations at sea.

Primacy they may have had over G2 in the 1970s but C3's detectives were ill-prepared to face a rapidly worsening conflict. There were two problems here, one to do with insufficient financial resources and the other with C3's centralisation at Garda Headquarters in Dublin. C3 was short of staff to process a steep rise in the number of intelligence files which were opened from 1972 onwards. In 1970 C3 opened 55 new intelligence files, in 1971 that number had risen to 89. In 1972 it was 1,595 and in 1973 it was 1,575. Yet the number of staff members allocated to the validation, analysis, assessment and distribution of intelligence in these files was kept to fourteen: one chief superintendent, one superintendent, one detective inspector, two detective sergeants and nine detective gardaí. Of the nine, two (and often three) were full-time typists (Finlay cited in Commission of Investigation 2007, p. 72). Mr Justice Finlay concluded that as a consequence of such inadequate staffing, a fundamental factor in efficient Garda intelligence, namely 'the filing, indexing and co-relation of information obtained' fell 'below the adequate and proper standard' (Finlay cited in Commission of Investigation 2007, pp. 70–1).

However, by 1974 there was alarm in the upper echelons of the force at the 'mere trickle' of information that was being fed to C3 from gardaí around the country (Commissioner, Crime Branch cited in Commission of Investigation 2007, p. 70). This exposed a notable frailty of C3's centralisation; its great dependence on the willingness and ability of members around the country to contribute intelligence. In their attempt to solve the problem by urging ordinary gardaí to file far more reports, top management helped boost the quantity of information at some expense of quality. Garda members began to fill them out in numbers. According to one senior officer some gardaí saw, in rallying to the commissioners' call, an opportunity to further their own promotional prospects: 'C.77s were like speeding tickets, a numbers game' (Author's interview). The system was reformed in the mid-1990s, so that each report had to carry the validation of the member's superintendent, and again in the wake of the Donegal controversy.[12]

C3's difficulties in these years may have been alleviated somewhat had the Special Detective Unit (SDU), the unit for operational duties, been adequately resourced. Mr Justice Finlay in his review of State security found the number of SDU detectives assigned to the surveillance of inquiry into subversive activities to be 'insufficient for the maintenance of a sufficiently good flow of intelligence' (Finlay cited in Commission of Investigation 2007, p. 71).

Despite these problems Garda seizures of weapons and arrests of republican extremists were ongoing. For example, some 29,000 rounds of ammunition, about 60lbs of gunpowder and seventeen rifles were uncovered at Dublin Port in July 1973 (Boyne 2006, pp. 108–9). There are two points to note here: firstly, for all its problems the Garda intelligence system still worked and delivered high-grade information; that it did and would continue to do so for the remainder of the Troubles was testimony to the dedication and bravery of many gardaí. Secondly, the force had by 1973 begun to develop what would become ongoing cooperation with the agencies of other states. The Dublin Port seizure was achieved through Irish detectives working closely with counterparts from the

Royal Canadian Mounted Police (p. 109). Over time the Garda would develop links with numerous other forces and agencies although, as the Eksund affair would show, cooperation did not always pay off as hoped.[13]

To the British authorities it was apparent from the early 1970s that because the border was impossible to seal off cooperation with the Garda was necessary to maintain reasonable security along it (Tonge 1998, p. 89; UK Ministry of Defence 2006, Chapter 3, p. 14; Chapter 4, p. 11; Chapter 5, p. 413). The RUC Chief Constable instigated closer relations with the Garda commissioner in 1974, the first such initiative in ten years (Ryder 2000, p. 132). Individual gardaí worked hard to maintain relations with their counterparts in Northern Ireland for good reason; the RUC was the State's main provider of intelligence on subversives resident in Northern Ireland, particularly loyalist subversives (Commission of Investigation 2007, p. 104).

Such routine contacts and cooperation at operational levels have continued to the present day and have overcome such potential crises as the conviction of a sergeant in C3 for passing secret documents to a British intelligence officer in 1972 and the revelation, in 1991, that a Limerick-based detective was a long-term agent for the Provisional IRA. But of more significance is the formal platform for security cooperation enshrined in the Anglo-Irish Agreement in 1985. The accord committed the Irish authorities to preventing, as far as possible, the use of the Republic's territory for attacks on Northern Ireland. Effectively, the Anglo-Irish security sphere took on, if it had not had it already, a special status in the priorities of the Garda. Notably in this period came indications of close Garda–MI5 cooperation (O'Halpin 1999, p. 334).

Closer Garda–RUC cooperation contrasted with the prohibition placed on contacts between Irish military personnel and their British counterparts in the North. The ban on fraternisation led to the farcical situation whereby the British Army was authorised to return fire at terrorists across the border, but its officers could not coordinate directly with Defence Forces units patrolling perhaps a few hundred feet away to the south. Instead British troops had to request the RUC to contact the Garda whose personnel would relay information to the Irish Army. With that said, officers of both armies had occasional informal conversations in the field (Jackson 2007, p. 112). In 2006 an official British review of Operation Banner, the military operation in Northern Ireland, concluded that 'joint Irish-British military operations along the Border … might have done much to deny PIRA its safe havens in the republic' (UK Ministry of Defence 2006, Chapter 3, p. 7).

It is worth considering, finally, another aspect of Garda security activity during the Troubles, which was driven by concerns that groups loyal to the Soviet Union were plotting to overthrow the Irish government and establish a revolutionary communist state. The Garda focused wide on the Irish left. It was the received wisdom among officers that Marxist activists linked to the Official IRA were, with dangerous purposes in mind, infiltrating key institutions. A senior CSB officer, in an interview for this study, referred specifically to the State broadcaster, RTÉ, where, he said, young broadcasters and producers in the 1970s and 1980s had been 'sucked in' and indoctrinated by a Dublin-based academic with extremist views. He continued:

> There was a sizable radical left wing. One side would be the bomb and the bullet. Equally lethal was the idea of infiltrating key organisations to over-throw the State – infiltrating the radio, television, the banks and, at the same time, lending their expertise to the Marxist-Leninist cause.
>
> People only think in terms of the bomb and bullet. You could bring down this country – and the Officials would have without the split in '69 – without a bomb or a bullet. (Author's interview)

Whether those holding influential positions in the Irish media and banking sectors wanted to or could have instigated revolution is not of concern here. Of interest is the serious consideration which the authorities gave to the threat that they were perceived to pose, that of disciples of an alien doctrine conspiring to overthrow the State.

Conclusion

The objective of this chapter has been to aid clarity by providing an overview of the Irish national security apparatus in its contemporary and recent histori-cal forms, but also a summary of arrangements in other states, most notably Sweden and Denmark. The Irish model is one of civilian responsibility for op-erational agencies; the Departments of Justice and Defence, respectively, are charged with administering, overseeing and supporting the work of the Garda and the Defence Forces. The Department of the Taoiseach, through its own offices but also by its chairmanship of the National Security Committee, acts to underpin inter-departmental and departmental-agency coordination on secu-rity matters.

A key characteristic of the National Security Committee is its civilian members' reliance on their frontline agency colleagues for all operational infor-mation and analysis coming before them. The civilians play the role of consum-ers but with no inclination to shop around for the perspectives on which the committee bases its recommendations to the government. The significance of this dynamic warrants the enquiry to which it is subjected in later chapters. So too is merited further examination of policy managers' sensitivities to Anglo-Irish security concerns and, perhaps more importantly, the suggestion that threat assessments to the National Security Committee are invariably benign.

When compared to the security and intelligence apparatuses of Nordic states the most striking features of the Irish case are the absence of a foreign and related SIGINT intelligence capability and the centralisation, in Dublin, of CSB. It is the official view that international agency cooperation provides a counterweight to the capability gap. In this regard during the Troubles the State pursued on-island terrorism with robust laws while its principal security agency, the Garda, assiduously developed relations with the agencies of other states to garner information. Like their Swedish counterparts the Irish authorities have displayed a pragmatic approach to the balancing of their claims to neutrality with their strategic need for intelligence. Moreover, deeper Irish participation in Europe's developing foreign and security structures provides a means through which Defence Forces intelligence personnel can enjoy a licence for intelligence collaboration comparable to that of the Garda counterparts, while Ireland retains her neutrality cloak.

However, Irish commitments to international cooperation do not necessarily imply a flawless or even desirable Irish intelligence apparatus. Here questions relating to the degree of benefactor reliance come into play, such as what biases it implies, how reliable is its flow, and so on. Hence, what the absence of a foreign intelligence entity means for Irish policy must be a matter to which this study applies scrutiny. So too must that of CSB centralisation. It proved problematic in the early years of the Troubles, with the absence and then the deluge of C.77 intelligence reports. What advantages does centralisation retain when, since the period of economic prosperity that began in the mid-1990s, the contours of the Irish demographic landscape have shifted? Is the apparatus tuned to the challenges of gathering intelligence in sprawling commuter towns or from within the migrant communities resident throughout the country?

In the next chapter, which is a literature review, the task of analysing these and other matters begins. Evaluating the scholarship of Irish security will help situate this study in relation to other work. It will, moreover, provide points of context for the analysis of empirical evidence in the subsequent chapters.

Notes

1   The legal and procedural underpinnings of Irish national security are treated at some length in Chapter 4. The main statutory instruments are the Defence Act 1954, the Garda Síochána Acts 1924, 2005; the Police Forces (Amalgamation) Act 1925.

2   Separate cross-departmental structures were put in place post-9/11 to deal with reactive security, i.e. emergency planning. These are dealt with at length in the course of Chapter 5, although it is worth re-emphasising that the main focus of this book is on proactive security, or attack prevention.

3   The title An Garda Síochána (The Guardians of the Peace) can be shortened to the Garda (pron. gar-dah). Members (plural) of the Garda are termed gardaí, e.g. three gardaí ran down the road (pron. gar-dee). Different rules apply in the singular, e.g. Garda Jane Smith ran down the road (capitalisation), or 'A garda ran down the road' (no capitalisation). The force is also referred to in English as the Guards.

4   On the eve of Britain's declaration of war in September 1939, Taoiseach Eamon de Valera introduced legislation to amend Article 28 of the Irish Constitution, allowing the Dáil to declare a state of emergency even though the State remained neutral. Thus, as Fisk puts it, the Emergency came into existence, 'a legally accurate but nonetheless euphemistic description for what, north of the border, was about to become the Second World War' (Fisk 1983, p. 101).

5   Staff members in the south unit cover the counties of Kronoberg, Kalmar, Blekinge and Skåne. The west unit covers the counties of Halland and Västra Götaland. The lower central unit encompasses the counties of Jönköping, Södermanland, Östergötland, Värmland and Örebro. Upper central unit watches over the counties of Uppsala, Gotland, Västmanland,

Dalarna, Stockholm and Gävleborg. Finally the north unit's area of operations comprises the counties of Västermorrland, Jämtland, Västerbotten and Norbotten.

6   It was alleged unsuccessfully that cabinet ministers, a G2 officer and a hard-line republican conspired with a Belgian businessman in the plot.

7   www.intelligence.gov.uk.

8   Issues of control and oversight of the agencies are treated further in Chapter 4.

9   In the latter regard FE claimed, prior to the US-led invasion of Iraq, that Saddam Hussein possessed WMD, an error that led ultimately to the resignation in April 2004 of Svend Aage Jensby, the defence minister of the Danish government which backed the invasion a year earlier.

10   The extent of Irish reliance on the agencies of other states is discussed at more length in Chapter 5.

11   The unit's aircraft based and maintained at Casement Aerodrome, the Air Corps HQ, are flown by Air Corps pilots with Garda observers. Tensions between the services that apparently resulted from the Garda's operational needs being at variance with the Air Corps' knowledge of the aircrafts' technical limitations took some years to smooth over (Author's interviews).

12   Among other misdeeds certain gardaí working in Donegal in the 1990s invented IRA arms finds and informers to engineer promotion and framed a prominent publican, leading to his imprisonment. A subsequent tribunal of inquiry identified serious and systematic problems of indiscipline and chaotic management throughout the force.

13   For a useful account of how the IRA managed to import into Ireland four shipments of weaponry prior to the Eksund seizure, see Moloney 2002, pp. 4–33. Boyne 2006 provides an exhaustive study of the covert arms trail to Ireland.

3

Political and financial pressures on national security

The previous chapter summarised the Irish national security apparatus, considered the State's responses to threats during the Emergency and during the Troubles and drew some comparisons between Ireland's frontline agencies and those of other states. Attention focuses now on the literature of Irish national security policy. This review will be divided into three sections to reflect what appear to be central empirical concerns of the authors. These are firstly, political pressure on the Garda Síochána; secondly, financial pressure on the Defence Forces; and thirdly, Anglo-Irish considerations in Irish national security policy. The objective is to situate the study in the constellation of Irish security scholarship and, in this vein, to show where existing work departs from and/or provides a context for this study's main arguments.

Political pressure on the Garda Síochána

The most influential literature on the Garda finds that government ministers can, and do, interfere with the operational duties of the force, especially at moments of perceived political crisis. This provides a supportive context to investigate the re-evaluation of Irish national security policy in an atmosphere of heightened political pressure. With that said, the literature on the force is sparse.

The first Free State government decided that the Garda should come under centralised political control rather than any localised system because the latter would prove easier for Anti-Treaty IRA elements to infiltrate (Brady 2000; Walsh 1998). This arrangement made the force answerable to cabinet via the minister for justice. The argument that cabinet control does not translate into interference in the Garda's operational affairs is a dividing line between studies of the force. McNiffe (1997), a former Garda inspector, states that the Garda commissioner has 'absolute authority in the internal management of the force' (p. 147). If so, then Garda management, in complete charge of their force, would have operated in isolation from political pressure. Walsh (1998), however, acknowledges 'the convention of operational autonomy' (p. 117). But, in contrast to McNiffe, finds that political interference occurs and is politically necessary for government (p. 119). He focuses on the Garda Síochána Act 1924 and Police Forces Amalgamation Act 1925 which, until 2005, provided the force's statutory underpinning. The acts vested in politically appointed ministers three key powers. These were (1) power over the appointment and dismissal of officers of the force (i.e. superintendent upwards); (2) power over force expenditure; and (3) power over the dispersal of the force. Most of these powers are preserved – and some strengthened – in the Garda Síochána Act 2005, which replaces the Garda Síochána Act 1924 and the Police Forces Amalgamation Act 1925. The 2005 Act is not treated in any of the relevant literature but is considered in Chapter 4.

Walsh argues that the minister for justice will use these powers to encroach upon the commissioner's operational autonomy from time to time as political need dictates.

> This may not accord neatly with the legal or constitutional theory governing the respective roles of the commissioner on the one hand and the government and the minister for justice on the other; but it must be an inevitable fact of life in a jurisdiction with a national police force. (p. 119)

He finds that the government's allocation of resources to the Garda amounts to an implicit statement by cabinet as to the actions that the force should take.

> The reality is that government does, and must, concern itself with the operational aspects of policing. The very fact that it must provide the force with the necessary legal, administrative and material resources to discharge its policing function implies that the government must have views, however broad, on the content of operational policies and priorities. These views will be reflected in the sort of resources that it makes available and in those that it withholds. (Walsh 1998, p. 115)

In the final analysis, government must interfere in the force because it is the government party(ies) and not the Garda which the Dáil holds to account for policing and security failures.

> The government must also be concerned with how the resources are applied. Ultimately, it will have to answer to the Dáil, and the electorate, for the manner in which the country is policed. Protestations to the effect that the force has been endowed with more resources than is necessary to provide an efficient police service will be to no avail if large parts of the country are experiencing an exponential rise in burglaries, vandalism and petty crime because, for example, Garda management has diverted too many resources away from beat patrol to road traffic control or the surveillance of subversive suspects. In such a situation, it is to the government, and not the Garda management, that the Dáil and the electorate will look for their pound of flesh. (p. 115)

Moreover, as noted above, pursuant to the Anglo-Irish Agreement, the State is under an obligation to do what it can to protect the interests of the nationalist minority in Northern Ireland and promote peace and security on the island as a whole (p. 119). Because the State does not have a security or intelligence service distinct from the Garda or the Defence Forces, 'it must follow that the government will lean heavily on the Garda in the discharge of its security responsibilities arising out of the Anglo-Irish Agreement and the situation in Northern Ireland' (p. 119).

Walsh (1998, pp. 115–19) finds that the government directed, not requested, the commissioner to comply with particular matters during a three-year period in the late 1980s. The commissioner was purposefully denied all discretion. The minister for justice of the day effectively usurped the role of the chief executive of the force. Indeed, at moments of perceived crisis the minister was the de facto chief executive, receiving daily and nightly briefings and issuing decisions (p. 118).

Other writers, mostly media commentators, are in broad agreement with Walsh that political interference occurs (Dunne and Kerrigan 1984; Joyce and Murtagh 1983; Mullan 2000; Ryder 2000). Most of these seek to address some well-known cases where drawbacks from political meddling have become especially apparent (unlike Walsh, whose examples refer to cases where no impropriety is purported (1998, p. 117). Careers of gardaí have been undermined on the word of parliamentarians disgruntled at the handling of operational matters (Joyce and Murtagh 1983). Garda leaders have conspired in political attempts to thwart the media, eavesdrop on members of the Oireachtas and suppress anti-government protest (Dunne and Kerrigan 1984; Joyce and Murtagh 1983). Members of the force have used brutal methods on suspects, apparently on the tacit urgings of government (Dunne and Kerrigan 1984). Garda management has been compromised by the perception of rank being a function of political allegiance over merit (O' Halpin 1999, p. 328).

Financial pressure on the Defence Forces

Prominent works on the Irish military emphasise that government-imposed financial 'starvation' has caused severe problems for the Defence Forces (Farrell 1997, 2001; Fisk 1983; O' Halpin 1996, 1999; Regan 1999). Several explanations are advanced as to why this 'starvation' occurred (Fisk 1983; O' Halpin 1999; Lee 1989; O' Regan 1999; Ward 1994). But scholars have also acknowledged that the Defence Forces can look forward to a more secure financial future with Irish engagement in NATO's Partnership for Peace and the European Security and Defence Policy (Horgan 1999; Ishizuka 1999; O' Halpin 1999). The point here is that the literature on the Defence Forces provides a backdrop for the study to explore an important line of enquiry. This is that senior military officers, when advising government after the 9/11 attack, did so as renewed doubt fell over the promise of financial stability for their organisation. A finding from them to the effect that Ireland faced a severe national security threat might well have worked against the blueprint for a greater overseas operational commitment which was intended to, at last, secure Army finances at realistic levels. Their advice to government was intelligence-led. But a consequence of years of financial starvation was a deeply flawed intelligence structure, out of which emerged analysis on which that advice was based.

The role and influence of the Department of Finance is a prominent issue in the scholarship on Irish national security and Irish governance generally (Fanning 1978; Farrell 1997, 2001; O' Halpin 1999; Regan 1999, pp. 138–9, 146–7, 162, 212, 215; Ward 1994). The department enforces government policy through a framework of legal and procedural arrangements. The Ministers and Secretaries Act 1924 is an important part of this framework. This act provides for the Department of Finance to grant prior approval to all public expenditure – including, of course, expenditure on national security (Fanning 1978; Farrell 1997, 2001; Ward 1994, pp. 114, 200, 217).

Farrell (1997; 2001) and O' Halpin (1999) criticise the Department of Finance's influence over national defence policy and, by extension, national security policy. The Army's 'dismal fate [in the State's first decade] was directly tied' to the rise of the Department of Finance (Farrell 1997, p. 112). The defence cuts ordered at Finance's behest were both 'excessive' and 'unreasonable'.

> Every single item of army expenditure, right down to telephone lines and spare parts for machine guns, required prior approval from the Department of Finance ... (which was) content to starve the army of resources. (Farrell 1997, pp. 112–13)

O' Halpin argues that since the State's foundation Finance has inflicted on the Defence Forces a form of 'control by starvation' (1999, p. 352; 1996, p. 411). Historically, it has not seemed to matter which political party is in power for it to occur.

> The army suffered under Fianna Fáil just as it had done under Cosgrave, deprived of men, equipment, and weapons, its only obvious practical role an internal security one, its warnings about the need for both the policy and the means to defend the state unheeded. (O' Halpin 1999, p. 149)

He suggests that Department of Finance officials have been allowed to weaken national defence even at crisis moments for State security. For example, with the Second World War looming, the government took the 'ominous if predictable' step of giving Finance a central adjudicating role over national defence preparations (1999, p. 161). The result was a 'mobilisation fiasco', in which the department engineered that the Army be reduced in size after hostilities commenced. Only later when Taoiseach Eamon de Valera ordered a call to arms – the prospect of British and German invasions of Ireland staring him in the face – did Finance's hold over matters weaken (1999, p. 164). Subsequent support from Finance officials for the national defence effort was reluctant if not begrudging. While G2 played a key role in counter-espionage, more generally the Defence

Forces suffered vast capabilities gaps to the end of the war (O' Halpin 1996, pp. 418–20; 2003). Indeed, as Fisk notes (1983, p. 160), 'so denuded of weapons' was it that maintaining neutrality was the only viable defensive option.

So, scholars' explanations as to why starvation has been allowed to occur relate mainly to political and economic pressures flowing downwards from government to the Defence Forces. Combined, they help to explain why the defence aspects of national security have failed to attract sufficient political and/ or official interest in curbing Finance's cuts. The explanations are as follows:

a) governments remained of the view that the Defence Forces must remain insignificant for the sake of stability of the State and Anglo-Irish relations;

b) a traditionally weak Irish economy could not sustain increased defence expenditure;

c) the character of the State's political system was such that defence was not an issue high on the political agenda;

d) governments made a politically and economically convenient assumption of friendly foreign assistance in the event of crisis.

As regards (a) – an insignificant military for the sake of the State's stability – the leading figures of the Free State government were, 'acutely aware of the perils of militarism, and of the need to keep soldiers firmly under the thumb of civil government' (O' Halpin 1999, p. 351). A large army might pose a danger to internal political and financial stability (O' Halpin 1999, pp. 84, 266). Government wariness in this regard appeared justified with a brief officer mutiny at the Curragh in 1924 (Lee 1989, pp. 96–105; O' Halpin 1999, pp. 45–51; Regan 1999, pp. 182–97). It was also accepted wisdom in government circles that a military force of significant size could be perceived as threatening British interests on the island of Ireland. Article 8 of the 1921 treaty set the Army's size at the same troop-to-population ratio as that applied to Britain's home-based forces (O' Halpin 1996, p. 411). Evidence from the author's interviews bears this argument out to some degree, with military commanders acknowledging 'divided loyalties' among personnel, particularly in the border region, during the Troubles (Author's interviews). Indeed, O' Halpin (1999) notes that in the mid–1930s, in the early years of the Emergency and, 'most dramatically', in 1969–70, 'cliques within the army or political circles broke the taboo against even contemplating the use of military force to gain control of all or part of Northern Ireland' (p. 352).

Evidence for explanation (b) – the inability of the Irish economy to support anything but a token defence – is also to be found in the early days of the State (Farrell 1997; O' Halpin 1996, 1999; Regan 1999). Massive expansion of the Army during the Civil War had placed a great burden on the public finances (Farrell 1997, p. 111). In 1924 the number of serving army personnel stood at 55,000 and the military budget at £11 million (pp. 111, 112). Government considered this in the context of the other burdens on the fledgling State (Regan 1999, p. 172). Moreover, ministers perceived the Army to be incompetent, inefficient and corrupt and ordered cuts accordingly (pp. 172–3). However, it seems that a move that began as a round of cuts to achieve defence reform became an enshrined practice in the management of the weak Irish economy (O' Halpin 1996, 1999). As the century wore on, defence budgets went instead to pay for public services of a more politically sensitive kind, such as health and education, which the State could barely afford to maintain. Government ensured that Irish defence policy over seventy-five years was the 'most convenient, malleable, and inexpensive of doctrines' (1999, p. 353).

It is worth noting that Farrell places considerable blame for what happened to the Army in the early State on the naivety of its most senior commanders, the general staff (Farrell 1997, 2001). He suggests that because military leaders failed to match their requirements to the government's economic and political 'realities', the Defence Forces suffered. This is an interesting backdrop against which to examine to what degree meeting such realities influenced the re-evaluation of policy, post 9/11. Farrell claims that in the 1920s and 1930s the general staff nurtured various ambitious plans to develop a fully equipped, conventional force, although there was insufficient financial support for it and it lacked strategic sense (1997, 2001). The generals floated these plans to unsympathetic 'civilian policy makers obsessed with controlling governmental expenditure' (2001, p. 67). He argues that the general staff, in the years prior to the Second World War, could have achieved more in their debates with Finance officials had they re-embraced War of Independence-style unconventional warfare. G2 and Finance officials supported this, arguably, more financially realistic guerrilla option (p. 69). By adopting it the Army would have been playing to their strengths and secured resources. But the general staff refused, leaving the organisation bereft of any workable organisational blueprint when the cutbacks began.

Regarding explanation (c) – the character of the State's political system – O' Halpin cites 'the strength of Irish democracy' to explain the 'emaciated and grievously underequipped defence establishment' (1996, p. 407). By this he suggests that Irish parliamentarians concerned themselves more directly with issues affecting voters 'on the ground' such as health and education provision. Defence was not a matter that was likely to swing the democratically expressed will of the people at election time. Other works focus more directly on political behaviour in Ireland's electoral system of proportional representation by single transferable vote (PRSTV) to multi-seat constituencies. For the Irish parliamentarian survival in a multi-seat constituency means first and foremost the practice of 'messenger boy' politics (Lee 1989, p. 84; Ward 1994). Laws and procedures that centre policy power in cabinet, yet leave ministers vulnerable to the same constituency pressures as backbench TDs and senators, amplify the effect (Ward 1994). Matters of great voter sensitivity like local employment or crime are central concerns of the messenger politician. On 'bread and butter' issues – not on national security – is the popular vote fought for and won in Ireland. National defence has not been able to gain significant political purchase in a sustained way. In interviews for this book military officers said it was because defence was a 'contingency' issue or something that did not affect the Irish public on a day-to-day basis.[1] Instead, the State maintains a military force for unforeseen eventualities and for esoteric diplomatic reasons like Ireland's place on the international stage (Author's interviews). Where defence and, more particularly, the Defence Forces have become the focus of political interest, it has typically been to do with keeping open budget-draining, militarily redundant barracks in marginal constituencies (O' Halpin 1999). But, in the main, the Defence Forces have consistently come off worse to demands for the parish pump in the highly politicised opportunity-cost calculations of government and opposition (O' Halpin 1999).

The final reason (d) offered for financial starvation is the claim of successive Irish governments that should any serious threat to defence of the island arise, Britain and, subsequently, the other members of the North Atlantic Treaty Organisation (NATO) will come to Ireland's aid (O' Halpin 1999, p. 350). The absolution this grants, in terms of investing in indigenous defence, is obvious. Only in the 1940s, when the protector looked like turning predator, was that assumption shaken to the point that serious independent action was undertaken (Fisk 1983; O' Halpin 1999).

In these circumstances – loath to send wrong signals into Anglo-Irish relations, averse to the cost of conventional defence, faced with competing constituency demands and resolute in their claim about other states coming to Ireland's rescue – successive governments have remained impassive to Finance's cuts. Consequently, there has been an absence of political momentum to prevent cuts continuing. But what of the role of the Department of Defence when it comes to insulating defence budgets from cutbacks and promoting substantive defence policy? Could the department most directly concerned with defence have done more to protect the interests of the Defence Forces?

Once again, the trail of evidence begins with decisions and actions taken during the State's early years (Farrell 1997, 2001; O' Halpin 1999). The first government had the daunting task of cementing civilian rule over the military, which meant demobbing thousands of unruly, poorly trained soldiers with rifle barrels barely cooled after fighting the Civil War. To achieve that objective the government made two major institutional decisions the outcomes of which remain largely intact to the present day. Firstly, and also as part of a wider bid to bring order to expenditure across the entire gamut of public policy, the Department of Finance was given power of prior approval over all public expenditure (Farrell 1997, p. 114). Secondly, control over all Army policy was vested in the Department of Defence (p. 115). This meant that

> Civil servants in the Department of Defence were able to offer their version of army proposals to the minister, and that was the only version he would see. It also gave defence officials remarkably broad powers, considering that almost all army policy proposals could be said to have had financial implications. (Farrell 1997, p. 116)

O' Halpin (1999) argues that the Defence Forces were badly damaged in this arrangement. His central allegation is that despite having a minister at cabinet, the Department of Defence has failed to generate significant defence policy which could have constrained the continuous defence cuts. Instead, the department has complied entirely with traditional government reluctance to get involved in major defence expenditure for the four reasons discussed earlier. Consequently, the Defence Forces have remained marginal to the concerns of government:

> While the presence in cabinet of the minister for defence suggested a key input at the appropriate policy level to ensure proper representation of the professional military view, it appears that few ministers for defence have had any substantive role in policy discussions relating to defence. Instead, they have been the political heads of an essentially executive agency required only to do the government's bidding, not to advise the government on what to do. Given the lack of a supporting policy focus within the department, that is perhaps not too surprising. (O' Halpin 1999, p. 344)

O' Halpin notes also how in the peacekeeping realm, officials at Defence have left their counterparts at the Department of Foreign Affairs to run a monopoly over policy decisions with a direct bearing on the deployments, and so on the lives, of military personnel.

> Its extraordinary diffidence on substantive policy contrasts not only with the role of comparable ministries in other European states, but with that of the Department of Justice ... which has emphatically denied to cede responsibility for policy to Foreign Affairs. (O' Halpin 2002, pp. 52–4).

A serving officer wrote that the Department of Defence's role was 'difficult to accept in either a national or international context' (Cudmore 2003, p. 55). He argued that Ireland held the unique distinction of being a state where the defence department would not undertake any direct responsibility for national security and, instead, focused on providing only a supportive role to various other departments (p. 55). The Department of Defence published a White Paper on defence in February 2000, but this failed to fill the vacuum for political or ideological principles for defence and by extension the defence aspects of national security (p. 56). The White Paper could have tackled the paucity of vision and blunted aspirations for military policymaking since 1924 (O' Halpin 1999). Instead, it provided 'a medium term policy framework from which defence policy can evolve to set a clear strategy for the next ten years' (Ireland, Department of Defence 2000, p. 91). In other words, it fudged.

Cudmore suggests that nothing has changed since 9/11. The only positive development for policy coherence he sees is the establishment of the Office of Emergency Planning (OEP), formed after 9/11 and, significantly, the State's only joint civilian-military office (Cudmore 2003). But the OEP may yet prove a mere talking shop with responsibility for reactive national security 'spread too wide amongst different government departments to allow adequate cohesion and accountability' (p. 58). The historical evidence is not encouraging in this regard. O' Riordan (1992) argues that Irish governments have rarely seen the value to themselves of emergency planning, despite the predictability of major emergencies and the rewards of advance preparation. Instead, they have left it to officials at the Department of Finance to take the short-term cost-based view.

> The most important of the factors that will determine the future of emergency planning in Ireland is the level of government commitment to the process. At present it would appear that this commitment is sadly lacking and the state of the public finances may be used as a reason for the postponement of any new initiative. However, the person who must eventually explain to a disaster tribunal why no ministerial attention or significant resources were made available for the emergency planning process over many years may very much regret such a decision. (O' Riordan 1992, p. 78)

What has the literature has to say in relation to the stability accruing to the Defence Forces from Irish engagements overseas? Scholars examine this in the context of various UN missions, as well as NATO's Partnership for Peace (PfP) and European Security and Defence Policy (ESDP).

Several authors suggest that periods of rejuvenation for the Army have coincided with government decisions to deploy Irish troops on overseas peace support missions following international pressure on Ireland (Horgan 1999; Ishizuka 1999; O' Halpin 1996, 1999). For example, according to Horgan, the Army's deployment in the Congo in 1960 'saw a major re-equipment of the Irish defence forces ...' (1999, p. 140).

Nevertheless, scholars emphasise that increases in expenditure have been relative to the financial starvation that has preceded them and have come only in response to obvious shortcomings in equipment or training. Until the late 1990s the State avoided spending on expensive military hardware and training to support overseas missions. Ireland's overseas profile flattered a 'bare-minimum' policy of defence investment (Murphy 2002; O' Halpin 1999). On this the Irish government went unchallenged by the UN whose civilian officials continuously demonstrated a lack of understanding of issues of equipment and training for lightly armed troops on the ground (O' Neill and Rees 2005, p. 60).

Consequences arose from the neglect, both in terms of the practical deployment of troops in numbers and the safety of individual soldiers serving in theatre. Stocks of equipment were so poor that those soldiers travelling to Lebanon in 1958, as part of the Irish contribution to the United Nations Observer Group in Lebanon (UNOGIL), were provided with duffle coats belonging to the Naval Service. Outfitters Millets of Capel Street, Dublin came up with 'something resembling a lightweight uniform' and the Fórsa Cosanta Áitiuil (FCA), the forerunner to the Army Reserve, provided a 'combat blouse pattern' bulls-wool uniform (Heaslip 2007, p. 88). Equipment shortcomings contributed to tragedy. In the Congo, at Niemba in November 1960, Irish troops, massacred by Baluba fighters armed with bows and arrows, had no signals equipment with which to radio their platoon headquarters for help (O' Neill and Rees 2005, pp. 60,

68–9).

The inclusion of 120mm heavy mortars in the arsenal of Irish troops serving in Cyprus (UNIFCYP) suggested that lessons were been learned in terms of the capacity to mount a serious military response (p. 99). But back in Lebanon the Irish contingent to the United Nations Force in Lebanon (UNIFIL) lacked the strength and heavy equipment to effectively carry out the tasks assigned to it (Murphy 2007, p. 187). An exceptional moment occurred at the village of At-Tiri in 1980 when Irish troops stood firm and successfully defended their positions in the face of hostile fire from the Israeli-sponsored *de facto* forces. The battle led to diplomatic action of consequence to the Defence Forces. The Security Council passed Resolution 467 (1980) which supported the tactical use of force by peacekeepers. It 'was the first occasion on which the Security Council found it necessary to make direct reference to the force's right to self defence' (Murphy 2007, p. 180).

The international prioritisation of the right of peacekeepers to defend their safety pointed in the direction of equipping soldiers to do so. The issue would become more clearly defined with the formulation of a new generation of post-Cold War peace enforcement strategies which required capabilities for robust military engagements (McDonald 1998; Moxon-Browne 1998; Murphy 2007). In Ireland the prospect of such encounters involving members of the Defence Forces was given legal form in the Defence (Amendment) Act 1993 (Murphy 2002).[2] The act and the UN resolution that preceded it, coupled with Irish engagement in the emerging architecture of EU security and defence, has given momentum for modest albeit continuing government investment in the Army since 2000 (Horgan 1999; Ishizuka 1999; Ireland, Department of Defence 2000). As we shall see later, the effects on Army strategy of having, for the first time, a more compelling institutional framework for investment have been considerable.

The financial benefits to the organisation aside, other advantages have arisen for the Defence Forces from international service. Most importantly it has provided 'an ideal training ground for an army of Ireland's size and resources' (Murphy 2002, p. 27). It has 'always been viewed as a welcome respite from the day to day barrack routine at home. It also boosted morale … has increased the wages and salaries of serving personnel by way of overseas allowances … (and) created a better public image of the army (pp. 27–8).

It 'remains a professional lifeline, providing variety, travel, extra money, familiarity with other armies, and some danger' (O' Halpin 1999, p. 343). Consequently, the stakes were high when Ireland's proposed membership of the NATO-led Partnership for Peace was subject to domestic debate in the late 1990s. Ishizuka laid out the costs for the Army of a decision to stay outside:

> In effect, the army has two options: to become an entirely home-based defence force acting in support of the Garda Síochána, or to find a new mission abroad … It can be concluded that, in terms of the military aspects, Ireland's participation in the PfP would manifestly contribute to the enhancement of the Irish defence forces in many areas: correction of defects in the defence

structure, improvement of equipment and officers' skills in decision-making and general leadership, and a training system more compatible with other European partners. (Ishizuka 1999, p. 194)

A former chief of staff, Lieutenant General Gerry McMahon, described as 'a low point which must never be allowed happen again', the curtailment of overseas missions during the particularly bloody years of the Troubles between 1974 and 1978 (O' Halpin 1999, p. 343). This remark provides an interesting insight into the Defence Forces' management preference for international rather than national security commitments. Serving Army interviewees concurred with Lt. Gen. McMahon's view (Author's interviews). Later on, primary source evidence will suggest that the generals 'got political' in this regard during the frosty rationalisation negotiations of 1999–2000. They tailored their bargaining positions to growing internationalised political pressures on the government for Irish participation in higher-tempo peace enforcement missions and deeper integration in EU foreign policy structures. They had moved on from their forebears' dreams of a major conventional home defence army. Instead, they signed up to a 'light infantry' force and negotiated to maximise its capabilities; for a modest (but steady) spend, met initially through the sale of superfluous barracks, the Army would be equipped and trained to satisfy demands for Irish participation in more dangerous operations overseas. Now, as O' Halpin notes, the Petersberg Tasks are the main drivers of Irish defence policy and planning and the Defence Forces are being re-equipped, re-trained and re-oriented accordingly (O' Halpin 2002, p. 55).

Tonra (2000) argues that deepening Irish involvement in international security through EU Common and Foreign and Security Policy is putting Ireland's traditional military neutrality under pressure. But a vociferous Irish NGO lobby 'remains a significant challenge' to Ireland's deeper participation in EU foreign and security policy (2000, p. 282; 2002, p. 35). This lobby finds scholarly expression in the works of Maguire (2002), who argues that EU 'militarisation' is anathematic to Irish neutrality, and McSweeney who proclaims the 'neutrality question' a 'moral obligation on each of us, which cannot be left to politicians and civil servants to answer' (McSweeney 1985, p. 179). If the lobby is that significant, it follows that it is also a challenge to what is increasingly meant to be the main generator of financial stability for the Defence Forces.

Anglo-Irish considerations in Irish national security policy

The literature points at two factors which appear particularly relevant to analysis of operational measures taken since 9/11. The first, already treated to some degree in the earlier discussion, is that over time Anglo-Irish cooperation on intelligence, policing, immigration and law has steadily improved. The second is that successive generations of Irish national security policy managers have sought to severely discourage immigration into Ireland. Strategic factors that have underlined cooperation and immigration control have included the threat of republican irredentism and the Common Travel Area between Ireland and the UK. There is no major point of departure between what this book claims and the findings of other literature in the field. What scholars say in relation to cross-border security will inform the critique of the agencies' capacities to respond internationally. Their conclusions around immigration will provide a context for evaluating how Irish policy since 9/11 meets the potential problem of terrorist cells emerging within the State's new immigrant communities.

The literature suggests that republican irredentism and threats to Britain associated with the Common Travel Area have, historically, been the primary strategic concerns of Irish security policy managers (Dunne and Kerrigan 1984; Meehan 2000; O' Halpin 1999). As already noted, the State's preference to tackle republican violence has been through a mix of legislation and British–Irish policing and intelligence cooperation. On legislation, the literature informs us, Irish governments began taking statutory measures against extremist republicans as far back as 1922, beginning with the Public Safety Act of that year (O' Halpin 1999, p. 27). The measures included internment without trial and trial by military court (Fisk 1983; Lyons 1973; O' Halpin 1999, pp. 27, 43, 79). By way of responding to the Omagh bombing of 1998, the Irish government again introduced severe statutory measures, passing the Offences Against the State (Amendment) Act 1998 (Mooney and O' Toole 2003). The act curbs the right to silence, thus the failure of an accused person to answer questions may constitute evidence against him or her of membership of an illegal organisation. It also makes provision for the confiscation of houses or land where weapons or explosives are found (Coulter 2000).[3] Civil liberties have been a casualty of the crisis laws, with 'the repeated and unashamed bypassing of constitutional safeguards in the name of public security' (O' Halpin 1999, p. 81).

On the criticality of cooperation between the Irish and British intelligence and policing agencies, O' Halpin's works capture the extent of intelligence-sharing between G2 and MI5 during the Emergency. In contemporary times CSB, as the lead 'on-island' intelligence agency, has operated jointly with MI5 and the US Federal Bureau of Investigation (FBI) against the 'dissident' republican group, the Real IRA (Mooney and O' Toole 2003).

As for policing cooperation, it had become routine by the end of the IRA's border campaign, as O' Halpin notes:

> The RUC and British police forces needed access to Garda intelligence, and the Irish government was plainly dependent on Britain and other friendly countries for information about arms smuggling and other republican activities outside Ireland, because it had no significant capacity itself to gather intelligence abroad. Similarly, the Irish authorities had little information on loyalist paramilitaries, who from time to time carried out cross-border bombings, and had no choice but to rely on the RUC for information. (O' Halpin 1999, p. 330)

Police force cooperation deepened after the Sunningdale Agreement of 1973 but cooled in 1979 amid anger in the ranks of the Fianna Fáil government at the apparent sanctioning of British Army 'hot pursuit' flights over Irish territory (p. 331). It is alleged that in this period British security services colluded with loyalist paramilitary groups conducting attacks in the Republic and Northern Ireland (Donohue 2006b). The 'Dowra affair' caused a lengthy rift between the Garda and the Royal Ulster Constabulary (RUC) which saw no contact between the then Garda commissioner and RUC Chief Constable for three years (Ryder 2000, p. 370). But scholars recognise the significant improvements in force relations following the signing of the Anglo-Irish Agreement in 1985 and the passing of the Extradition (Amendment) Act 1987 (Mooney and O' Toole 2003, pp. 293–8, 304–5; Meehan 2000, p. 69; Mullan 2000, pp. 133, 139–41, 145, 154, 159; O' Brien 1999, p. 205).

All of this is useful in terms of evaluating the State's capacity to counteract terrorism from a cross-border perspective. But scholars also note the reluctance of Irish security policy managers to unduly provoke traditional anti-British republican sentiment. This has at times constrained, or at least coloured, policy. For example, the most extreme laws intended to deter those tempted to take up arms to force a united Ireland were frequently relaxed (O' Halpin 1999, p. 351). Similarly, a key reason for the decision to stay neutral during the Second World War was simmering popular anger at the British 'occupation' of Northern Ireland. Fisk argues that the Irish government feared that an alliance with the British military could spill over into a civil war (1983, p. 415). As Murphy points out,

> Irredentist sentiment, devoid of any real understanding of the Northern Ireland situation, was ardent and universal in the Southern state in the strongly nationalist atmosphere of the 1930s. There would have been opposition to participation in 'England's wars' in any case but public opinion would certainly not countenance such involvement 'as long as England unjustly occupied our six counties' to paraphrase popular sentiment. (Murphy 2000, p. 12)

After the war the government used neutrality as a bargaining chip to further other interests such as membership of the EEC (Bhreathnach 2002, p. 249; Keogh 2000; O' Sullivan 1994, pp. 169, 204). But neutrality was maintained, although made peculiar by Irish membership of the UN and EEC. Successive cabinets feared the domestic backlash a military alliance involving the Defence Forces and British armed forces would trigger. As Keatinge (1984) notes, neutrality held its place alongside 'reunification and the restoration of the Irish language in a triptych of traditional populist symbols' (p. 108). Its potency in domestic debate had directly influenced security policy.

Immigration control is an important area because since 9/11 Irish policy managers have emphasised the risk of terrorist cells emerging from within the State's new migrant community. However immigration control has been treated as a matter of great importance to Irish national security since the foundation of the State (Meehan 2000, p. 11; O' Halpin 1999, pp. 76–7, 81, 131–2, 203, 292–7, 337).

It was seen to create problems for Irish and British security alike. Anyone landing in Ireland from a foreign country could 'make their way unsupervised into the United Kingdom' via the Common Travel Area (O' Halpin 1999, p. 75). It appears some pressure from the British side resulted in the Free State enforcing a highly restrictive British-compiled passport 'blacklist' (pp. 76–7). However, as Meehan argues, the Common Travel Area was not a leftover of imperialism but something that stood to Ireland and the UK's mutual advantage. It helped to facilitate, for example, the UK's insatiable appetite for Irish labour. Tourism agencies on both sides of the border lobbied to have removed certain restraints placed on freedom of movement during the Second World War and, in practice, a liberal approach was taken (Meehan 2000, p. 26; O' Halpin 2008, p. 260). British and Irish officials realised both the dangers of open access within the outer perimeter of the islands' borders and the impracticalities of securing the long, straggling border between Northern Ireland (Meehan 2000, pp. 11–12). It was felt that the better policy would be to allow free movement underpinned by close co-operation between British and Irish security and policing agencies. In this regard, it was largely accepted that 'undesirables' landing in Ireland would travel to the UK (2000, p. 27). Dubious measures were taken in the name of preventing impediments to open access. At Shannon Airport it was the norm to deny those seeking asylum any access to legal advice; instead they were pushed back on to the aircraft from which they had alighted (O' Halpin 1999, p. 296).

However, the concern to prevent Ireland's use as a back door for an attack on the UK has not been the sole arbiter of Irish government thinking on immigration policy, according to scholars. Goldstone (2000) argues that Social Darwinism and theories of 'less desirable' immigrants were prevalent among Irish political and official elites in the early decades of the State (p. 118). Goldstone, O' Halpin (1999) and Wylie (2000) agree that Jews were viewed with particular unease, subjected to a working assumption that they would not, or could not, assimilate and so would fan the fires of racial disharmony. Frequently, this was cloaked in pious servitude to Roman Catholic beliefs (O' Halpin 1999, pp. 132–3).

Goldstone (2000) emphasises that the desire among officials to restrict Jewish immigration in the pre-war years was not unique, but also a familiar theme in British, Canadian, South African and US administrations (p. 117). However, she ascribes to Irish officialdom in the 1930s, 'covert anti-Semitism [that] was far more common, particularly among Irish civil servants, that [sic] has been accepted' (p. 119). O' Halpin claims that the view of Jews in national security circles was rarely short of conspiratorial if not fantastic and fixated on tales of greed and wealth (1999, pp. 294–6). Wylie notes that hostility towards Jews remained prevalent but hushed up after the Second World War (2000, p. 140). Strikingly, however, even the credentials of a shared Christian heritage were not enough to overcome Irish bias. Such were the poor conditions of lodgings offered to (Roman Catholic) refugees of the Hungarian uprising of 1956 that many chose to leave the country, even returning home (p. 295). O' Halpin (1999), pointing to the record of the authorities, was sceptical about the Refugee Act

1996. It was billed at the time of its enactment as 'groundbreaking'. But, to O' Halpin, it remained to be seen, 'whether this new-found liberalism will continue or whether government will pander to public unease by shutting the gates once more' (p. 337).

Conclusion

The most influential literature on the Garda finds that government ministers can, and do, 'lean heavily' on it, especially at moments of perceived political crisis. The minister for justice will even assume the role of de facto chief executive, directing operations. Equally, military scholars argue that the Defence Forces has come under severe financial pressure for most of its existence, even at moments of serious uncertainty over the security of the State. Matters in this regard were set to improve two years prior to 9/11 with Irish accession to NATO's PfP and a deepening military commitment to EU Common Foreign and Security Policy (CFSP). But the attack sparked an evaluation that relied for its defence inputs on the intelligence apparatus of a still-starved military and, conceivably, by its outcome could have seen the Defence Forces ordered to steer a course away from the promised financial stability of foreign operations. These constitute important contextual considerations for the analysis to come.

Over time Anglo-Irish cooperation on intelligence, policing, immigration and law has steadily improved. The Anglo-Irish Agreement of 1985 and the Extradition Act 1987 have provided a framework for stable mutual assistance. It is important to remember what led security co-operation to continue despite difficult and bitter episodes. Perhaps the greatest single factor was preservation of the Common Travel Area through which goods and unemployment flowed in the interests of both states. Moreover, neither state could deny the case for shared intelligence against enemies who waged most of their war within Northern Ireland but saw no legitimacy in a twenty-six county state. The Irish and British governments' shared history of and response to threat is an important baseline on which to consider the capacity of the Irish agencies to act transnationally in the pursuit of terrorism; this will be developed in Chapter 5.

The desire to preserve the Common Travel Area helped place immigration at the core of Irish security policy. Scholars have also revealed how at times Irish policy managers have used the national security imperative to mask unsavoury notions about immigrants. Official thinking was replete with sanctimonious devotion to a strain of Catholicism, by which other races and creeds were simply intolerable lest they blemish the perfection of Irish society. As for the role of politicians in mediating their officials, most acquiesced to what went on and, indeed, some stood as its loudest cheerleaders (O' Halpin 1999, pp. 223, 294).

The evidence about immigration will help to analyse how Irish policy since 9/11 meets the potential problem of terrorist cells emerging within the State's new communities. Among the issues to be explored will be whether the Irish immigration regime encourages, or discourages, disaffection towards the State;

whether it encourages or discourages racism; and how it conditions Ireland's reputation abroad.

This chapter has sought to provide various contextual points of reference by deriving key themes from the existing literature. These can be found in the conclusions which scholars have derived from the political control of the Garda, the financial woes of the Defence Forces, Anglo-Irish security dynamics and the Irish authorities' approaches, official and otherwise, to immigration. Chapter 4 will examine how the agencies' ways of dealing with financial and political pressures on them may have affected, or may perhaps affect, security policy after 9/11. This analysis will be done using a model of historical institutionalism.

Notes

1   The concept and practice of contingency planning is dealt with further in Chapter 6.
2   The Act is discussed further in Chapter 4.
3   The act permits detention for questioning to be extended to three days which is significant in an Irish context but must also be seen in comparison with British anti-terrorism law, which, by means of the Terrorism Act 2006, provides for pre-trial detention of twenty-eight days.

4

9/11: a critical juncture?

Introduction

This study contends that when the Irish security and intelligence agencies were ordered to re-evaluate national security policy after 9/11 they did so in an atmosphere of heightened financial and political pressures on their organisations. Serious policy weaknesses occurred. Furthermore, several problems of policy persist. In Chapter 3, the findings of leading scholars suggested that Irish policy managers in the frontline agencies were subject to continuous financial and political pressures. This was so even at moments of perceived crisis for the security of the State. The major consideration here is whether the ways that the agencies have learned to deal with these pressures contribute to policy weaknesses after 9/11.

Historical institutionalism is used to pursue this line of enquiry. The specifics of historical institutionalism were discussed in Chapter 1. But, to summarise, it is associated with the identification of path dependencies and critical junctures. New or re-evaluated policy is rarely detached from long-standing policy making traditions and outlooks. Path dependencies are about organisational reliance on familiar routines and practices of appropriate behaviour. Self-reinforcing or positive feedback processes in the political system bolster path dependencies. Often these paths will reinforce or defend the actors' positions in the face of threats. But established paths are shot through with power relationships that privilege some interests and ignore others (Bulmer and Burch 1998; Hall and Taylor 1996; March and Olsen 1996; Pierson and Skocpol 2003).

Some institutions are highly formal, such as constitutional laws. Others are less formal, like organisational codes and guidelines that build up over time, often in order to avoid unfavourable outcomes (e.g. financial cutbacks) (Hall and Taylor 1996, p. 938). However, policymaking is not always about the pursuit of reliable routes. Historical institutionalism can also account for occasional moments of significant transformation, known as critical junctures, where behaviour moves to a new trajectory or pathway (Bulmer and Burch 1998, p. 605). But scholars using the approach emphasise that positive feedback mechanisms reinforce the recurrence of a predominant pattern. Hence, the policy process is frequently characterised by a powerful inertial 'stickiness' (Pierson and Skocpol 2003, pp. 701–2).

A common route used by scholars adopting the historical institutional approach is to examine policy as an outcome of the formal structures under which policy managers operate, the procedures they follow and the routines, norms and conventions embedded in their organisational structure (Hall and Taylor 1996, p. 938). In this vein, Bulmer and Burch use 1) formal institutional structure, defined in terms of constitutional–legal rules, formal organisations, and positions; 2) processes and procedures, which facilitate the day-to-day functioning of the institutions and govern the networks of relations which spread out from them; 3) codes and guidelines, which set out conventions for handling business; and 4) the cultural dimension, which relates to the norms, values and identities that are constructed systematically around individual institutions and within organisations. Employing Bulmer and Burch's configuration (1998), this chapter will work to the following plan: firstly, as regards formal structures it will consider the statutory frameworks underpinning the Garda and Defence Forces. In Chapter 3, we saw from Walsh (1998) that the two acts governing the Garda provided for political control over the force. Consequently, it was necessary for government to intervene in the Garda, even in operational matters. This prompts the question, how might this interference – and the Garda's long-standing ways of dealing with it – have impacted on policy re-evaluation after 9/11? Furthermore, the Garda's statutory framework was revised in 2005. So what, if any, were the implications arising for security policy? In relation to the Defence Forces, the first section will deal in particular with the Defence (Amendment) Act 1993. Murphy (2003) argues that the passing of this act was a highly significant moment for the organisation because it provided for Irish military participation in overseas peace support missions of a higher tempo than before. It was followed by a difficult period of restructuring and cutbacks during which the Defence Forces were remodelled for the more demanding roles now set out in law. This greater commitment of Ireland's small Defence Forces to international security begs a further question: had their intelligence pointed to the need to so do, was there sufficient capacity, even willingness, among the organisational management to also deliver a major commitment to national security? What, therefore, has the 1993 act meant for national security policy since 9/11?

The section dealing with processes and procedures needs to address two important matters. Firstly, if the agencies re-evaluated policy in an atmosphere of heightened political and financial pressures, did these or other pressures weaken the vital process of gathering and analysing intelligence to inform the outcome of the re-evaluation? Are the structures such that they could cause analytical shortcomings in the future? Secondly, it is noticeable that the appointments process within the Defence Forces limits access to the top management structure to Army officers.[1] Has this arrangement ensured that the military inputs to national security policy have reflected joint, 'tri-service' perspectives (i.e. Naval Service, Army, Air Corps)? What, if any, are the effects of this arrangement on the distribution of financial and/or political pressures?

The analysis then moves to consider codes and guidelines. Here, it seeks to identify links between the policy choices facing agency managers and their budget constraints and obligations to government. The objective is to consider to what degree their established ways of dealing with these limitations have affected the re-evaluation of national security policy after 9/11. Was the re-evaluation of policy also about 'balancing the realities' between operational, political and financial needs, and, if so, what were the compromises made? What scope exists for such balancing to impact on future policy management?

Finally we turn to culture: in the years since 9/11 much has been made of the need to radically improve the Garda's culture of management and discipline (Dáil Debates, 2006b, pp. 13–18). Shortcomings in these regards matter because of the risk to the credibility of Garda evidence in terrorist trials and to public cooperation with counter-terrorism efforts (Tribunal of Inquiry 2004, 2005, 2006a, 2006b, 2006c). This study needs to assess if the remedies taken are sufficient to contain doubts over the integrity of the Garda and the system of control that the force works within. It does so with reference to similar problems which have occurred in Sweden and Denmark. In relation to the Defence Forces, other scholars have pointed out that the financial starvation of the organisation has been ongoing and severe. This chapter explores whether this has served to bring about a culture of organisational threat within the Defence Forces. If so, what are the implications of this culture for the re-evaluation of national security policy?

Formal institutional structure: An Garda Síochána

The most influential literature on the Garda finds that government ministers must interfere with the operational duties of the force especially at moments of perceived political crisis (Brady 2000; Dunne and Kerrigan 1984; Joyce and Murtagh 1983; Mullan 2000; Ryder 2000; and Walsh 1998). This lends credence to the proposition that pressure was exerted on the Garda during the re-evaluation of policy post-9/11, although it says nothing about whether pressure at this time was unusually high, or caused policy weaknesses. These are matters for the remaining chapters. In this section some of the scholarly evidence supporting the claim of political interference is revisited. Doing this sets the ground for the discussion to extend to the statutory framework for the Garda, introduced in 2005, and whether this framework is problematic for national security policy.

Walsh (1998) focuses on the Garda Síochána Act 1924 and Police Forces

Amalgamation Act 1925, which together provided the statutory basis for the Garda until 2005. The acts vested in politically appointed ministers three key powers. These were firstly, power over force expenditure; secondly, power over the dispersal of the force; and thirdly, power over the appointment and dismissal of officers of the force (i.e. superintendent upwards). He demonstrates that parliamentary accountability for these powers has encouraged continuous political interference in, and pressure on, the force (1998, p. 115). Such interference may have played a positive role after 9/11, with the Fianna Fáil and Progressive Democrat (FF/PD) Government leaning on the force to take effective action against any terrorist threats in the face of the opposition and media outcry. Indeed, at another moment of perceived crisis – in the aftermath of the Omagh bombing – the same FF/PD government actively interfered by de facto directing Garda management to deploy additional gardaí to the border (pp. 85–6).

However, the statutory structure left the door open to a less beneficial outcome. Walsh finds that the Garda management appointments procedure reflected 'a strong bias in favour of government influence over the force' (p. 20). Government's power of appointment (and dismissal) extended from the highest to the lowest officer rank, and so to direct operational command level. This indicated 'a desire to subject [officers] to a test of political as well as professional acceptability' (p. 20). Hence, when it came to re-evaluating policy after 9/11, the Garda's input was left entirely to personnel whose current and future promotional and appointment prospects depended on government opinion of them. It is conceivable that in these circumstances the Garda input would reflect, however partially, what officers might think the government would want to hear, as distinct to what would actually be required from a national security perspective. Such behaviour would reflect a path dependency, the Garda's pursuit of the familiar as a safe and possibly profitable bet.

In the course of interviews for this book no member of the Garda or figure of equivalent standing and insight claimed that political pressure influenced the Garda's task of evaluating national security policy. In the absence of such evidence we can only conclude that those gardaí involved in the process of advising the government after 9/11 were led by the available intelligence and their past experience of the Troubles. But that is not to say that such were the formal and informal structures in which the force had to operate that political and/or financial pressures were not bearing down on the gardaí concerned at that time. Nor is it to say that their accommodation of these pressures did not lead to optimum advice that was both responsible and sound. Neither is it to say that such pressures could not, at some future point, come to dominate matters with calamitous consequences.

In this regard, the Garda Síochána Act 2005, which replaced the 1924 and 1925 acts, and related procedural changes modified the promotional system to allow external assessment of candidates. Significant as a move to external review was, it did not constitute a critical juncture. Final government control over appointments and dismissals was maintained. Those for whom gardaí were formulating advice were also those who would cast final approval on their career advancement. Hence, the potential remained for Garda perspectives on national security policy to reflect the career calculations of Garda officers, that is, what officers thought their overseers wished to hear. That this possibility exists adds credibility to this study's claim that there are persistent policy problems even if progress has been made.

In addition the 2005 act, among its other provisions, obliges the Garda commissioner to keep the minister for justice fully informed of matters related to the security and policing of the State, whenever required. The minister may, with the approval of Cabinet, issue to the commissioner 'written directives concerning any matter relating to the Garda Síochána' (Garda Síochána Act 2005, s.25 (1)), save where it may 'limit the independence of a member … in performing functions relating to the investigation of a specific offence or the prosecution of an offence …' (s.25 (3)). The commissioner must comply with any such directive and parliamentary scrutiny is not provided for where the directive relates to national security (s.25 (2)). While perhaps necessary in extreme circumstances, this latter power provides carte blanche for a compromised or incompetent minister to engage in corrupt political control that is damaging to national security. By removing parliamentary oversight, it appears to constrain the ability of gardaí to challenge such unreasonable, inappropriate or even dangerous commands. That the State's primary national security agents are vulnerable in this way suggests another persistent problem for national security policy: political expediency may, in the future, overcome strategic need.[2]

In summary, the Garda was vulnerable to government pressure when conducting the re-evaluation of Irish national security policy after 9/11. It was open to officers with responsibility for the review to see it as being in their best interests to tell the government what they believed it wanted to hear, as distinct to the actual situation. This not at all to suggest that they did so but that a weakness existed in the legislative framework under which they operated which could nurture such behaviour. This weakness was not adequately addressed by the Garda Síochána Act 2005 which may, through Section 25, have been exacerbated by the act.

The assistance of the historical institutional model here is notable. The Garda's statutory underpinning encouraged path-dependent behaviour among senior officers which centred on satisfying government political priorities in order to safeguard promotions and budgets. The government's bringing forward of the Garda Síochána Act 2005 was a critical moment in this regard, one which might have heralded change and lowered the stakes for senior Garda decision-makers but which, ultimately, failed to translate into a critical juncture.

Formal institutional structure: Defence Forces

Prior to 9/11, the most significant amendment to Irish law on defence came with the Defence (Amendment) Act 1993. The act was instigated by international pressure on the Irish government to permit Irish military participation in a new generation of peace support missions (Author's sources). The ending of the Cold War had seen a doctrinal shift in military affairs away from policing-style peacekeeping operations – the mainstay of the Irish military overseas – to higher-intensity peace enforcement (Moxon-Browne 1998; McDonald 1998). The passing of the act allowed for Irish military participation in United Nations Operation in Somalia II (UNOSOM II), a Chapter VII peace enforcement operation.[3] As Murphy argues,

> It marked a watershed in Irish involvement in peacekeeping activities, and a realisation that Ireland could be left behind in the changing nature of the international security environment, unless it too adapted to events. (Murphy 2003, p. 24)

But after successive decades of budgetary starvation, the Defence Forces were sorely unprepared for future missions (Farrell 1997; O' Halpin 1996, 1999). How close Ireland was to getting left behind was hammered home when a leaked report by consultants described the Defence Forces as 'badly structured, too old, poorly trained, and inappropriately equipped' (Murphy 2003, p. 24). The Price Waterhouse report had 'important implications for participation on UN operations, because deficiencies in training would also undermine operational capacity on the ground' (p. 24). The realisation that the Defence Forces were now in such a poor state as to reduce Irish influence abroad, coupled to UN pressure on the Irish Government, prompted action. The government committed itself to reorganise the Defence Forces as an 'all arms conventional force' (p. 24).

Hence, the 1993 Act was a transforming moment, a critical juncture, after which funding was ploughed back into the Defence Forces and its management set about re-designing force structure, ethos and training. The entire Defence Organisation became tied into a policy focus on the new generation of overseas mission. In other words it began to operate along a new path dependency. With that said, a bitter seven-year restructuring process ensued before the Defence Forces emerged ready for action. And when restructuring was completed it left the military establishment (approved number of personnel) at 10,500 plus and an optional 250 in training. This was significantly below what the then chief of staff, Lt. Gen. David Stapleton, had said was the bottom line figure to meet Irish military commitments overseas (Dáil Debates 1999).

Most of the funding went to the Army, because government decided that the funds accruing from sales of barracks to fund military reform in the medium term would be such that the State could not afford to also re-equip the Air Corps and Naval Service beyond their current capabilities (Ireland, Department of Defence 2000). During 2001 the investment programme to reduce the Army to a better-equipped, three-brigade, light infantry force, compatible with modern international (i.e. NATO) force structures, was underway (Author's interviews). Some optimism was apparent that modernisation and concomitant investment would continue so long as there was pressure on government to improve Irish military capabilities overseas (Author's interviews). Then came 9/11 and a government-ordered re-evaluation of national security policy against the threat to Ireland from transnational terrorism.

The order implied a fundamental dilemma for Defence Forces' management who were both party to the re-evaluation and responsible for the continued effectiveness of their organisation. A conclusion from the review that Ireland faced a significant national security threat could have forced a second change of the military's primary focus and, thus, unravelled progress that had been achieved over several years with considerable pain. The diligence of those officers who partook in the evaluation is not questioned here. But a process whereby the order to review national security placed in doubt the organisational well-being of one of the key agencies party to that review was, clearly, suboptimal on several fronts.

Firstly, heavy commitments to their national security roles had rarely proved rewarding for the Defence Forces, either financially or professionally (O' Halpin 1999). Immediately prior to 9/11 this had become a source of some discontent. In 2000 Lt. Gen. Stapleton (unsuccessfully) suggested that government should end the Defence Forces' commitment to gendarmerie-style Aid to the Civil Power (ATCP) duties (Murray 2000). These had been a staple task during the Troubles but were a major drain on resources. Cash, prisoner and commercial explosives escorts against paramilitary attack took up an estimated 30,000 personnel days in 1999, a year after the signing of the Belfast Agreement. General Stapleton said that resources could be better spent on training military personnel for Ireland's growing overseas duties demands (Murray 2000). Secondly, one arm of the organisation, having just undergone its significant programme of change, was on the cusp of realising perhaps the most financially secure phase of its history. Was it now, a year later, to turn away from the militarily relevant international security tasks that lay ahead in order to re-focus its scarce resources on policing-style national security tasks? (Author's interviews). Thirdly, at a more extreme level, when last a significant national security threat was declared (in the mid-1970s) government suspended all overseas missions (O' Halpin 1999, p. 340). In this regard, the comments of a former Chief of Staff, Lt. Gen. Gerry McMahon, are worth recalling; the suspension of overseas duties between 1974 and 1978 was 'a low point, which we can never allow to happen again' (O' Halpin 1999, p. 343). Another senior Army officer emphasised, in the course of an interview for this book, that the Defence Forces had a clear preference for international over national security taskings – especially in the context of ongoing financial pressure.

> In order to train soldiers, to keep in touch with that, we must have a broad range of international experience. In order to equip them we must purchase equipment wisely and scales of equipment will be purchased initially to meet our overseas requirements with small training holdings at home. Later on, if additional sums become available, we will be able to buy some greater holdings, which will allow home training [to] feature more significantly. I would say that continued participation in international peace support operations is critical for the Defence Forces. (Author's interview)

As it turned out the review found no major threat to national security and, thus, no reason to alter the Army from its present course. Reflecting the new order, by 2007 Special Forces soldiers of the Army Ranger Wing (ARW) were continuing to develop their skills on anti-terrorist special operations but much more emphasis was been placed on preparedness for taskings abroad. As a reporter of the Defence Forces' official magazine put it:

> Up to the end of the 1990s the main focus of the Defence Forces was Aid to the Civil Power (ATCP) and a lot of the ARW's capabilities focussed on this area, mainly assisting the Garda Síochána with anti-terrorist operations. Consequently most of their training was similar to that of foreign special police units such as GIGN in France or GSG9 in Germany. Since 2000 the focus has changed significantly ... Today's focus is more on convention-al operations and particularly in being prepared to deploy overseas. This change of focus manifests itself in the training carried out at home and in the exchange programmes with other Special Forces units, which are now more likely to be the likes of the French parachute regiment or the Dutch Royal Marines, rather than the police units mentioned earlier. (Bourke 2007)

The emphasis on overseas service had also been extended to the Army Reserve. A reorganisation plan envisaged 2,600 of the State's 12,000 reservists being offered training up to the level of full-time soldiers, in preparation for overseas service.[4] Reservists would also conduct, on a routine basis, ATCP operations. This seemed to suggest that in time, while the permanent Army concentrated on overseas missions, mostly unpaid, part-time soldiers would take their place in duties defined broadly enough to encompass everything from flood relief to anti-terrorist patrols (Defence Forces 2004b; Ireland, Department of Defence 2000a; Irish Times 2004b). The appropriateness of this in the face of a major national security threat would, surely, have been open to doubt with the concomitant implication this would have had for major Permanent Defence Forces (PDF) deployments overseas.

Processes and procedures: An Garda Síochána

This section examines the Garda's gathering and analysis of intelligence to inform the re-evaluation of policy after 9/11. It does so from the perspective of processes and procedures which facilitate the day-to-day functioning of the in-stitutions and govern the networks of relations which spread out from them. It looks at the problems/strengths, if any, that political control over the Garda con-tributes to this important work and makes two arguments. The first is based on the Garda procedures around counter-terrorism cooperation with UK Security Forces. This cooperation points favourably at the State's capacity to participate in joint operations to protect the two islands from terrorist activities. National security policy is effective in this area. Less positive is the second argument. The essential point made is that the Garda's dependency on the security and intelligence agencies of other states for intelligence is problematic for national security. This is a matter unlikely to change for cost and political reasons. But the inherent weakness in the process calls into question the validity of intelligence used to draw up the official threat assessment on which policy after 9/11 has been based. At the root of the issue is the absence of a dedicated Irish foreign intelligence entity. This is relevant to the study's claim that problems of policy persist. In most cases, security intelligence available to the State remains vulnerable to the vagaries of other states' interests.

Principally because of the Troubles in Northern Ireland, the Garda is not a newcomer to multi-agency cooperation against terrorism. In the previous chapters, scholarly evidence showed that cross-border security and policing relations between the Garda and RUC/PSNI gradually improved. The Anglo-Irish Agreement was an especially important development, providing a political framework in which cooperation would take place. The Garda also traded intelligence on republican paramilitaries and left-wing activists with counterparts in the Club of Berne, the confidential gathering of European domestic security agencies, and at other forums. In turn, the Irish were kept in the loop of intelligence-gathering across Western Europe (Author's interviews). Irish republican activities in the USA gave rise to CSB forging stronger relationships with the FBI and CIA than might otherwise have been the case (Author's interviews). All these agency relationships, honed throughout the Troubles, remain in operation. The force is party to Interpol and Europol. Through the Department of Justice it services the EU Internal Working Party on Terrorism and the 'Clearing House' mechanism for listing suspected terrorists. Via the Departments of Foreign Affairs and Justice, it receives intelligence reports from the EU's Situation Centre (SitCen). CSB also operates memorandums of understanding (and officers hold regular meetings) with various security agencies, including the agencies of Saudi Arabia and Israel, and conducts bilateral contacts with security staff at foreign embassies in Ireland. A senior garda cited bilateral contacts with the Russian Embassy as an example (Author's interviews). In all these regards it is worth noting Herman's conclusions as to the benefits of intelligence-sharing between the agencies of states. There is always more information potentially available than any agency can collect by itself. Sharing allows agencies access localised intelligence outside their areas of operation. For states that do not have a major SIGINT capability, cooperation provides the means to access it (Herman 1996, pp. 204–18).

But how did the Irish arrangements play out after 9/11? The most significant activity appears to have taken place at Anglo-Irish level. Senior Garda officers and officials of the Department of Justice suggested that for some time after the attack Anglo-Irish security dialogue focused on the need for closer cooperation in regard to the Common Travel Area (Author's interviews). Consequently, the emerging Irish policy centred, once again, on the traditional concerns of British and Irish security policy managers. This can be explained on three grounds: the Anglo-Irish Agreement had bound the State to cross-border security cooperation to promote security on the island as a whole. Secondly, the authorities in both jurisdictions were conscious, through intelligence and experience, of the ongoing threat from republican terrorists and the possibility of links to their internationalised brethren. Thirdly, to take Walsh's argument, the government was politically accountable for the Garda (Walsh 1998, p. 119). The opposition might well have inflicted political damage on the government had it not emphasised a long-recognised security weakness, on-island terrorism. In such circumstances the government was bound to support the Garda's security efforts in the Anglo-Irish sphere, especially the budgets that these efforts entailed. In the language of historical institutionalism, the Anglo-Irish sphere was a dependable path for the government and the Garda to follow.

The degree by which this mutual dependency has impacted upon institutional innovation within the Irish national security apparatus is a matter worth pausing on. Some insight comes from reaction to a suggestion, made in 2003 by minister for defence Michael Smith, that a new security and intelligence entity apart from the Garda could benefit the State. His intervention caused a stir in government, the minister's own officials decrying it as inappropriate while emphasising that any proposal for a new security agency was a matter for the Department of Justice to bring forward (Author's sources).

In this settled institutional setting, the existence of strong cross-border intelligence cooperation is continuously emphasised but a major gap in the State's intelligence apparatus – a stand-alone foreign intelligence agency – remains (Author's interviews). The absence of this competence, costly as it may be, raises uncomfortable questions over the reliability of threat assessments underlying Irish policy. There is no mechanism to act as a counter balance, or amplifier, to Garda and G2 analyses of what they receive. They have, at best, a limited capacity to bring to the table alternative or 'disruptive' intelligence. Nor is there anything to dilute their control over the dissemination of intelligence information, domestic or foreign. In this context, the comments of a senior Department of Foreign Affairs official are revealing:

> I think there is a tension always between government agencies dealing with issues of this nature. Terrorism and crime in general are seen as areas where the gardaí has a lead role. I think it's fair to say that it can be difficult at times to get information out of them. I would say that it's not only our department that has difficulty. I would say that the Department of Justice itself has difficulty ... I don't think Ireland is unique in that at all, but it's certainly something that can be improved if a decision is taken at a high level to do so. (Author's interview)

Such a foreign intelligence mechanism can take at least two forms. It can be one that collects foreign intelligence and processes it for final delivery to all relevant stakeholders. Less ambitiously, it can be one that simply better coordinates CSB and G2 intelligence-sharing. The former would address what a senior Foreign Affairs official described as 'the problem that Ireland faces and any small country faces that doesn't have an external intelligence agency – we don't have any raw intelligence at all of our own' (Author's interview). Without such first-hand information, CSB and G2 are vulnerable to recycling the group wisdom of the security collectives from which they feed, tailored perhaps by their experience of the Troubles. However, the establishment in the foreseeable future of a foreign collection agency would, undoubtedly, mark a critical juncture not least because it would contradict decades of low spending on security. Assuming, therefore, it is an unlikely prospect we must presume that CSB and G2 vulnerability to the quality of what others share will continue indefinitely. In comparison with the Irish set up, Swedish policy managers have at their disposal the HUMINT analyses of SÄPO and MUST but also SIGINT collected by Sweden's Forsvarets radioanstalt (FRA). In Denmark, state security service PET operates rather like the Garda in its heavy reliance on international cooperation. But decision-makers can compare what turns up from this cooperation with information which DDIS, the foreign intelligence service, both collects and processes.

As for the second option, that of the establishment in Ireland of an intelligence coordination entity, a senior Army officer and senior Department of Foreign Affairs official, interviewed separately, proposed a stand-alone agency that would draw into one complete source, information from a wide range of competent agencies and sources (Author's interviews). The Foreign Affairs official suggested that domestic intelligence-sharing was irregular and patchy, adding that EU security structures only partially alleviated the problem:

> To a certain extent [they do], but they can't replace a national competence. We're interested in the threat to Ireland, not the threat to the EU in general and there are differences and variances and I think there is a strong argument in favour of having some sort of agency, of that type, here … making it clear that it has a remit to draw information.
>
> We are missing the information that perhaps gets given to the gardaí through Europol or through Interpol or through some other bodies that I'm not aware of that the gardaí sit on and share information on. I'm sure there is information coming through those sorts of channels that we never see. Likewise, they may never be seeing the stuff that we produce in Brussels. As I say, we send it to Justice, but I have no idea, quite honestly, how far it goes then. (Author's interview)

The senior Army officer envisaged a statutory agency located within the Department of the Taoiseach from where it could ensure the cooperation of relevant public bodies and cultivate goodwill from others, including missionaries and NGOs:

> I think the pulling together of Foreign Affairs, Army intelligence, Garda intelligence and other areas … There are Irish people in sensitive areas all over the world, be they missionaries or NGOs or anything like that, who are extremely well informed as to what's going on … I think that we would move on to another level of security intelligence in this country and it would have fallout. It would have economic intelligence, industrial intelligence, everything that a modern state needs. (Author's interview)

In contrast, Garda interviewees stoutly defended the existing arrangements. A senior CSB officer claimed that the force's systems had worked before to counter international support for the IRA. Furthermore, he argued, the Garda's dual responsibility for law enforcement and security prohibited it from engaging in a murkier world of intelligence alliances and, thus, provided it with a freer hand to go after information:

> Our security agency is bound by the rules and regulations of the law of the land, here as in any policeman down in Mayo or Galway. We in Crime and Security don't have a special dispensation, nor do we look for it. So all our analysis, all our responses are based on Irish law and operating within the strictures of that, not in the strictures of politics … as some agencies do … So, for that reason, we're not tied into any agencies in the sense that we would speak to the Israelis, the Palestinians, the Americans.

But, he conceded that,

> We have that safeguard [but] that's not foolproof. You might rightly say we're still open to the influence of others. (Author's interview)

Senior G2 officers were in qualified agreement that Irish reliance on the agencies of other states for intelligence was a problem. G2 is heavily dependent on the largesse of other EU intelligence agencies for the information that comes to it. According to one officer,

> You have to remember that in the EU, there are a number of former super-powers still playing out rivalries and it would be simplistic to think they are going to share all information … (Author's interview)

However, he added that,

> If a piece of information comes up in terrorism, where it comes down to that, there is information sharing … We're not necessarily seeking all that information, only what will impact on this country, where the Defence Forces are based, or where they will be based. That's the way we try to structure it and if we make a request to somebody, we tell them it is for Ireland, and to filter it.

As to whether they would be vulnerable to 'buying into' the perspective of others, a senior G2 officer said, 'we can receive a lot of reports; we might look at them in an entirely different way to other countries' (Author's interview).

To recap, well-developed Anglo-Irish cooperation suggests that security policy is geared towards the broader protection of the two islands. On the Irish side, this cooperation reflects obligations under the Anglo-Irish Agreement, an awareness of the bloody capabilities of on-island terrorism, but also the government's reliance on successful Garda operations to offset political criticism and the Garda's dependency on the government for budgets, promotions and so forth. Ireland's reliance on the security and intelligence agencies of other states is a policy problem which could have negative consequences in the future but is unlikely to be resolved. While CSB and G2 officers claim that existing arrangements work quite well, they are, nevertheless, a compromise at the root of the intelligence system underpinning Irish security policy.

Processes and procedures: Defence Forces

This section deals with procedures governing the top command hierarchy of the Defence Forces. It will argue that the current regime around appointments to the general staff poses a significant problem for national security policy. After 9/11, military input to the policy re-evaluation was, although diligent and well-intentioned, in effect an all-Army affair and key outcomes reflected a 'land bias'. Army dominance of headquarters appointments exacerbated the problem. This situation is ongoing, despite Ireland being an island state with sovereign control over sections of some of the busiest maritime and air corridors in the world.

The Defence Forces' general staff is made up of the three most senior officers within the Defence Forces. They are the chief of staff (a three-star general) and two deputies (both two-star), one in charge of operations and the other, support. This permanent configuration omits one-star generals. Consequently, the Air Corps, which is under the command of a brigadier-general, and the Naval Service, under a commodore, are not directly represented at the top tier. In addition, Army personnel are usually appointed to fill most, if not all, the appointments at DF Headquarters. Significantly, senior officers of both 'lesser' services point to a tradition of 'land bias' within the military's decision-making. Such was the case, they said, despite the sovereign territory extending seawards to a 12- mile limit (the Irish Sector of the European Exclusive Economic Zone measures 165, 200 sq. mls. according to Department of Marine figures supplied to the author) and airspace through which transited 70 per cent of civil air traffic between the USA and Europe (Air Corps 1998). One senior Naval Service officer said,

> In the overall planning process, from a military point of view, we think in one environment. Obviously I have an organisational perspective to put forward but I think any lay person, any international commentator looking at the Irish security scene, would see that from a defence services point of view, we think in a land environment only … strategic decisions are being made with a certain sea blindness. (Author's interview)

This would suggest that the structure of the general staff facilitates a dependent path for the Army, one whereby its priorities and interests (and the interests of its officers) are dominant over those of the other services. One obvious manifestation of land bias in practice after 9/11 was the military representation on Ireland's aviation security committee formed after the attack. Rather than appoint one of its aviation specialists, the general staff appointed an Army colonel. A senior Air Corps officer offered this view:

> One of our gripes, if you like, is that there is an aviation security committee and who is on it: an army officer. So there's nobody who knows anything about [military] aviation representing Ireland Inc. on Ireland Inc.'s top aviation

security level. So okay, that is because DFHQ and the chief of staff's attitude is, 'no, I'm responsible as chief of staff for security, and I'm sending one of my own staff'. That's grand, he can do that … [But] there are people who run this committee and I often wonder do they ever scratch their heads and say, 'why don't we have an Air Corps guy here?' (Author's interview)

The configuration of the general staff means that the Army dominates military representation at government level. The chief of staff is the Taoiseach's military advisor and the chief of staff always comes from the Army. At the National Security Committee he is expected to advise on all spheres; land, sea and air. Yet, when interviewed, very senior officers of the Naval Service and Air Corps had little or no knowledge of the National Security Committee or what its functions were (Author's interviews). It is also significant, in terms of their day-to-day circulation in the centre of power, that the headquarters of the two minor services were decentralised from Dublin city centre in the 1990s. The Naval Service was most acutely affected, its headquarters transferring to the Naval Base at Haulbowline in Cork.

Worth noting too is how, in the course of the fieldwork for the study, the Naval Service was mentioned only once by non-Naval Service respondents. The sole comment came from a senior Department of Defence official, who said:

> The navy is mainly involved in fishery protection. Ninety-five per cent of its work is fishery protection. All its ships are armed with guns. There is a capability. I think that's about it. (Author's interview)

The interview constituency encompassed senior officials and officers from the Departments of the Taoiseach, Defence, Justice and Foreign Affairs, the Garda and the Defence Forces (all branches). The failure by so many senior officials and officers to mention the maritime sphere, in the context of discussing their approaches to Irish national security, appears especially strange when set against Ireland's strategic position as an island state. Indeed, the chief of staff, Lt. Gen. Jim Sreenan, in a speech to mid-ranking DF officers in May 2005 during which he paused on the challenges posed by international terrorism, made no explicit mention for naval options. He said:

> 9/11 2001 changed everything … So we need to consider very carefully what the military can contribute and what we, the Defence Forces, can bring to the table and this must be a focus for us in the development of our forces. Clearly it points us in the direction of improving our intelligence effort and our air defence, further developing our special forces (ARW) and our CBRN capability as well as looking at possible military roles in consequence management following a terrorist outrage. (Sreenan 2005)

But perhaps this is no more curious than the size of the Naval Service, which in its entirety consists of eight small ships (the largest, as of 2007, displacing 1910 tonnes fully laden), with a strength of approximately 1,000 personnel. This tiny force is tasked with maintaining control over a vast expanse of Irish and European waters, through and over which criss-cross trade shipping lanes and aviation corridors of global economic importance. To be more precise, the Naval Service area of operations encompasses the Irish Sector of the European Economic Zone (EEZ), measuring 165,200 sq. mls. (427,900 sq. km) as already noted, and the total designated Continental Shelf of 254,300 sq. mls. (658,700 sq. km).[4]

In summary, the top command structure of the Defence Forces is problematic for national security policy. So too is the tendency to have Army personnel fill most of the appointments at Defence Forces Headquarters. Even in Ireland's relatively small security apparatus some voices apparently, if unwittingly, get prioritised and others marginalised. This reflects how established path dependencies are shot through with power relationships that inevitably privilege some interests and ignore others (Pierson and Skocpol 2003). The net result appears to be decision-making that is dominated by 'land-bias'. Army dominance is based more on that service's numerical size than on Ireland's strategic positioning as an island state with responsibility for key shipping lanes and international commercial aviation corridors. In terms of what this study seeks to argue, this state of affairs does not immediately translate into a problem for national security policy. But it is difficult to see how, in these circumstances, policy can be framed to reflect Air Corps or Naval Service perspectives on transnational terrorist threats. For an island state that is remarkable.

Codes and guidelines: An Garda Síochána

The next two sections seek to identify less formal and visible codes and guidelines under which Irish agency managers operated when deciding the direction of security policy after 9/11. This section investigates the Garda management decision made in the wake of 9/11 not to make transnational terrorism a key priority for the force. The decision prompts a number of important questions. To what degree did convention(s) within the force influence matters such that the primary operational focus remained on the more familiar on-island terrorist groups (e.g. Provisional IRA, Real IRA, Continuity IRA)? How did conventions regarding the handling of financial/political pressures play out after 9/11? Could these conventions pose a problem later on? What are the implications for policy?

In the course of an interview for the study, a very senior Garda officer confirmed that transnational terrorism was not a major expenditure priority for the force. CSB was more concerned with disrupting on-island terrorist groups (e.g. Real IRA, Continuity IRA):

> We are not now into the business of spending public money to any great extent in relation to the areas now we're talking about [countering trans-national terrorism].
>
> [But] I can assure you from a Garda point of view, the gathering of intelligence on the various terrorist groups that we have on this island is pretty big and we have a hell of a lot of people engaged on that work, every single

day of the year. It's an unspoken area, for all the right reasons. You only read about it when there's a success in the area. But the amount of man hours that will go into something, to actually arrive at that success, can be enormous. (Author's interview)

Again, Garda managers made their decision by looking at the intelligence before them and considering their long years of exposure to the Troubles. Nevertheless, events coincided with a sudden and dramatic downturn in the Irish economy. The characteristics of this downturn are worth summarising with a view to the implications for what can be concluded regarding political control of the force. Ireland had experienced a remarkable turnaround in the public finances during the 'Celtic Tiger' years preceding 9/11. Exporters enjoyed massive growths in business. The information technology and biotechnology industries were thriving. Increased employment and a concomitant healthy tax-take followed on. However, 9/11 and a countrywide anti-contamination operation to contain the spread of foot-and-mouth disease earlier in the year contributed to a sharp economic reversal. By November 2001 a senior correspondent with *The Irish Times* was writing of how the 'boom-time government' was 'struggling to manage an extraordinary reversal of economic fortune, as a general election approaches' (Brennock 2001). That same month the government's book of estimates was published. It made for grim reading. Whereas in 2000 the estimate for public spending increased by 13 per cent and on Budget Day went up by 21 per cent, in 2001 cuts were made in the current expenditure budgets of many departments. Major infrastructure spending stalled amid expectations of a budget deficit and a rise in unemployment. Although spending on the Garda was increased by 4 per cent (to €917 million), the Department of Justice's budget fell by the same percentage (to €235.5 million) (Hennessy 2001). In June 2002, as the re-development of security policy continued, a secret document produced by the Office of the Minister for Finance warned ministers of 'substantial risks' to improved economic prospects. The document, entitled 'Memorandum for the Government Economic and Budgetary Strategy 2003–2005', required a 'difficult to secure reduction of €900 million in the cost of running the existing level of public services'. The memo cautioned that spending in excess of a Budget Day 2003 envelope of €1.9 billion would involve 'increases in taxation', creating 'political difficulty' and 'unavoidable adverse effects' on the economy (*Irish Times*, 2002). In December 2002 the cabinet confirmed that it would not be honouring its pre-election promise to hire 2,000 extra gardaí. The minister for justice, Michael McDowell, blamed the sudden change in economic circumstances:

> People will say it is a commitment that wasn't honoured. But we did not realise earlier this year that there was going to be a budget deficit of €1.3 billion. It's not a broken promise to people. It would have been worse if we endangered the public finances. (Dooley 2002)

The general secretary of the Association of Garda Sergeants and Inspectors (AGSI) said it was 'extremely disappointing' that cover would be reduced dramatically at a time when policing was becoming ever more challenging (Dooley 2002). The force came under pressure to prioritise the most essential activities in response to the economic situation. A senior CSB officer indicated that this caused difficulties for security and policing sections alike.

> Well, we're like all the police sections, we're struggling. We could do with much more. But what you have to do realistically when your feet are on the ground is that you have your resources and you design your response accordingly … But it's like everything else. You're stretched to the pin of your collar to make do. (Author's interview)

This all suggests that during the initial re-evaluation of policy between September 11 and approximately October 3, when critical decisions were made, the Garda was operating under heightened financial pressure. Granted, the evidence presented here only goes back as far as November 2001, or some seven weeks after the agencies' threat assessment and the decision to concentrate on emergency planning was made public. But it stretches credulity to suggest that the Irish authorities did not calculate on leaner times ahead for Ireland's export-dependent economy in the immediate aftermath of a major shock to the global civil aviation industry. The Foot and Mouth Disease outbreak had had an effect on the country's finances earlier in the year. In government, cutbacks were the order and tough choices were being made over what to prioritise and what to downplay.

So, what guided senior Garda management when deciding which objectives to pursue? It is not disputed here that intelligence and past experience were their critical guides. The 9/11 attack came only three years after dissident republicans demonstrated their killing capacity at Omagh, in August 1998. The Garda knew well the destruction and trauma that Irish terrorism was capable of causing. As a senior CSB officer said, 'don't forget that we're conditioned by the potential multiple loss of lives'. However, as Walsh suggests, government held the burden of accountability for the force and the power over its budgets, appointments and deployments (Walsh 1998). It is therefore not unreasonable to suspect that satisfying government priorities was a convention to which Garda managers had to be sensitive. Arguably, it could be a very influential one given the potential costs to senior gardaí. A key security priority for government – all-island security – had been enshrined in a binding treaty in 1985. This had meant tackling the IRA, its allies and adversaries even before the Agreement. When the Garda did this well, the opposition were denied important ground to criticise the government's stewardship of the force. That, in turn, helped safeguard the Garda's budgets, appointments and deployments. But the Garda's statutory basis raised the stakes for management if they de-prioritised a politicised imperative – operations against republican subversives – and something terrible occurred. For example, ministers could try to contain political pressure arising from the terrorist event by removing the Garda officers responsible for the decision.

How did on-island terrorism considerations play out in national security policy against transnational networks? By 2002, or relatively soon after 9/11,

Garda management adopted the view that, in the main, CSB would pick up intelligence on transnational Islamic terrorism networks in their intelligence operations against dissident republicans. A senior Garda officer involved in that decision defended the move:

> People involved in terrorist organisations, whether it be internal terrorist groups, they have a tendency to actually relate to terrorists from other jurisdictions. Even at the height of the Provisional activities, you will find that there was a connection going back to ETA in Spain. You'll find linkages, even in the procurement of munitions you will find that they are going into Eastern Europe and places like that. So they tend to find their own people in other countries, and if, for instance, there is some activity here, you will find unless it's just purely fundraising, if it's anything more other than fundraising, you will find that you will have terrorists here talking to or meeting let's say terrorists from other jurisdictions in this country. So, that's why I say you generally pick them up. (Author's interview)

Management's decision enabled the force to maintain a good grip on domestic terrorism and its potential internationalised linkages. But it amounted to a second-best option to also maintaining dedicated monitoring of transnational terrorist suspects, backed up by close sharing of information with intelligence personnel monitoring the dissidents. Costlier as this re-balancing would have been, taking the 'double-up' route amounted to a gamble that the warning signs of transnational activity would always be seen through the lens of domestic-focused operations.

By 2007, with the economy growing again and the Garda Vote at €1.445 billion (up from €1.355 billion in 2006 and from €917 million in 2002), financial pressure on the Garda was no longer such an acute issue (Ireland, Department of Justice 2006). There was some media evidence of an active Garda Middle Eastern Desk (Brady 2006b). Yet transnational terrorism continued as a matter of secondary importance. The minister's annual priorities for the force gave primary emphasis to dissident republican groups. 'Monitoring' and 'taking appropriate action against those who supported international terrorism' was only an additional concern (Ireland, Department of Justice 2006). Once again it is not disputed that intelligence and past experience led the decision. But it is also clear that Irish government concern with Northern Ireland-related terrorism is enduring.

In summary, the Garda re-evaluated security policy while the State was under heightened financial pressure in the immediate aftermath of 9/11. Garda managers were faced with difficult prioritisations. Intelligence and past operational experience led their decision-making but they had to operate in a structure whereby, as Walsh has argued, they also had to consider government's political priorities. A management decision saw CSB ordered to gather intelligence on Islamic terrorists in operations against dissident republicans. Put in conceptual terms, the statutory and political framework concerning the Garda was such that the prioritisation of violent dissident republicanism amounted to a dependable path for the force to follow, even though it was also experience-led. The question thus arises as to what would happen at some future point were these factors to diverge (rather than run in parallel, as we accept they did after 9/11). Senior Garda officers could find themselves in a very difficult, if not impossible, position. This is hardly to the good of national security.

Codes and guidelines: Defence Forces

This section will assess a remarkable code expressed among senior officers of all three services within the Defence Forces. It is that national security threats are only acknowledged at the highest levels of the Defence Organisation, when there is a realistic chance that the means will be made available to meet them. This implies that the process of deciding security policy is seriously defective. Consequently, there is a need to investigate the claims of these officers, in the context of the argument that policy after 9/11 suffers serious weaknesses. The investigation will first examine evidence to do with the effects on the Defence Forces of the economic slump that occurred in 2002. It will ask whether the acknowledgement of threats to Irish national security was affected by this downturn. It will then consider equipment procurements made since then. Did these reflect any failure to recognise stated threats? Finally, it will look at military aviation strategy going back to 1998. Is there evidence from this that the most senior military and departmental decision-makers overlooked credible warnings of threat put before them?

A senior Army officer, referring to Irish national security policy, said, 'We only recognise as much threat as we can afford' (Author's interview). A senior Air Corps officer, speaking in the same context, said:

> We don't see the threat. We don't even gear up properly to see if there is a threat out there because if we see something we might have to deal with it, and that would cost us … there has been a positive decision to do nothing in some areas … the eleventh of September actually had no real effect on what happens here. (Author's interview)

A senior Naval Service officer, said:

> It should not be a case of refusing to allow factors to be considered in the formulation process because they might be costly in financial terms. Such an approach is a classic case of situating the estimate rather than estimating the situation.

He added,

> I do understand that policies cost money. However, there is the question [of] should we be in the situation that we know as much as we can about the situation, from the highest level possible, that is not guided or directed by the fear of what something might cost, or the politics of what somebody might think? … You [should be] doing it in the national interest … not by petty politics or financial constraints. (Author's interview)

These officers, each interviewed separately, did not suggest that intelligence personnel, or their overseers, had deliberately tailored their analysis of threat to reflect defence budgets. (Indeed, at least one of them was a former intelligence officer.) Instead, they articulated a codified belief that broad gaps could exist between precautions viewed as necessary by those charged with drawing up, setting and implementing 'appropriate' expenditure and the security needs of the State, as identified to top management by subordinate albeit senior and experienced military strategists. What was the evidence to suggest this played out during the downturn in the Irish economy after 9/11? Did obvious pitfalls emerge?

It is worth noting at the outset an anomaly that Herman refers to between the thrust of intelligence provided and what senior policy-makers interpret it to be telling them. He notes: 'If intelligence is used, users consciously and unconsciously *select* from what is presented to them ... Even diligent users who pay attention to everything interpret intelligence's careful expressions of uncertainty and alternatives in light of their own prejudices' (1996, p. 142). The decisions they take will reflect these prejudices but often be at a remove from actual strategic need as identified in the intelligence. They may instead take a narrow, even dismissive approach to implications other than those which they judge to be necessary.

As Herman might have it, a tradition of prejudice against increased defence expenditure has characterised Irish security policy. This was, perhaps, the dominant decision-making context in which the Irish military leadership had worked almost since the foundation of the State. It is highly likely that within hours, if not days, of 9/11, Defence Forces' management braced for an economic downturn and thus, a scaling-back of public expenditure. As noted earlier in respect of the Garda, the Celtic Tiger economy was in failing health even before the attack. There was an obvious correlation between the well-being of an export-led, small, open economy and an unprecedented attack on the security of the global aviation industry. Responsible defence managers would have had to have planned ahead for the effects of pressure on the public purse in the strategies they devised 'going forward'. Of course, the key strategic decision facing Defence Forces management was that which government thrust on them on the afternoon of September 11: to re-evaluate national security policy.

With all that said, the Defence Forces actually escaped the worst of the spending constraints that government put in place in the months after 9/11. The Defence Estimate for 2002, released two months after the attack, was €734.8 million, representing a 4 per cent decrease on the 2001 figure (Ireland, Department of Defence 2001b).[5] But this decreased allocation needs to be seen in the context of exceptional expenditure during the previous year on a new Naval Service ship (approximately €25 million), buildings and equipment. Excluding these figures, the Estimates for 2002 allowed for a net increase in the Defence Vote of 2.8 per cent (Ireland, Department of Defence 2001b).[6] In the context of the 'extraordinary reversal' in the public finances and the tradition of cutting Defence budgets, this was a reasonable outcome (Brennock

2001). It seems fair to suggest that the insulation of the Defence Forces from the worst public sector cutbacks was, at least partly, due to the organisation having only just come through a difficult review and restructuring period. Moreover, the now remodelled Defence Forces needed additional resources to carry out the more robust international overseas missions which the government had re-committed itself to support in the defence White Paper of 2000 (Ireland, Department of Defence 2000). However, the question that surely faced Defence Organisation management was how long could it be before cutbacks impinged? Sure enough, economic deterioration continued throughout 2002, prompting the Department of Finance to warn of expenditure reductions right across government (*Irish Times*, 2002a). All departments were ordered to prioritise core concerns and reduce budgets accordingly (Cusack 2002b; Donohue 2002a).

The Department of Defence, with the agreement of the general staff, was among the first to comply (Cusack and Brennock 2002). The Defence Estimate for that year was cut to €707.6 million, representing a 6 per cent decrease on 2002.[8] The minister for defence, Michael Smith, noted that as a consequence, 'some programmes of lesser priority will have to be delayed' (Ireland, Department of Defence 2002b). These lesser priorities, decided 'following negotiations with the military authorities', included a contract for medium-lift helicopters worth in the region of €100 million which was cancelled (Ireland, Department of Defence 2002b; Donohue 2002b). Investment in G2 was kept static until at least mid-2003.

Significance is to be found in what was chosen as suitable for cutbacks. The choices made represented the weakening of national security capabilities but the maintenance, if not expansion, of the ones needed for international security operations. The helicopters were set to make a direct contribution to national security preparedness, by providing enhanced 'casevac' (casualty evacuation) and rapid air deployment of special forces capabilities (Author's interviews). The decision not to increase G2 resources was made despite the agency's attempts to step up its 'on-island' work against transnational terrorist networks (Author's interviews). Only in late 2003 was 'considerable effort put into developing our systems and processes and co-ordinating our efforts with our partners', which translated as sending intelligence officers overseas for training and liaison with other agencies (Sreenan 2005; Brady 2005b).

In contrast, while these national security capabilities went by the wayside, provision was made for a further twenty-five MOWAG Piranha III armoured personnel carriers (APCs), primarily for new overseas roles (the government had an option on forty) (Hennessy 2003). These were to add to the forty already in the fleet since 2000 at a cost of €50 million. By 2005, the Army's Piranha complement stood at eighty, comprising fifty-four APCs, nine close reconnaissance vehicles (CRV), eight command vehicles, six medium reconnaissance vehicles (MRV), two ambulances and one recovery variant (Connect 2006). The go-ahead was also given for a programme to replace anti-armour weapons needed abroad. Onto this, there was the €8 million spent, in the two years previously, on specialist transport cargo and troop-carrying vehicles and new VHF radio equipment for soldiers on the ground (Ireland, Department of Defence 2002b). So, it seems that by targeting the cuts at spending programmes centred mainly on national security policy, defence management kept intact those programmes that were needed for overseas missions. This meant that the Defence Forces could continue to service the government's deepening obligations towards international security. It also meant that the Army, the only service that stood to benefit directly from these new missions, for example in terms of its equipment and training, avoided the worst of the cutbacks.[9]

The cancellation of the helicopter contract needs to be seen in the context of the official view that re-equipping the Naval Service and Air Corps beyond current capabilities would use up money required to modernise the Army. This would defeat the purpose of restructuring (Author's interviews; Ireland, Department of Defence 2000, pp. 39, 45). It was a pragmatic position in the context of the Defence Forces taking on new and robust international security missions – the new dependable path. But in terms of strengthening and improving national security policy, it amounted to 'a decision to do nothing' (Author's interview). The costs to aviation security of the official view are examined in more detail later in this chapter. More generally, the spending cuts add weight to suspicions that military inputs into security policy are Army-dominated to a degree that is problematic.

To recap, the general staff's advice to government provided no stimulus whatsoever for equipment growth in the Naval Service and Air Corps beyond current capabilities. This was despite the services' obligations to defend Ireland's vast aviation and maritime responsibilities – and their obvious lack of capabilities to carry out these duties. The most senior commanders of both services, as one-star officers, lacked the necessary rank and thus appointment to influence the official position. Expressed in conceptual terms, they were not in a position to alter the direction of decision-making corresponding with a major path dependency from which the Army had most to gain. Of course, the obvious counter-argument to this and Herman's claim of interpretative prejudice is that even had the minor services had greater process access, the outcome would have been the same because it was intelligence-led. In Chapter 5, however, the effectiveness of the intelligence structure from which the analysis came, is placed at issue.

Interestingly, national security expenditure was moved up the order of priorities when the financial outlook improved later in the decade. In November 2006 the minister for defence, Willie O'Dea, announced that the Defence Budget in the Estimates for 2007 was €1.005 billion (gross), which represented a €46 million (4.6 per cent) increase on the previous year (Ireland, Department of Defence 2006b; Newman 2006). Earlier in 2006 the Air Corps had taken delivery of the first of four Agusta AW 139 utility helicopters at a cost of €50 million. Although smaller than the medium-lift helicopters cancelled in 2002, their purchase three years later, in January 2005, nevertheless provided the State with enhanced airlift capabilities (Ireland, Department of Defence, 2006). It was confirmed in December 2006 that the government was taking up the option of a further two AW 139s (RTÉ News 2006). Also that year, two light-utility Eurocopter EC135 helicopters were procured largely for training purposes (Ireland, Department of Defence 2006). In September 2006 the minister confirmed that the department was in negotiations to purchase for the Naval Service a new €100 million multi-role vessel (MRV) (*Irish Independent*, 2006). The limit of an eight-ship flotilla would remain but the bigger 'blue-green' ship (called such for its capacity to support multiple land and sea operations) promised some improvement in Irish national security at sea (Author's interviews). It could also provide a platform for the Naval Service, as an operational unit, to get a greater slice of the action on international security missions.

Expenditure to service the Army's overseas priorities continued in this period. For example, €36 million was spent on fifteen more MOWAG armoured personnel carriers for 'Surveillance and Reconnaissance roles on overseas missions' (Ireland, Department of Defence 2006b). However, the headline spending suggests that when funding for international security commitments is considered safe (e.g. in a period of relative financial security), national security expenditure is increased. If taken as a general trend, a clear weakness exists in national security policy-making: in times of financial pressure but low security threat, the interests of national security will fall second to the overseas interests of the largest and best-represented service. The price is to the State's development of naval and airborne national security military capabilities which, when considered in the context of high-tech ships and aircraft and training the people to man them, take time to build to minimum effectiveness. Assuming it is a price paid on the basis of intelligence analysis that indicates a consistently low level of threat to the State, it follows that the structures of intelligence must be well calibrated indeed.

The apparent weakness in the argument that Irish national security suffers in weakened economic conditions is that between 1999 and 2001, during which time the Irish economy showed signs of slowing down, some €51 million was spent on two ships for the Naval Service (Ireland, Department of Defence 2002b). Moreover, in 2002, while the Air Corps lost its contract for medium lift helicopters, provision was made for the purchase of eight new training aircraft. However, on more detailed consideration, quite different conclusions can be drawn from these procurements. The LE Roisín and LE Niamh replaced two Naval Service patrol ships that had reached their thirty-year maximum operational lifespan (Author's interviews). Procurement to maintain the Irish flotilla at its existing small size was unavoidable, especially given the State's obligations vis-à-vis fisheries patrols in EU waters.[10]

As regards the eight training aircraft, their procurement exposes a good deal about policy weaknesses at the expense of far-sighted security management. In 1998, three years prior to 9/11, senior Air Corps officers, in a document to government, highlighted terrorism as one of the dangers that would be faced by the State in the emerging security climate and, in this context, warned against a further running down of military aviation capabilities. They argued:

> The continuing lack of any capability to police and monitor sovereign airspace is a serious deficit in the State's commitment to its own security, and therefore to the security of its neighbours. (Air Corps 1998, p. 17)

They also pointed to speed as one of the key characteristics to conduct successful air interception missions. In 2000 the Air Corps lost all armed jet capability when the last of its five ageing and lightly armed Fouga Magisters was mothballed. Delays in buying replacement aircraft resulted in the Corps' jet pilots losing their combat-jet ratings. Apart from a handful of flyable Cessnas, of the type familiar to private flying clubs the world over, but which could be modified to carry light armaments, the Air Corps' only other combat aircraft, post-2000, were seven SIAI-Marchetti SF 260 WE Warriors. The Warrior is a relatively slow turboprop trainer totally unsuited to interception of a 9/11-type assault. As one senior Air Corps officer put it:

> A 200 mph aeroplane trying to catch a 600 mph aeroplane … you might as well give them a sling shot and a bow and arrow and put them up there. (Author's interview)

Sixteen months after 9/11, in January 2003, the Irish government placed an order for eight Pilatus PC–9M Advanced Turboprop Trainer aircraft to replace the seven Warriors and to some day act as a platform for pilots to train up to subsonic trainer jets. The PC-9M has a service ceiling of 38,000 ft and a maximum *diving* speed of 400 mph (667 km/h, mach 0.73). Fully armed, it carries two 0.5 inch machine guns and two 2.75 in folding fin aerial rocket pods. Hence, while their lead strategists had warned in 1998 that the protection of Irish sovereign airspace from terrorist attack required a modern jet interception capability, the Air Corps were re-equipped in 2004/05 to a degree not incomparable with the major combatants in the later years of the Second World War.

A senior Army officer was robust in his defence of the general staff decision not to support the development of a jet-based, aerial patrol capability, after 9/11. He cited the high cost of so doing:

> Other countries have pilots on alert, in their bases, ready to go should that take place. But to do that it's not just a pilot and a plane. It's a large number of pilots, and a large number of planes, and that is not the end of the story. You then need a huge interceptor guidance system to control those aircraft in the air. You are looking at billions of euros to construct such a capability and I don't think the threat in this country justifies that type of interceptor capability.

He insisted instead that the Army's ground-to-air capabilities were sufficient to Ireland's limited resources and defensive needs.

> So, what we have to do is pinpoint likely targets that we could defend, in a well-constructed manner, by a mixture of guns and missiles on the ground. That we have put in place since September 11th. (Author's interview)

These ground-to-air capabilities were built up in 2001, when the Army received a small number of surface-to-air (SAM) missiles and associated guidance equipment and soldiers were trained in their use. The mobility of these platforms makes them favourable to tactical deployment at installations of high value such as airports. They were deployed in and around Shannon Airport and Dromoland Castle in County Clare for the EU/US Summit of June 2004. However, reliance on them alone leaves Ireland without any form of high-speed air cover above their service ceiling – approximately 10,000 feet (Author's sources).

In considering the merits of this strategy it must be noted that it is one conceived by the Army and, in procurement terms, benefits the Army. It reflects the path dependency on overseas missions. Air Corps management were, unsurprisingly, opposed to it but were not sufficiently empowered to do anything about it. Nor were the Defence Forces sufficiently resourced to fund an alternative (Author's interviews). In relation to what the study claims, reliance on ground-to-air missiles is a strategy that leaves open a clear gap in security policy. That is unless intelligence shows, accurately, that there is little or no risk above a certain altitude. This assessment must remain so in the very long term given the length of time it takes to procure aircraft and train personnel to fly them. (Again, the validity of the intelligence process is examined in Chapter 5.)

Quizzed in relation to the State's 10,000 feet response limit, a senior Department of Defence official said that in an emergency the government would 'call in an air force' (Author's interview). According to seemingly well-informed media reports, the air force burdened with protecting Irish airspace – a wide corridor that runs from the Atlantic directly eastwards to the UK and Europe – would be the British Royal Air Force (RAF) (Clonan 2005). Other interview respondents corroborated these reports (Author's interviews). But while convenient and certainly cost effective in the face of traditionally low Irish political support for major defence spending, the government reliance on the RAF has been called into serious question. A top-ranking Air Corps officer said that the corps had informed the general staff and government officials that under the terms of the Convention on International Civil Aviation, signed in Chicago in 1944, only a commissioned officer of the Defence Forces could attack a civil aircraft in Irish airspace (Author's interview). The Air Corps' view was that RAF personnel, in attacking an aircraft with potentially hundreds of civilians on board, would place themselves in contravention of the convention and, thus, Irish and international law. The Air Corps warned the government that Irish diplomatic clearance to RAF pilots might not prove sufficiently watertight should passengers or people on the ground be killed. They also warned that scrambling a force of RAF aircraft could prompt suicide hijackers en route to a target in the UK or mainland Europe to 'go in glory' into a random Irish target (Author's interview). It is not known whether emergency powers legislation first drafted in early 2003 provides for combat actions by foreign forces against civil airliners in Ireland's sovereign airspace.[11] Even if it does so provide, no realistic attempt is being made to address, by building indigenous aviation capabilities, a sudden but unforeseen emergency requiring a high-speed Air

Corps intervention in the near future.

In summary, senior officers of all three services within the Defence Forces claim significant differences between what is officially accepted as threat and the State's actual national security requirements. It is important to emphasise that no evidence is presented here to imply that if there were an imminent threat of attack identified tomorrow, the State would not act. Whether it could act quickly enough, or sufficiently, are entirely different matters because warnings from military strategists within the Defence Forces of the need to equip for threats existing, or coming down the line, appear to have been ignored. This is especially clear in relation to military aviation strategy. It is worth noting that Air Corps management estimates that regaining jet aviation pilot and maintenance capabilities to prevent and intercept threats could take many years (Author's interviews). Impossible to ignore here is the make-up of the general staff and the Army's dominance of military inputs to national security policy formation. Through curtailing expenditure on national security capabilities amid the economic decline in 2002 the all-Army general staff preserved, for as long as possible, expenditure on equipment for overseas mission readiness. The evidence does not add up to recklessness or a lack of professionalism on their part or on that of their intelligence experts and civilian overseers. Rather, in the language of historical institutionalism, one must suspect that not least because the minor services lacked sufficient channels of influence, the leadership conformed to the tendency within responsible organisations to stay on a dependable path. In this case against a backdrop of financial uncertainty they stuck to a course that reified the interests of the major service over those of the others. Nothing is in place to prevent this recurring into the future with, perhaps, dreadful consequences for national security.

The cultural dimension: An Garda Síochána

In the years since 9/11, although not because of it, there has been an unprecedented focus on how to reform the Garda Síochána. Government has focused on instilling 'a culture of performance management and accountability' in the force (Dáil Debates 2006b, pp. 13–18). This is in response to findings from tribunals of inquiry and other official investigations of serious indiscipline and weak management running throughout the force. Whether these problems place in doubt the Garda's capacity to pursue and prosecute successfully cases against suspected terrorists, is a matter of significance to this study's claim that there are serious shortcomings in policy. The effectiveness of measures to improve the discipline and management of the force is also relevant in terms of whether problems of policy persist, as this study argues they do. To address these issues, this section will proceed as follows: firstly, the nature and extent of the problems will be mapped out. Secondly, the discussion will analyse what remedial measures have been put in place in the force. It will consider if these measures will help to ensure the force can deliver effective anti-terrorism outcomes.

In 2004 and again in 2005 and 2006 a judicial tribunal of inquiry concluded that indiscipline was widespread within the force, and management was unable to contain it (Tribunal of Inquiry Set up Pursuant to the Tribunal of Inquiry (Evidence) Acts 1921–2002 into Certain Gardaí in the Donegal Division 2004; 2005; 2006a). It reported, in blunt terms, that the Garda was 'losing its character as a disciplined force … Ultimately, the gradual erosion of discipline … will sooner or later, lead to disaster' (Tribunal of Inquiry 2004, p. 490). The tribunal found an Omerta-style practice of silence throughout the force, whereby officers and members covered for each other and refused to acknowledge wrongdoing. In the course of proceedings at a separate tribunal of inquiry into alleged Garda misconduct – the Barr Tribunal – the Chairman, Mr Justice Barr, accused members of the Garda of being incapable of admitting to any faults in their work (Kelly 2004b). Similarly in 2007 the Chairman of the Garda Complaints Board, Dr Gordon Holmes, said that he had 'emphasised in the past and continue(s) to emphasise the total inability of the gardaí, where a genuine *bona fide* mistake has been made, to offer apologies for that mistake' (Edwards 2007a). Such inability was disputed by the Garda commissioner, Noel Conroy (Edwards 2007b).

Gardaí have been found to engage in a range of misconduct, from beating-up suspects to making bogus explosives and firearms finds so as to engineer promotion. In the five years to 2003 approximately €6 million was paid out, mainly in out of court settlements, to some seventy victims of alleged assault and wrongful arrest by gardaí (Coulter 2003a). Senior judges have accused gardaí of playing fast and loose with the judicial process (Coulter 2004a; Brennock 2004). Among the allegations in this regard is that gardaí repeatedly tell lies under oath. In one notable instance detectives working for CSB were found by Mr Justice Barr to have fabricated evidence and to have 'persistently lied on oath' in the trial at the Special Criminal Court of a person charged in relation to the Omagh bomb attack of August 1998. In January 2005 the Court of Criminal Appeal, acknowledging the perjury, ordered a complete retrial. According to observers, the Irish courts are treating Garda evidence with greater scepticism than before (Coulter 2002). Such additional scrutiny may lead to fairer, more just and, thus, more secure convictions of those guilty of terrorist acts. But it may also make the task of successful prosecution more difficult. In this regard, Irish anti-terrorism law attaches considerable weight to the opinion of a garda. For example, the Offences Against the State Act permits a court to convict a person on the basis of the opinion of a chief superintendent that the individual has engaged in terrorist activity. Clearly the greater the doubt there is about the integrity of Garda evidence, the higher the risk to the efficacy of powers provided for under anti-terrorism law.

Senior Garda officers deny that the problems within the force have corroded the public's willingness to cooperate with its members (Author's interviews). As one senior officer said:

I think that the people out there, for all the right reasons, would see us as a

service that they can trust – I would hope – and that information would flow
from them to us. (Author's interview)

The fact that some 7,000 people applied for membership of a new Garda reserve
force in 2006 supports their claim (Dáil Debates 2006b, pp. 13–18). However,
opinion poll evidence is at best divided, with several polls suggesting a loss of
public confidence in the force, particularly in urban areas and among younger
people (Ireland, Department of Justice 2002; Brennock 2004). In 2006 the Fine
Gael front bench spokesman on justice said:

> The alarming circumstances now exist where some members of the public
> second guess the motivation of Garda decisions, doubt the *bona fides* of indi-
> vidual members and question the honesty of the force.

He was speaking during a Dáil debate that saw the opposition parties united in
the claim that public faith in the Garda had been damaged. He continued:

> Refusal to reform, along with the failure of systems to prevent corruption,
> mismanagement, rising crime and falling detection rates, have been respon-
> sible for the decline in confidence in the Garda. (Dáil Debates 2006b, pp.
> 13–18)

In what follows the discussion addresses why indiscipline and poor management have grown under the system of political control over the Garda. It analyses whether that system is providing an appropriate remedy to put right these
issues as they may affect security policy. It comes at these issues on two fronts:
firstly, by introducing historical evidence suggesting that indiscipline within
the force accelerated in the early years of the Troubles and, secondly, by evaluating whether government accountability to the Oireachtas on Garda matters
works in the interests of reform.

Widespread indiscipline in the Garda did not shoot up overnight; the
problem has been dated to the escalation of the Troubles in the early 1970s
(Keating in Coulter 2004a). The high rate of violence in that period made it politically difficult for the government to account to the Oireachtas for its successful stewardship of Garda enforcement of law and order. It also brought about
pressures at Anglo-Irish level for a more effective anti-terrorism response. To
alleviate the strain, government sent signals to the force that crackdowns were
required, even if these involved taking shortcuts on normal standards of human
rights (Dunne and Kerrigan 1984). According to the minister for industry and
commerce in the Fine Gael/Labour government of 1973–77,

> I'm satisfied that the nods and winks that were given to the gardaí at that time
> gave rise to the culture that we have today. (Keating, in Coulter 2004)

The convictions of six suspected republican terrorists for a train robbery in
March 1976 near Sallins, Co. Kildare, was generally accepted as a notorious
example of deceitful, but also brutal, practices by members on the security side
of the force (Coulter 2004a). The case offered the first glimpse of an unofficially
tolerated 'Heavy Gang' of detectives, whose task was to beat confessions out of

suspects. Dermot Walsh also identified the Troubles as a starting point for these and other difficulties, in comments to *The Irish Times*.

> The gardaí were allowed to engage in those activities because the State, and a lot of ordinary people, did not want to undermine or demoralise them in their fight against subversion. (Walsh, in Coulter 2004a)

In another intervention in the same newspaper, he said:

> The gardaí were allowed to think they were bigger than the law itself. Their self-perception was that they were the law and, as long as their activities were aimed at subversives and organised crime, they were not to be brought to account. (Walsh, in Coulter 2003a)

This all suggests that the system of political control has directly contributed to the growth of indiscipline within the force. To alleviate the political pressure it was under, government indicated to the Garda that it wanted results – and fast. This signal was sent to a force whose officers depended on cabinet approval for their promotions and which depended on government to fix budgets and for dispersal of personnel (Walsh 1998). An unforeseen consequence was a blind eye turned in many quarters to decaying discipline. Despite this, can the system of political control deliver remedies for indiscipline and mismanagement and the problems they imply for national security policy? Official policy as set out in a law to reform the force, the Garda Síochána Act 2005, is that it can. Measures provided for under this act and initiatives announced to accompany it, as well as a proposal to enhance parliamentary scrutiny of the Garda, are investigated in this chapter.

As already noted, by 2006 government was committed to introducing into the force, 'a culture of performance management and accountability' (Dáil Debates 2006b, p. 14). To this end, a year earlier the Oireachtas passed the Garda Síochána Act, sections of which were introduced above. The act provides for a range of measures aimed specifically at improving discipline and supervision. The headline changes are the introduction of a Garda Ombudsman Commission to investigate complaints against the force and a Garda Inspectorate to oversee standards. The ombudsman is independent of government but constrained in its capacity to conduct certain enquiries. For example, in the event that its officers wish to search a Garda station, the station must first be informed in advance. The ombudsman's powers relative to those of the Police Ombudsman of Northern Ireland are contested (Reid 2005). The inspectorate reports directly to the minister and is therefore open to the accusation that it is not fully independent. Other measures provided for under the act and (by 2008) introduced in addition to it were:

a) the appointment of a four-person civilian expert group, chaired by Senator Maurice Hayes, to provide advice to the Garda commissioner on change;

b) revised procedures for handling human intelligence;

c) the development of a Garda professional standards unit, to address performance, effectiveness and efficiency in the force;

d) the establishment of local policing committees, involving discussions between Garda officers at local level and local authority representatives;

e) the creation of a deputy Garda commissioner position to lead a change management team;

f) obligations on members to account for their actions and a new Garda disciplinary code, the latter aimed at preventing lengthy judicial cases against disciplinary procedures;

g) external expertise to provide input into a merit-based promotion system (but with final say on appointment remaining with the cabinet);

h) a 'whistleblower's charter' to protect members reporting misbehaviour by others within the force. (Dáil Debates 2006b, pp. 13–18; Ward 2006b)

At the time of writing none of these changes have been in existence long enough to evaluate their contribution to policy with any real value. For example, the impact is yet to be seen of the civilian expert group's recommendations of sweeping changes including fast-track promotions for outstanding young gardaí and personal coaches for senior officers (Lally 2007b). Some indication of the way of things came with a comment by the head of the Irish Human Rights Commission in 2007 that the Garda was at 'the beginning rather than the end of the journey' towards human rights-led reform (Manning 2007), although the Garda management journal, *Communique*, presented an upbeat assessment (Fitzgerald 2008).

Furthermore the scope and design of the Ombudsman Commission and Inspectorate appear problematic. One constant amid the change is that the government retains ultimate responsibility and accountability for the force. The system of political control is practically the same one that has been blamed for helping to instigate the problems that the management and procedural revisions are intended to remedy. For instance, the commissioner is now the accounting officer for the finances of the Garda since the passing into law of the 2005 Act. But the government has stronger powers to issue direct orders to the force and if these relate to national security – however defined – has greater scope to evade accountability. The nods and winks of the 1970s may take the form of secret directives from the minister under Section 25 of the act.

But a secret directive from the minister is, arguably, an extreme case. It does not necessarily follow from it that political control cannot deliver a 'culture of performance management and accountability', and so remedy the issues for national security policy caused by discipline and management problems within the Garda. What is the intended regime in more routine circumstances?

In November 2006 the minister for justice, Michael McDowell, who brought forward all of the reform measures discussed so far, announced that consultation was to begin on the establishment of a new Oireachtas security and policing committee. This was necessary because the existing Committee on Justice,

Equality, Defence and Women's Rights was 'overloaded on other matters'. So it could not ensure 'direct Oireachtas accountability for the Garda' (Dáil Debates 2006b, pp. 13–18). Is a dedicated committee, coupled with the usual parliamentary scrutiny in the Dáil and Seanad, likely to lead to the reassurance of accountability that national security policy requires? Analysing this point requires us to consider again the burden of accountability on government which, as Walsh (1998) argues, political control over the Garda entails.

It falls to government to account to the Oireachtas for its stewardship of the force, within the chambers of the parliament and at committee level. This has political consequences which underpin why governments need to interfere in the running of the Garda 'on their watch' (Walsh 1998, pp. 115–19). It follows that government members must be cautious about what they say and do publicly in relation to serious problems within the Garda. Prior to the tribunals making their findings government members routinely avoided admitting to shortcomings in the force. Instead, the official line was that where indiscipline arose, gardaí could investigate gardaí and the matter would be satisfactorily resolved (*Irish Times Breaking News* 2004).

The Fianna Fáil/Progressive Democrats government of 1997–2002 initially refused to establish a tribunal to investigate serious allegations of Garda indiscipline and mismanagement in the Donegal Garda division (Dáil Debates 2006b; Tribunal of Inquiry 2004, 2005, 2006a). It must be added that they cited possible prejudicial implications in respect of cases before the courts to defend their initial refusal to establish a tribunal. Nevertheless, an opposition spokesperson on justice, Alan Shatter, an experienced lawyer, condemned the government's 'unpardonable foot dragging' on the matter (Labanyi 2002). The same government was opposed to the introduction of a Garda ombudsman, along the lines of that introduced in Northern Ireland, to investigate police wrongdoing (Dáil Debates 2001). The FF/PD government of 2002–07 relented in this regard in the wake of Judge Morris's warning that Garda discipline was breaking down (Tribunal of Inquiry 2004, p. 490). Out of this came the ombudsman commission and inspectorate of Garda standards in the Garda Síochána Act 2005. The government emphasised that reforms to the force were having the desired effect following the publication of three Morris tribunal reports in 2006. The problems were in hand. The minister for justice told the Dáil in 2006 that the Garda Síochána Act was

> The catalyst for the most fundamental reform and transformation of the force into a modern police service in which we can all take pride ... The government has acted firmly and radically to ensure the culture and organisation of the Garda Síochána is fully fit for purpose ...

In the same key Dáil Debate, he said:

> I draw to the attention of the House that a veritable transformation is taking place in the Garda Síochána. It is not the same old force; it is a changing force in a changing Ireland. All the things are happening for the better. (Dáil Debates 2006b, pp. 13–18)

This uncompromising optimism, while perhaps well founded, also has to be seen in the context of the political risks for government in admitting to shortcomings in its reform measures. Doing so would leave the door open to opposition criticism over a matter of considerable public concern. In these circumstances Garda management, vulnerable to political control, cannot feasibly disagree with the minister's assessment. They would be at odds with centralised political control. This seemed to be what Sinn Féin TD, Aengus O' Snodaigh, had in mind when he told the Dáil that:

> Given that all top ranking positions are dependent on the minister's favour, it is no wonder that the Garda Síochána has refused to recognise and rectify the scale of abuse. (Dáil Debates 2006b, pp. 13–18)

The question arising for national security policy is whether reform can be really maintained when it is in the interests of both the Garda and government to play up changes made in the reform policy process but downplay problems. If it cannot be achieved then a significant problem for national security policy persists; the credibility of the State's main national security agency could, once more, be at issue.

More particularly, what are the implications for the question set out earlier: can an Oireachtas committee provide accountability? An opposition spokesperson, Jim O' Keefe (Fine Gael), suggested that in such circumstances of mutual government–Garda interest, an Oireachtas committee was insufficient to future needs. Current Oireachtas standing procedures exacerbated the issue:

> As somebody who has been a member of this House for a long time, and who is a member of the Joint Oireachtas Committee on Justice, Defence and Women's Rights, I know it is not possible, under present procedures, to have Oireachtas oversight. (Dáil Debates 2006b, pp. 13–18)

Writing in a Garda representative association publication, a serving member of the force, Garda Michael O' Boyce of the Donegal Garda division, drew a blunt conclusion:

> Better to face into an election pretending that you have reformed An Garda Síochána rather than actually set in train a process that will deliver the necessary reform. In other words, real reform of An Garda Síochána takes second place to political expediency … It seems the only way to implement true Garda reform is to establish an independent Garda authority and allow them to appoint the commissioner. (O' Boyce 2006, pp. 14–15)

Support for an independent Garda authority was voiced by justice spokespersons of three opposition parties in the Dáil debate on Garda reform in November 2006. Jim O' Keefe suggested that the authority should be modelled on that of the policing authority for Northern Ireland (Dáil Debates 2006b, pp. 13–18). Labour's justice spokesman, Brendan Howlin said the authority, 'would approve an agreed policing plan for the country and must agree with senior Garda management on the level of resources needed to implement this agreed work plan' (pp. 13–18). According to the spokesman for the Green Party, Ciarán Cuffe,

> To date, one of the most glaring omissions from the minister's raft of reforms concerns the establishment of an independent Garda authority. I understand that the minister has stated that he considers both himself and the government to be acting as a Garda authority. However, this does not go far enough. (pp. 13–18)

Irrespective of the advantages or disadvantages of an independent Garda authority, it is a prominent feature in evidence suggesting that the reform process is not all it should be. In regard to this and all of the evidence so far, it is worth noting that it is not only in Ireland that political control has proved inadequate to the task of maintaining acceptable standards of management and discipline within state security services.[10] Weller (2000) notes how three of the four Scandinavian countries, the exception being Finland, have faced a series of major controversies in connection with the operations of their security and intelligence services. In Norway, for example, in the mid-1990s the 'inadequacy of ministerial control' over the state security service was clearly revealed. The service, POT (Politiets overvåkningstjeneste, since renamed as Politiets sikkerhetstjeneste or PST), was found to be colluding with the Norwegian Labour Party which had been in power throughout much of the period. Among other things it conducted illegal surveillance of Norwegian citizens.

In this context of malfunction, it is striking that the various Scandinavian security intelligence agencies are subject to a range of controls not unlike those operating in Ireland. As Weller notes:

> Responsibility over the security and intelligence agencies is exercised in many ways, including the direct issuance of directives and, less directly, in the form of control over such items as personnel and budgets. (2000, p. 174)

Here it is useful to focus briefly on Denmark as an example of a state where a security agency under both political *and* parliamentary committee control strayed outside the boundaries of acceptable behaviour. On behalf of the government, the minister of justice supervises and provides directions to PET, the Danish security service. The minister has set down that the director of PET is obliged to keep the minister informed of general as well as specific issues of importance. Under the Garda Síochána Act 2005 the commissioner is similarly obliged. But unlike the Dáil the Danish Parliament, the Folketinget, has parliamentary control of PET through a special parliamentary committee set up under Act no. 378 of 1988 with the role of 'supervising the Danish Defence Intelligence Service (FE) and PET'. The committee consists of five MPs who are appointed by the five major parties of parliament. Under law the committee must be informed of the general guidelines governing the activities of PET and must be told of important matters of security or foreign political issues that are relevant to the activities of the intelligence services. In return the members are bound by confidentiality on what they hear.

A further mechanism of control, designed to assuage public anxiety, is the government-appointed Wamberg Committee, the function of which is to conduct checks on intelligence files that PET opens on individuals or organisations. No such entity exists in Ireland. The committee must approve new files on Danes and foreign nationals resident in Denmark that the service requests to be registered. The committee meets six to ten times a year at PET's offices to review cases and decide whether the criteria for recording them have been met. It also takes a random sample of old files to establish whether the deadlines for deletion are being kept.

Despite coming under a system of ministerial control like that operating in Ireland, but also parliamentary and semi-independent external oversight in excess to that proposed by Minister McDowell in the interests of Garda reform, PET has run into serious controversy. In 1999 the Danish minister for justice, Frank Jensen, established an inquiry into allegations that the agency was involved in widespread illegal surveillance activities throughout the 1960s and early 1970s. Documents emerged suggesting that the surveillance continued after an order was made for it to stop and that PET had infiltrated at least one political party (Weller 2000, p. 179). Similarly negative findings were reached in respect of Sweden's SÄPO by an inquiry established following the assassination of Prime Minister Olof Palme. The agency was found to have routinely acted outside political control and to have violated standards of civil rights (p. 177).

This evidence indicates, in summary, that political control of security and intelligence, be it in Ireland or elsewhere, can run at odds with effective discipline, standards and, by consequence, public faith in the agencies concerned. Moreover parliamentary control, intended to interrupt bias in ministerial control and thus act as a higher standard of accountability, can be out-manoeuvred with apparent ease. In the Irish case the dark revelations from Donegal further underlined serious shortcomings in the political control of the Garda. But subsequent management reforms have not been 'followed through' with substantial changes to the system of control and accountability which helped to cause the problems in the first place. With the system left intact, those whose job it is to pursue and prosecute terrorists continue to operate in a system whereby discipline and management can be undermined at the highest levels, and those in highest power can be put at political risk by admitting problems. This constitutes neither a critical policy juncture nor the greatest possible reassurance to sceptical members of the judiciary, or the public, as to the future integrity of Garda evidence and the force in general. This is a persistent problem for national security policy, with potentially very serious effects.

The cultural dimension: Defence Forces

In this section, a culture of organisational threat within the Defence Forces is analysed in the context of whether or not it has presented problems for the formulation of national security policy after 9/11. The origins of this culture lie in the practice by successive Irish governments of financial starvation of the Defence Forces. The key points to be derived are whether the traditional sense of threat was a factor relevant to the re-evaluation of security policy and so, perhaps, represented a weakness within it, or was it the case that détente at the most senior military and official levels following the bitter White Paper controversy helped to ensure that perceived threats were adequately addressed?

Perhaps unsurprisingly, given the history of very limited government expenditure on the Defence Forces, a culture of organisational threat is discernable throughout the three services (Farrell 1997; Murphy 2003; O' Halpin 1996, 1999). The remarks of a senior Air Corps officer exemplify the phenomenon:

> I can see a range of threats and a range of abilities that I believe that I have. I report them to the military commander who says 'no fucking way' because I'll get all the money and he'll get nothing. He puts it to the Department of Defence who says 'we don't have the money anyway, so you can fuck off'. You know our whole system is … the dynamic of the pie. (Author's interview)

The clearest manifestation of the organisational threat culture is the sensitivities felt within the Defence Forces around the commitment of the Departments of Finance and Defence to defence policy (Author's interviews). This was a matter that occupied practically all military interviewees for the book except for Army officers working daily at close quarters with officials. Most of these sought to emphasise that relations were 'back on track' (Authors' interviews).

Relations between the civilian official and military sides of the Defence Organisation appeared to be sour indeed in the years leading up to 9/11 and the policy re-evaluation that followed it. In 1999 a proposal, apparently originating in the Department of Finance, to reduce the Army from three brigades to a single brigade and to reconfigure the Naval Service and Air Corps as an unarmed coastguard service (Author's sources), sparked predictable anger. The minister and Department of Defence were at best ambiguous about where they stood on this (Author's interview 1999). Perhaps the lowest point came with the publication of the White Paper on defence in 2000. Widely expected to lay out the State's first concrete defence strategy, the paper instead provided for the cutback of another 1,000 military personnel (Ireland, Department of Defence 2000a). It confirmed the Army's development into a light infantry force. Yet on its publication, the Chief of Staff, Lt. Gen. Stapleton, confined himself to saying the paper would be implemented. He expressed no welcome for it. 'The white paper is a decision of government and always the Defence Forces will implement a decision of government' (Brennock 2002). The secretary-general of the Department of Defence, David O' Callaghan, publicly acknowledged that damage had been done to relations between the civil and military sides: 'We have all learned from this. We have to have a look at the relationship and that has been agreed' (Brennock 2000a).

Throughout the period, the Defence Forces and their representative associations waged an intense campaign of briefings to the media about the department's intentions (Author's sources). The then minister for defence, Michael Smith, told

The Irish Times that at two meetings he left the chief of staff and his two deputies 'in no doubt as to my feelings on what was going on'. The Defence Forces openly fighting a public relations battle against the government was, he said, 'not the way to do business'. He said he was 'throwing out a warning for the future' about this. An internal Department of Defence memo also criticised the behaviour of Defence Forces' management. It stated that 'the leaders of the Defence Forces responded with a ruthless and skilful subterranean campaign to thwart their democratically elected superior' (Brennock 2000b). Several years later a senior Army officer told the author that within the Defence Forces there remained suspicions that a) the Department of Finance retained the objective of reducing the Army to a single brigade and b) that Defence could not be trusted to stop them (Author's sources). A last-minute concession that the Department of Defence granted during the White Paper negotiations is noteworthy here. The paper was revised after publication to include, among other things, a guarantee that there would be no more cuts in personnel numbers for ten years. That guarantee was breached two years later with the post-9/11 expenditure 'adjustments'. It is also worth noting, in the context of the broader discussion on the general staff, that the White Paper revisions vested in the chief of staff the power to decide where the cuts would come (Brennock 2000a).

It is difficult to see how these strained relations could have been to the benefit of open debate and agreement in the policy re-evaluation that came after 9/11. However, Department of Defence officials and senior Army officers at Defence Forces Headquarters said that relations had moved on considerably since the paper's publication (Author's interviews). That, in itself, is problematic. Could the desire to maintain repaired relations after such a bitter and public falling-out have constrained what policy options against transnational terrorism it was feasible to explore? For example, was it realistic to seriously consider a major increase in spending to begin the lengthy process of capability-building to counter identified aviation and maritime security weaknesses, given that the official side had proposed demilitarising the Naval Service and Air Corps to save money a few years earlier? Such an outcome would have involved top managers of the Defence Organisation moving to an entirely new institutional pathway. They did (and perhaps could) not and, consequently, the dangers highlighted in 1998 remain unaddressed.

Conclusion

Conceptually, the model of historical institutionalism used here – a four-part scheme providing for formal and less formal institutional behaviour – has helped to identify and explain the significance of key moments in the development of Irish policy. The Defence (Amendment) Act 1993 was quite clearly a critical juncture. After it the Defence Forces, and especially the Army, embarked on a new pathway which centred on eventual participation in more robust but organisationally reinforcing overseas missions. The escalation of the Troubles was also a critical juncture after which successive governments, in their own interests, failed to address growing Garda indiscipline.

Empirically, financial pressures hung over the agencies as they conducted their review of policy in the period immediately after 9/11. It was in this context – but doubtless led by available intelligence – that the Garda's top managers made a number of significant decisions including one to channel the main share of counter-terrorism resources at the dissident groups. However, this increased the risk that intelligence on transnational networks would be missed. Their almost exclusive reliance on the agencies of other states for foreign intelligence left CSB vulnerable to their goodwill and accuracy. (This was not a choice within the gift of the Garda but a structural constraint within which they operated.) The State continues to have almost no hand in the foreign intelligence on which its national security policy is largely based. Hence the intelligence process underpinning policy is, perhaps seriously, suboptimal.

The system of centralised political control, as it currently stands, poses difficulties for national security policy. It leaves open the possibility that at some point in the future, senior gardaí will acquiesce to improper political influence with whatever consequences this may have for national security. The system has already failed to prevent the widespread indiscipline and management problems in the force. The remedies for these problems, instigated since 2005, are incomplete. In essence, gardaí continue to operate within an arrangement that while improved in several respects may still facilitate systematic wrongdoing. In such instances, trials of serious terrorist suspects may fail.

The military structure for senior and top-level appointments is such that Army perspectives dominate at the expense of those from the other services. A significant weight of evidence suggests that threats, as identified by military strategists, have been left aside. Acknowledgement of aviation and maritime threats to national security seems to have been especially poor. Moreover, it appears that after 9/11 efforts to preserve a détente within the highest echelons of the Defence Organisation further constrained the build-up, over some years, of potentially vital national security commitments. A system whereby serious action is not taken to remedy evidently major weaknesses identified by expert specialists represents a clear shortcoming for national security policy. In the next chapter the operational outcomes to have emerged out of this and other problematic structures are more closely examined and critiqued.

Notes

1   This process is not something that is germane to financial and political pressures. But, arguably, it has implications for how financial and political pressures are dealt with.

2   In early 2008, the government introduced a whistleblower system to protect gardaí when reporting suspected wrongdoing. But whether this will apply in relation to matters treated under Section 25 of the 2005 Act or whether its remit will extend to the office of the minister is a matter that remains to be fully established.

3   UNOSOM II was established in March 1993 under Chapter VII of the UN Charter which

sets out actions that may be taken to curb threats to peace and acts of aggression. The specific mandate of UNOSOM II provided for enforcement measures to establish throughout Somalia a secure environment for humanitarian assistance. To that end, UNOSOM II was to complete, through disarmament and reconciliation, the task begun by the Unified Task Force for the restoration of peace, stability, law and order. UNOSOM II was withdrawn in early March 1995.

4   This plan for the overseas deployments of reservists was postponed in 2009, amid a public service recruitment freeze in Ireland introduced in response to the economic recession that year (Brady 2009).

5   Measures supplied to the author by the Department of Marine, Communications and Natural Resources.

6   Whereas €734.8 million was the figure provided by the Department of Defence, the Defence Forces Annual Report 2002 put provision for all Defence Subheads at a slightly higher €755 million of which 94.45 per cent was expended (Defence Forces 2002a, p. 52).

7   The Defence Vote refers to sanctioned expenditure for the pay and allowances of Defence Forces personnel and their supporting civilian staff, for what is officially termed 'defensive equipment', for the equipment, fuel and maintenance needs of the Air Corps and Naval Service, for repairs to and maintenance of land, for barrack expenses, building capital, military transport, compensation payouts, administration, 'other non-pay military expenditure', the Civil Defence Board, the Irish Red Cross Society and Coiste an Asgard (the State's sail training organisation under the aegis of the Department of Defence).

8   The Defence Forces Annual Report 2003 put the figure for all Defence sub-heads in the 2002 Book of Estimates at €722.491 million, of which 97.3 per cent was expended (Defence Forces 2003a, p. 37).

9   There are two matters to note here. Firstly, it was intended that the light infantry model, provided for in the White Paper on Defence 2000, would operate with air and naval support from the military services of states other than Ireland. The second point is that while the Army avoided the most serious post-9/11 cutbacks, the government announced in late 2003 that the Defence Forces' establishment would be reduced below the level agreed in the 1999–2000 restructuring negotiations (Lally 2003b).

10 Negotiations for the €100 million ship (multi-role vessel) in 2006 came about in identical circumstances. It was to replace another vessel due to reach its maximum service limit between 2007 and 2009 (Ireland, Department of Defence 2006b).

11 According to the author's sources in various government departments, the legislation deals primarily with key emergency planning issues such as continuance of government power in the event of a catastrophic nuclear, biological or chemical (NBC) incident. The legislation will remain 'on ice' unless there is a serious increase in the level of threat to the State. At that point, it will be brought before the Oireachtas for immediate ratification.

12 For information on the structures of control over the Scandinavian agencies discussed here the author has drawn from their official web sites, details of which are listed in the bibliography.

5

The threat to Ireland and the security response

Introduction

This chapter will analyse security policy against what the frontline agencies say are the threats facing the State. In so doing, the extent of policy problems and how these are linked to political and financial pressures on the agencies will be further investigated. Buzan's model of threat intensity will underpin the analysis. It provides three elements of state which must be protected – institutions, territory and most importantly, the binding idea that binds citizens to the authorities. Moreover, it offers a broad set of criteria to support a critique of policy responses to identified threats. These criteria are specificity of threat, range of threat, probability and consequences and the historical dimension. Specificity of threat refers to the nature of threats to the state. Are threats specific – i.e. do they have a clear focus and source? Or are they diffuse in nature? For example, do the processes of responding to threats represent points of vulnerability (Buzan 1991, p. 134)? Range of threat is about the nearness of a threat spatially and in time, i.e. whether it is about to occur (p. 135). Probability and consequence acknowledge that threat assessments are usually gambles involving a calculation between the probability of an attack occurring and its fallout (p. 136). It helps to examine the strategies that security agencies use to shorten the odds when assessing threats. Finally, there is the historical dimension. Historical experience will influence assessment of threat; memory can amplify sensitivities or dull expectations (p. 137). Using these four criteria as focal points to underpin a critique of security policy in response to threat does not represent a fundamental departure from what the model was designed to do – identify threat intensity. The criteria lead to the state's view of threat, which in turn, leads to policy. Here, the State's view of threat is not disputed and we are simply tracing and then evaluating policy to emerge from that.

This chapter will proceed in accordance with the following plan: under specificity of threat, the first criterion of Buzan's model of threat analysis considered will be the advice on the level of threat and how to meet it, which the Irish agencies drew up for government after 9/11. It will then identify reasons why senior policy managers concluded that immigration to Ireland presented the nearest major risk to Irish national security from transnational terrorist groups. Thirdly, it will set out and discuss the implications arising from the way that the Irish agencies calculate threat to the State on the basis of its 'target value'. Finally, it will address the capacity of the security agencies to gauge threat in the context of change over time. This discussion will deal with a key aspect of CSB's on-island intelligence-gathering process in the context of shifting population patterns and the reform of the Garda. Each section will set out and then critique policy since 9/11 and/or the thinking underpinning it.

Specificity of threat

An assessment of threat to the state, the purpose of the intelligence process from collection onwards, is meant to locate threats in terms of their specificity and diffusion (Buzan 1991, p. 134; Herman 1996). In the wake of 9/11 the government ordered the security agencies to re-evaluate their assessment of threat to the State. Ireland is not considered to be the specific target for attack of any international terrorist group or network (Author's interviews; Brady 2006b). This has been a consistent conclusion of all threat assessments delivered by the Irish security agencies since 9/11. However, diplomatic and multinational corporate holdings on Irish territory are classified as being at a higher risk (Author's interviews). Furthermore, the agencies and their government overseers urge 'vigilance' (Author's interviews). But overall the likelihood of an attack in Ireland is considered to be low (Author's interviews). The comments of a senior official of the Department of the Taoiseach sum up the official view:

> We are an integral part of the Western world. We host significant US investments. We are, clearly, fully part of the European project. So in that sense, in a broader way, we are part of a Western culture that may be seen as problematic. It's not as if we're in some sort of cocoon of isolation. We're also very close to our neighbouring island, which would, of course, see itself as being more in the frame of action, and we have seen the pattern of secondary strikes. I mean Bali and Australia … And then, one has to complement that with specific information, intelligence and assessment, which would not suggest, thus far anyway, that there is any reason to believe that we are in any sort of significant risk space. But it does underline the need for continuing vigilance and preparation. (Author's interviews)

It is worth noting that the agencies' conclusions have been unswerving despite well-publicised warnings to Irish national security since 9/11. Anti-war groups, politicians and commentators have claimed that Ireland is a terrorist target because the United States government uses Shannon Airport in Co. Clare to transport hundreds of thousands of military personnel to Iraq and Afghanistan (Boyd-Barrett 2005; Kyle 2005; Whelan 2006).[1] Anjem Choudary, the main UK spokesman for the radical Islamic group, Al Muhajiroun, warned in 2005 that the decision to allow US military personnel through Shannon provided Muslims with the right to attack Ireland (McCaffrey 2005). In 2006 a controversial Islamic cleric, Omar Bakri Mohammad, urged that Dublin Airport be attacked, during a secretly taped conversation with members of a British anti-terrorist group, Vigil (Brady 2006b). But the Irish government has not wavered in its position. In November 2004, when some 20,000 US military personnel were transported through Shannon, Taoiseach Bertie Ahern told the Dáil that the link between the airport and America's war efforts was 'not an issue' that concerned the National Security Committee (O' Halloran 2004). Almost a year later, in the wake of Choudary's claims, Mr Ahern said that Ireland was not facing substantial risk (McCaffrey 2005). In 2006 the minister for defence, Willie O' Dea, said, in reply to Omar Bakri Mohammad's warning, that the risk of attack on any target in Ireland remained low (Brady 2006b). A seemingly well-briefed reporter maintained this line in the wake of the 2007 attacks on London and Glasgow (Brady 2007).

When interviewed, several senior government officials and officers of the frontline agencies (both cohorts including members of the National Security Committee) concurred with the official view (Author's interviews). When asked why, they claimed that 'benign' Irish foreign policy helped to offset the risk of attack. According to a senior official at the Department of the Taoiseach:

> We are not a location, a country which has been cast in any particularly negative role vis-a-vis those that are likely to be initiating terrorist attacks. In that sort of geopolitical sense we would have lots of credits in the eyes of those people who might be looking at the world through that perspective. We're not a major power. We don't have a significant international military presence; such as it is, it's entirely benign and principled. So, for all of those reasons one would say, 'on the side of the angels', if you like, in terms of our international profile. (Author's interview)

A senior Defence official said that Irish foreign policy was perceived in the Middle East to be 'pro-Palestinian movement':

> You have to understand where we are in international affairs. We're not regarded as a threat to anyone. We are a very small country. We're a neutral country. We have a good reputation as a supporter of the UN, particularly in peacekeeping ... So, in as much as anyone in the Middle East would have thought about Ireland, it would probably be a benign view. I certainly don't think we would have been regarded as very pro-Israeli. I think quite the contrary in fact ... I think we're probably more pro-Arab, certainly more pro-Palestinian movement than we would be pro-Israel. So, we have no reason to feel threatened. (Author's interview)

A CSB officer said that terrorist networks would come down against attacking

Ireland lest it jeopardise Irish overseas development aid:

> Well, again what you have to take into account is that Ireland has a very strong tradition of help and aid in developing countries and countries where a lot of the terrorism came from or potentially came from. And you'll find that there's slick enough people involved in these uprisings and coup d'états in a lot of these countries. They know where their bread is buttered and what side it's on and who to attack and who not. So strategically if I were a despot out in Africa somewhere, where I was going to get humanitarian aid, and I see a small country over there, Ireland has a good record on that. 'Strategically, is there any point bombing them, or killing them? No. They are more an advantage to us to keep them on side'. (Author's interview)

While the threat assessments have classified Ireland as being at a low risk of attack, seemingly well-briefed journalists have reported the presence in Ireland of a 'hard-core' of around a dozen transnational terrorist suspects. These individuals were said to be in contact with known activists based in the US, Europe and elsewhere and required close monitoring. There were also some thirty or forty sympathisers to radical Islamic causes living within the State. Intelligence sources denied the suspects in Ireland were, 'part of an operational cell … [but were] re-organising their logistics support and ready to help out any emerging operational cells in other countries'. Their main roles were to fundraise and supply 'identification documents, driving licences, insurance and assistance to asylum seekers' (Brady 2002, 2004a, 2004b). One report stated that one of the alleged masterminds of the July 2005 attack on London, Mohamad Meguerba, was radicalised in Belfast while living in Dublin. He apparently came to the State in 1997 from Algeria and subsequently married an Irish woman (Brady 2005a). The report cited 'security officials' as saying that marrying was one method used by *jihadis* to obtain citizenship in host countries.

It was subsequently reported that two suspected *jihadis* who US forces captured in 2005 held Irish passports. Others had used Ireland as a location to take a break from the frontlines in Iraq and Afghanistan (Brady 2005). The reports suggested that radicals linked to five groups provided these logistical supports. The groups were the Egyptian Islamic Jihad and al Gama'at-al Islamiya (IG), the National Front for the Salvation of Libya, the Groupe Islamique Armée (GIA) of Algeria and the GIA breakaway, the Groupe Salafiste pour la Prèdiction et le Combat (GSPC). Other reports claimed that a suspected financier of radical Islamic causes lived in Ireland. He was named as Bin Muhammad Ayadi Chafiq. It was also claimed that the Mercy International Relief Agency, which US intelligence agencies linked to transnational terrorism, was discovered operating in Dublin and that between 9/11 and June 2003, the Central Bank of Ireland froze bank accounts belonging to six transnational terror suspects (Cusack 2002b; Lally 2003). One report claimed that radicals were attempting to recruit Irish-based Muslims to fight against the US-led occupation of Iraq (O' Toole 2004). Up to thirty radicals in Ireland were former *mujahidin* in Afghanistan or in the Balkan conflicts during the 1990s, according to this report. Other reporters stated that an Algerian-born couple arrested under British anti-terrorism laws at Holyhead Port in Wales in August 2006 were naturalised Irish citizens. The report cited a Garda source as stating that police in Holyhead seized a laptop computer and a disk containing bomb-making instructions. The woman, who had been staying for some time at an address in Clondalkin, west Dublin, had travelled to Wales – where the two were to meet – on a ferry from Ireland. The couple had four children, at least one of whom was born in the Republic. The arrested man was based mainly in Britain (Lally and Mac Cormaic 2006).

Manifestations

The Irish agencies, having concluded that there is no specific threat against Ireland, have concentrated on more diffuse threats. They have placed significant emphasis on policy to improve reactive (i.e. post-attack) security rather than proactive security. This section deals with the decision made to overhaul the State's administrative arrangements for emergency planning, the management framework that emerged as a consequence, the objectives set for that framework and the outcomes that resulted from it.

Members of the National Security Committee said that the first 'concrete recommendation' they made immediately following 9/11 was the establishment of an administrative framework to better oversee Ireland's emergency planning efforts (Author's interviews). As a senior Department of Defence official put it some two years later:

> Our nearest neighbour, including possibly Northern Ireland which would be part of the UK, would be a key target … You know, what if there was a terrorist attack on Sellafield? What would happen? What if there was an outbreak of smallpox introduced in the UK? (Author's interview)

Days later, on October 3 2001, that framework had taken shape. The Task Force on Emergency Planning was established under the chairmanship of the minister for defence. Senior officers of the frontline agencies were among those given seats on this committee. At first the minister convened meetings daily, although as time wore on this dropped off to once a month (Author's interviews). The task force receives similar intelligence briefings to the National Security Committee and compiles a secret annual report for cabinet. The minister for defence is permitted to 'call in' other ministers to discuss emergency planning matters concerning their departments (Author's interviews). Officials said that this power was used to inject urgency after the initially sluggish efforts of other departments and agencies (Author's interviews). The Office of Emergency Planning (OEP) was established as a logistical aid for the task force to provide general oversight and coordination. This represented the first time that a joint Department of Defence/Defence Forces office was put in place (Author's interview). The Department of Defence official chairing the Office of Emergency Planning also chairs an Inter-Departmental Working Group on Emergency

Planning. The membership of the working group extends to all government departments with roles in emergency planning, as well as public authorities and frontline agencies that support the activities of those departments. The working group is intended to act as a forum for joined-up discussion to generate strategic guidelines for responders and to carry out the requests of the task force. The National Security Committee assists the emergency planning structure by 'formally confirming' that the operational supports for the frontline agencies, including those related to emergency planning, are – in the agencies' own judgements – satisfactory. If they are not, the committee acts to ensure the agencies receive what they require (Author's interviews). An objective of the revised planning structure is to introduce internationally benchmarked 'broad guidelines' for the numerous actors within the emergency planning community. This is in order that they might approach their testing, operational and reviewing procedures in a standardised manner (Author's interviews). It is also policy that planning includes 'low level' emergencies, such as wintertime flooding in Dublin.

In the two years following the review officials and ministers insisted that the new emergency planning structure was working and generating arrangements sufficient to Ireland's needs (see for example, Smith 2004). Developments flagged as the most significant included:

a) the investment by the Department of Defence in 9,500 protection suits, respirators, biological agent detectors, screening kits, and group and personal contamination equipment for use by emergency agencies in the event of a major radiological, nuclear, chemical, or biological incident;

b) the upgrading by the Radiological Protection Institute of Ireland (RPII) of its monitoring stations;

c) new facilities for the National Disease Surveillance Centre (NDSC);

d) the locating of Ireland's first National Bio-Terrorism Unit at a Dublin hospital;

e) the procurement of vaccines and antibiotics for smallpox and other virulent biological threats;

f) investment in decontamination equipment for the Defence Forces, the fire services and regionalised Health Service Executives;

g) desktop and field emergency planning exercises at local, national and cross-border levels (e.g. between the Garda and the PSNI);

h) the establishment of both Civil Aviation and Maritime Security Committees and their overseeing of strengthened aviation and port security measures;

i) circulation to hospitals and health professionals generally of information relating to diagnosis and treatment protocols in the event of any serious radiological, nuclear, chemical, or biological incident.

Additionally, protocols for emergency communications between Irish and UK government departments and agencies, in particular, were put in place; so too were procedures for government continuity in the event of a major disaster (Author's interviews). It was envisaged that the National Security Committee could act as a conduit for officials to communicate with the Taoiseach or cabinet members if their minister – the normal channel – became unavailable (or was killed). According to one senior Defence official:

> We would recognise that in an emergency one would need the shortest possible line to the top, whoever that happens to be. So, we have to provide a framework for that to happen. (Author's interview)

In preparation for such an extreme event drafts of emergency powers legislation have been drawn up, in secret, by officials at the Department of Justice (Author's interviews). Officials said the legislation was intended to deal with circumstances such as an attack on cabinet involving numerous deaths, the need to quarantine-off large areas and panic movements of the population. A senior Justice official provided a glimpse of the measures which have been provided for:

> Emergency powers are one area that would be our territory here. Now, if the public saw the kind of emergency planning legislation you would have to introduce for extreme situations, national diarrhoea would break out, because it's a total breach of anything that you would consider to be acceptable in accordance with human rights in a normal situation. But, you would have to take pretty draconian powers, whereby governments could take pretty serious measures against looters in an extreme situation. Now, that legislation is on somebody's plate to be drafted and put away, essentially. (Author's interview)

Senior officials also identified the need to develop means of communication with the public in the event of an extreme emergency. The senior Justice official said that

> One of the problems that we identified or that I'm worried about, having attended these meetings and not having been at them before, is that we will have a wonderful set of plans sitting in a safe somewhere, but how does Jack Citizen find out about it when it happens. How do you communicate information to the public without frightening the bejaysus out of them? That's a balance that we haven't worked out. (Author's interview)

In March 2007 the minister for defence, Willie O' Dea, promised a public information campaign 'to explain in ordinary layman's language' how emergency planning worked in Ireland. He also announced the imminent completion of a national emergency coordination centre at Agriculture House, Kildare Street, Dublin. The centre would provide ministers and senior officials with a facility from where an emergency response could be coordinated (Collins 2007). An information booklet on emergency planning was delivered to households in 2008.

Critique

The discussion now turns to the revision of Ireland's reactive security policy in the context of the political environment in which this revision occurred. Three key issues arise from the changes made. These centre on 'joined-up' government control of national security policy, command and control arrangements in response to an emergency, and the prevailing agendas and traditions of the relevant departments and agencies. This section also compares and contrasts the outcomes of the emergency planning review after 9/11 with those of a second significant review completed in 2006. The two sets of outcomes are evaluated against the study's key argument.

Ireland's reactive security was not a major priority for government from the mid-1960s up until late 2001 (O' Riordan 1992, p. 43). Much of what passed for major emergency planning, especially at a national level, was thought out during the 1950s and 1960s and the results left to gather dust. For two weeks after 9/11 the government paid little or no attention to the re-examination or improvement of these arrangements (Author's interviews). The situation changed rapidly amid public outcry over the comments of a junior government minister on a morning radio talk show in late September. As a senior Department of Defence official put it:

> In the context of defending the population against a direct attack of the international type against Ireland, I think there wasn't a huge level of consciousness in relation to it. But that, of course, changed significantly in the fairly immediate aftermath of 11th of September because of the nuclear Joe Jacob issue. (Author's interview)

Joe Jacob was minister of state for nuclear safety in the Fianna Fáil/Progressive Democrats government. In an interview on the Marian Finucane morning talk show on RTÉ Radio 1, a fortnight after 9/11, he appeared clueless as to how the National Emergency Plan for Nuclear Accidents would work in the event of a terrorist attack on the Sellafield nuclear facility in Cumbria (Jacob 2001). Recalling the aftermath of the interview, the official continued:

> I was speaking to him [another minister] that afternoon and I said: 'the current score on Joe Duffy is Irish public, thirty, Joe Jacob, nil.'[2] It was that kind of scale of event that got worse and worse and worse because of the ridicule to which he exposed himself that day … Joe Jacob, more than anything else in my view, galvanised the government into taking some position in relation to it. And that then resulted in the establishment of the Office of Emergency Planning. (Author's interview)

An immediate outcome of the political pressure generated that day was the decision to distribute iodine tablets to every household in the country. It had been suggested that the ingestion of these tablets could counter the effects to humans, especially to children, of a radioactive plume crossing the Irish Sea from the Sellafield nuclear reprocessing plant in Cumbria, UK. Hours after Mr

Jacob's interview the minister for health, Micheál Martin, gave another media interview in which he said that the State had ample stocks of the tablets for public distribution in the event of a nuclear emergency (Fahy and Donnellan 2001). A day later it emerged that most of the national stocks were several years out of date (Anderson 2001). Eight months after deliveries of the new batch to Irish households it was revealed that thousands had not received them (Hogan 2002). As one analyst noted, those who had were provided with accompanying literature that failed to mention any provision for the taking of tablets at schools, leaving parents to wonder what would happen to their children were a jet to hit Sellafield on a weekday morning (Kenny 2003, p. 220). Parents could be both comforted and alarmed at the advice of a senior British Nuclear Fuels scientist, Rex Strong, who claimed that an equivalent amount of iodine to that contained in the tablet could be obtained by eating two kippers (p. 222). But he warned that the consumption of iodine could be dangerous to the health of people in certain population sectors.

The credibility of the government response came into further doubt when it emerged that the 2.1 million tablets that were apparently circulated were useful only against the radioactive isotope, Iodine 131, which Sellafield ceased handling some years earlier (O' Brien 2004). Subsequently the government was forced to consider recalling the entire batch amid concerns about their deterioration after their March 2005 best before date. The expiration of these tablets' use-by date so soon after distribution suggested the date was either overlooked or ignored by those under pressure to deliver. A government-appointed expert group later advised that the tablets' shelf-life could be extended until 2009, subject to yearly monitoring (Wall 2006). In April 2008, the minister for health, Mary Harney, advised the public to dispose of any remaining tablets as risks 'that may have existed' in 2001 had been reduced (O'Regan and Heffernan 2008).

The iodine affair can be explained as the outcome of the government's panicked reaction to political pressure over the claimed disarray in emergency planning. But this pressure also led to more fundamental consequences. Foremost among these was the government's decision that the management of emergency planning needed immediate overhaul. The new management structure was put in place in days. For example, the Office of Emergency Planning was established a week after the Jacob interview, on October 3 2001. However, while it was achieved with speed the new structure split top-level responsibility for the overseeing of reactive security from that of proactive security. Since 1982 the Department of the Taoiseach was the lead department both for what overseeing of emergency planning there was and for the National Security Committee, such as it was.[3] Paradoxically, this element of joined-up government was divided in the immediate aftermath of terrorists exposing gaps in the institutional expression of US security with ruthless effect. Moreover, while the official Irish threat assessment prioritised reactive over proactive security, Ireland's new arrangements demoted emergency planning within the hierarchy of government departments from Taoiseach to Defence. As a policy action, giving lead responsibility to Defence ran against the grain of arrangements in most other

EU states in which reactive security was perceived as a matter of prime-ministerial remit. As a Defence official put it:

> We're probably a little unique within the EU as having emergency planning being placed in the ministry of defence. Most of them tend to be in a centralised department, such as the ministry of the interior, the ministry of the environment, [or] such as in practically all of them, a cabinet office where it is seen as being sufficiently important to justify the personal intervention of the head of government. (Author's interview)

Aside from splitting lead responsibility for proactive and reactive security, the re-evaluation of security policy left intact, and in some cases added to, complex lines of operational command and decision-making in the event of an emergency. Various government departments were left holding lead responsibilities for major emergency plans. The State's overall Major Emergency Plan fell between the Departments of the Environment and Local Government, Health and Children, and Justice. But the Department of Health and Children was the lead department for the Contingency Plan for Biological Threat. The Plan for Dealing with Major Oil Spillages from Vessels came under the Department of Communications, Marine and Natural Resources. So too did the Plan for Dealing with Marine Search and Rescue. The Department of Transport held lead responsibility for the Plan for Dealing with Security Situations Involving Aircraft or Airports. The National Emergency Plan for Nuclear Accidents was the responsibility of the Department of the Environment and Local government. At the operational level, each of the regionalised Health Service Executives (HSE) had its own major accident plan, each local authority in the State's twenty-six counties maintained separate major emergency plans and each Garda division was required to have ready a major incident plan.

These plans were expected to draw together a multiplicity of independent management components should a major incident occur. The nuclear accident plan provides a good example of how things were intended to work out at national level. An emergency response coordination committee would be brought into immediate session in a central control room. An official from the Department of Environment would chair. In assistance would be representatives from departments and agencies, including the Departments of the Taoiseach, Agriculture and Food, Defence, Health, and Marine and Natural Resources, as well as representatives from the Food Safety Authority and the Garda. The committee's role would be to provide to cabinet advice on the practical issues and implications associated with the recommendations of the Radiological Protection Institute of Ireland (RPII). A committee of ministers would also be established, chaired by the minister for environment and consisting of ministers including those for health, agriculture and food, marine and natural resources, and defence. But with so many diverse actors coming together in sudden formation and in circumstances of extreme pressure there was at least some scope for problems of cohesion to arise, even where exercises had occurred.

In this regard, rivalry and turf wars over emergency planning had marked interactions between several of the key players in the past (O' Riordan 1992). Additionally, the likely hierarchy between advice that the emergency committee might provide to their lead minister – the minister for the environment – and any competing advice that the Taoiseach might receive from his advisors on the NSC, was unclear. At a regional/local level, while each of the primary response agencies had devised plans, the Garda, HSE and local authorities operated to different geographical boundaries. Hence, it was at least conceivable that in an emergency, multiple Garda, HSE or local authority plans would clash although, subsequently, Garda boundaries were modified in a manner that mirrored those of county councils.

Some senior officials defended the need for an elaborate management structure on the basis that a single-agency approach would work only when threats could be precisely predicted and the elements essential to that brought together (Author's interviews; Smith 2004). They cited the foot-and-mouth disease crisis of 2000 as an example of how cooperation between departments and agencies of different backgrounds could be harnessed together to work effectively at short notice. Moreover, they pointed to the smallness of the Irish emergency planning community relative to other states, the typically Irish way of doing business informally and the use of a common language throughout the State. Laudable as these arguments are, they are problematic. Most obviously, the benefits of common language, less formal business practices and smallness of community combine as cogent grounds in favour of dispensing with a structure of innumerable small pieces.

However, the most engaging rebuff to the patchwork approach came from interview evidence of frontline agency specialists. These senior officers suggested potential for serious command and control lapses, resulting in unnecessary dangers and delays. The comments of one senior Army officer encapsulated this concern:

> We were saying 'clear lines of command and control'. It's what we believe in and how we operate. Now, that is not necessarily the way it would be looked at in the area of emergency planning ... We have made our points known about it and we have seen the kind of fudge ... Someone has got to be in central control and there has got to be clear lines up and down. And we have put forward our views on this and they have not been necessarily taken ... It is the most fundamental thing in any operation, clear lines of command and control. Without them the whole thing dies. (Author's interview)

A third problem to arise out of the new structure was that it had to 'work around' prevailing agendas, or long-standing traditions of the departments and agencies under its remit. Two examples are useful here, the first to do with the Department of Health's remit for policy and the second with Army dominance of the Defence Forces. Firstly, several interviewees were exercised at what they saw as the failure of officials of the Department of Health to embrace emergency planning responsibilities. It was claimed that officials at Health were, as one Defence official put it, 'not well prepared, frankly' (Author's interview).

Tensions had arisen because as far as officials at Health were concerned their remit only extended to health policy. Operational responsibility fell to the Health Service Executive (HSE). Officials at the Department of Defence and senior Defence Forces officers said that this called into question the effectiveness of cabinet-level decision making over a major health emergency (Author's interviews). According to a senior Army officer:

> Now we'll muddle through. I think Agriculture handled the Foot and Mouth thing very well. The anthrax thing, it got through okay … But from that, it was apparent that if there was to be something in the future happening, you can't put it to somebody who says they're not an executive department they're a policy department. If there was an emergency in that area I would be concerned that we'd work it through, but there would be muddle and confusion in the beginning, which shouldn't be there, certainly based on the lessons we should have learned. (Author's interview)

Secondly, as noted in the previous chapter, the government established a National Civil Aviation Security Committee after 9/11 which reported through the Irish Aviation Authority. But an Army officer rather than an Air Corps officer was appointed to represent the Defence Forces on this committee. Hence, the forum for deciding the State's aviation security policy was denied direct input from military aviation specialists even though military jet escort of suspect civil airliners subsequently became a common tactic internationally.

In terms of the study's main argument it seems that reactive national security policy after 9/11 was weak on three fronts: government responsibility for reactive and proactive security was split, practitioners lacked clear lines of emergency command and control, and existing traditions and agendas within the policy community constrained the new management structure. But do these problems persist or were they remedied in a significant adjustment made to the regime of emergency management in 2006? In late May 2006 a new framework for major emergency management was brought to cabinet for approval (Ireland, Department of Environment 2006; Hogan 2006; O' Brien 2006). The framework replaced 'The Framework for Co-Ordinated Response to Major Emergency' which had been in place since 1984. Major emergency plans in all local authority areas were based on this document. The purpose of the revised framework is to act as a blueprint for the 'principal response agencies' (Garda, HSE and local authorities) at local level to update their major emergency plans. For example, it sets out how to ensure that appropriate inter-agency coordination arrangements are in place and provides common terminology, 'to facilitate coordinated and safe working' (Ireland, Department of Environment 2006, pp. 13, 32). The Department of the Environment described it as 'the foundation block for the development of a new generation of major emergency plans by the principal response agencies' (see 'What We Do – Fire Services and Emergency Planning', www.environ.ie; Ireland, Department of Environment 2006, p. 11).

The framework places significant emphasis on preparing lines of command and control to take effect locally at the scene of both regional and national emergencies (Department of Environment 2006, pp. 43, 54, 58–63, 74). It provides for the appointment of scene-of-emergency controllers of operations from each of the principal response agencies and an overall on-site coordinator. At regional level it requires the agencies to come together in defined regions to form regional steering groups on major emergency management to coordinate the inter-agency aspects of major emergency preparedness and management. It also recognises the problem of differing geographical borders, stating that where such a situation arises,

> There should be only one controller of operations for each of the three principal response agencies and it is necessary to determine from which unit of the principal response agency the controller of operations should come. (p. 55)

However, the framework does not address the split in government management of reactive and proactive national security – an unsurprising failing considering its purpose as a blueprint for regional and local emergency planning. A more direct criticism of it is that it has further complicated the emergency management structure at national level in two ways. Firstly, a National Steering Group has been established as part of the framework in order to oversee consistent implementation of the emergency plans and to facilitate key decision-making nationally in the event of an emergency. This new body overlaps in its functions and membership with the Office of Emergency Planning and the Inter-Departmental Working Group on Emergency Planning. For example, the Office of Emergency Planning has responsibility for the coordination of the various departments and agencies in their planned responses to emergencies.[4] The steering group is the body entrusted with the overseeing of the agencies' development and maintenance of their emergency plans. It is also the coordinating body through which departments decide which one has lead responsibility for a particular emergency (Ireland, Department of Environment 2006, p. 63). Whereas the inter-departmental working group is engaged in 'examining issues at national level relating to the activation of major emergency plans', the role of the steering group is to 'develop, maintain and update the new framework in light of the experience of its application and report on these issues to the Government Task Force on Emergency Planning'.[5] The only clear difference is in which minister chairs which committee. The Department of Defence provides the chairpersons for the task force (the minister for defence) and the Office of Emergency Planning (a senior Defence official). Both are designed, with the support of the inter-departmental working group, for open communication between all relevant departments and agencies. The steering group provides membership to the Department of Defence and the Defence Forces, as well as to the three principal response agencies and their parent departments, but is chaired by the minister for the environment.

Aside from overlapping function, the steering group contributes to an unwieldy and awkward system of departmental management of declared emergencies. When an emergency is called, it falls to each principal response agency to inform their parent departments (Ireland, Department of Environment

2006, p. 63). The departments, 'in their role as members of the National Steering Group', have to 'consult and agree' among themselves which department should hold lead responsibility and, thus, whose plan should be activated. Where the determination is that the lead department is a government department other than one of the members of the National Steering Group, the chair of the National Steering Group (or a person acting on his/her behalf) is expected to inform both the lead department and the lead agency of the designation.

Where there is difficulty in designating a lead department in accordance with these arrangements, the Department of the Taoiseach is contacted by the chairperson of the National Steering Group to determine the matter. 'When designated, the lead government department will be responsible for activating its own internal emergency/crisis management arrangements and making contact with the relevant Local Coordination Group ...' (pp. 63–4). There is no reference in the framework to what will happen in the event that the Department of Health is designated the lead department (i.e. whether its officials will continue to be constrained by their policy remit). But in acknowledgement of the problem has been formed the National Public Health Emergency Team, which manages the public health emergency responses of the HSE and the Department of Health; the secretary general of the department acts as the team's chair. In terms of addressing what the study claims, therefore, the 2006 framework makes significant progress on improving command and control at local and regional levels. However, problems persist insofar as there remains a split in top-level government control of the management for national security policy. In addition, an already convoluted emergency management structure at national level is further complicated.

Range of threat

This section deals with factors that the frontline agencies believe bring risk nearer to Ireland. It focuses, in particular, on border security and various measures taken to modify Ireland's immigration regime since 9/11. The discussion examines, among other things, agency concerns around 'sleeper cells' of terrorists operating within the State.

The majority of key decision-makers interviewed argued that the Common Travel Area was the most significant issue in Ireland's proactive security architecture after 9/11 (Author's interviews). They claimed that it raised the risk of Ireland being used as a logistical base for launching attacks elsewhere or for taking shelter afterwards. As a senior G2 officer put it:

> From where we sit, Ireland has the potential to be the base for logistical operations and without logistical back-up, no military operation will succeed. (Author's interview)

Senior respondents said that the dramatic rise of immigration into Ireland since the Celtic Tiger economic boom of the 1990s brought matters into sharp relief. The number of asylum applications to the State increased from some 400 in 1995 to 11,643 in 2002 (Author's interviews; Lally 2006b). As a senior Department of Justice official put it:

> The main gap, or worry, is in relation to immigration … You could have people with fifteen or twenty aliases that come to the attention of the guards and quite who they are is unknown or very difficult to establish. Now, if you ally that with the fact that we've got a Common Travel Area with the UK there is potential there for terrorists to go unspotted, as it were … (Author's interview)

According to a senior garda,

> The fact that so many are coming in and there is so little known about them, you could have among them somebody that could create a lot of problems not alone for this country but for a lot of countries. (Author's interview)

A senior military officer took a similar line:

> The movement of asylum seekers would conceivably provide a cover for any-thing; the freedom of movement between Ireland and Britain, open borders. (Author's interview)

A foremost concern among interviewees was that immigration would be used as a cover for the establishment in Ireland of 'sleeper cells'. These cells of terrorists would take time, perhaps years, to absorb themselves into migrant or domestic communities. A senior Department of Justice official said that the possible attainment of an Irish passport to use as cover when mounting a future terrorist mission made targeting Ireland an attractive 'sleeper' option.

> I mean these people clearly play a long game and if you reach a situation where you stay here long enough to be naturalised, you become a traveller who isn't as likely perhaps, on an Irish passport, to attract attention as on others. So, we're conscious of that and taking our own measures in terms of how we decide naturalisation cases. There would be certain people that we'd have to look at closely before we'd agree to that. (Author's interview)

The official said that 'clearance arrangements' governing certain public sector appointments served as a barrier against infiltration into the institutions of the State (Author's interview). But interviewees expressed concern around immi-grants taking up study or work opportunities, particularly in the fields of elec-tronics and engineering, in either the public or private sectors. The granting of visas to overseas students is also viewed with suspicion (Downes 2005). In these regards, a senior Garda officer said one of the lessons from 9/11 was that the Garda had to ensure cooperation with employers and third-level colleges.

> Okay, is there anything they know about these individuals? It may very well be high-tech jobs, particularly in relation to engineering, electronics, all that area. It is very important that they would play their part if, for instance, they ever became suspicious of any individual they have employed … We would

be talking to employers [asking], 'is there anything we should know'; third level colleges, the very same, 'what are individuals studying', particularly in relation to the areas I just mentioned because they are the people that could cause problems. (Author's interview)

Manifestations

In the fifteen months after 9/11, to December 2002, asylum applications into the State reached a level that was probably unimaginable less than a decade beforehand (Lally 2006b). The Irish government responded with wide-ranging legislative and institutional changes. Interviewees agreed that when these changes were being drawn up the need to prevent immigration access being used by transnational terrorists was a central concern (Author's interviews). The legislative measures consisted of the Immigration Acts 2003 and 2004, and the Irish Nationality and Citizenship Act 2004. (Another act passed in 2000 and, thus, prior to 9/11 provides a crucial arm of the overall framework that has been subsequently developed.) Ostensibly to streamline existing instruments and procedures the Immigration, Residence and Protection Bill was prepared in 2008. The principal objectives of the Immigration Act 2003 were twofold: firstly, to constrain immigration by providing for carriers' liability and, secondly, to comply with Irish obligations on immigration into member states under the Schengen Agreement. The act places a financial liability of €3,000 per offence on airlines, ship operators and any other carriers who transport individuals without travel documents or with incorrect ones. The Illegal Immigrants (Trafficking) Act 2000 imposes even heavier penalties including a possible ten-year jail sentence on anyone convicted of knowingly facilitating the entry into the State of a person who they know to be, or has reasonable cause to believe to be, an illegal immigrant or a person who intends to seek asylum.

The minister for justice, Michael McDowell, said of the Immigration Act 2004 that it was focused on,

> the need to control the movement of people who are engaged in international terrorism, the capacity to stop them at entry points and monitor their behaviour in the State, and the capacity of the Garda to identify who is and is not here by demanding identification. (O' Halloran 2004a)

Among its provisions, the Act empowers immigration officers to refuse entry to the State to applicants who are not in possession of a valid passport/other equivalent document. Officers may also deny people suffering from certain severe mental illnesses. Anyone who comes by sea or air but lands anywhere other than an approved port is deemed guilty of an offence. The master of a ship or pilot of an aircraft must detain on board non-nationals refused entry by an immigration officer. Those giving lodgings to a non-national are in breach of the law unless they 'take reasonable steps' to ensure that their guest is registered with the authorities. Whether they be non-nationals, mariners, pilots or householders offering bed and board, anyone guilty of an offence under the act is liable, on summary conviction, to a fine of up to €3,000, a twelve-month prison term, or both. According to some critics, the 2003 and 2004 Acts create, among other problems, a barrier to entry for asylum seekers forced to flee their home countries without passports or using false ones. The Acts fail to recognise that some asylum seekers may have no choice but to travel on 'people smuggling' routes and give wide discretion to gardaí to treat people with added suspicion on the basis of their racial background (Irish Refugee Council 2004). Similar concerns were expressed with regard to the 2008 bill; the United Nations high commissioner for refugees and the Irish Roman Catholic bishops were among those to sound notes of concern about its provisions, especially in the area of refugee appeals (Brennan 2008; Coulter 2008).

The government also introduced measures to discourage 'welfare tourism' by limiting State entitlements open to foreign nationals in the period while their applications to remain and work in Ireland were being processed by the Irish authorities. In tandem with the Immigration Act, the government amended social welfare legislation to the effect that asylum seekers were placed in 'direct provision' housing and given small allowances. Previously, they were entitled to rental allowances on the dwellings of their choice and benefits such as children's allowance (Lally 2006b). The government did, however, subsequently agree to implement an EU Council Regulation extending social welfare benefits to all legally resident third country nationals (O' Halloran 2007b).

In the same year that the welfare restrictions were introduced the Irish Nationality and Citizenship Act 2004 was enacted. The Act provides that a child born in Ireland to non-national parents is entitled to citizenship if one of the parents has lived lawfully in the State for at least three of the four years preceding birth. Prior to its enactment the State successfully pursued a Supreme Court action which overturned the automatic right to residency for non-national parents of Irish-born children. A referendum was passed that amended Article Two of the Constitution withdrawing automatic citizenship rights by sole virtue of birth on the island of Ireland.[6]

These measures are important in national security terms when seen in the context of 'sleepers' targeting Ireland. Indeed, the legal affairs correspondent of *The Irish Times* wrote after the referendum's passing:

> The message from the government and the raft of legislation and initiatives is clear – Ireland is threatened by people coming to our shores, and we need to restrict this as much as possible. (Coulter 2004c)

Aside from changes to legislation, the outcome of the re-evaluation of national security policy after 9/11 also led to a strengthening of the State's main immigration control agency, the Garda National Immigration Bureau (GNIB), to a degree that had not been envisaged previously. The bureau was established in May 2000 amid what certain government figures described as a 'flood' of immigrants into Ireland. The new entity was placed under the authority of the assistant commissioner for national support services but directed by a detective chief superintendent. In its original state it was allocated a staff of 37 personnel including a detective superintendent and detective inspector. In early 2001 its staff number was increased to 69 and some 60 Garda immigration officers at Dublin Airport were brought under its command in order to streamline the immigration service (Haughey 2001a, 2001b). But by far the greatest increase came in April 2002, seven months after 9/11. The minister for justice, John O' Donoghue, announced that an additional 200 gardaí were to be fully assigned to GNIB. When asked had the threat of transnational terrorism since 9/11 driven this development a senior CSB officer replied, 'Oh it has yes, in a big way, yes' (Author's interview). This was corroborated in the remarks of other senior officers and officials.

Public spending estimates for 2007 indicated that the government's emphasis on security through immigration control had not tapered off almost five years after 9/11. Spending by the Department of Justice on immigration and related services by the Irish Naturalisation and Immigration Service and its associated bodies was estimated at €136.5 million. In comparison, spending on prisons was pegged at €38.8 million. Expenditure on information technology – a 'key support for successful policing and crime fighting' – was put at €38.4 million. The Department's total for immigrant integration measures was €3.2 million. It set aside €1 million to support the National Action Plan against Racism (Ireland, Department of Justice 2006).

A year later the Irish government signalled that the State would, in the near future, introduce a system of electronic passport controls at airports and sea ports. The new system would involve the gathering of data from the machine-readable zones of passports so as to better track suspect movements. Britain's decision to enhance security against terrorist attack by introducing its own electronic controls, under a project called e-borders, prompted the Irish move (Author's contacts, Department of Justice; Collins 2007). Significantly, the Irish government's position was that the new Border Information System would 'converse' with that which would operate in Britain; the traditional exchange of information would continue (O' Halpin 1999).[7] However, this masked an important policy difference between the governments. The UK authorities sought to apply e-borders to passengers who were resident within the Common Travel Area and so to extend its operations to the Northern Ireland border. Irish officials considered application within the Common Travel Area unfeasible on three grounds: firstly the shortness of journey times between Ireland and the UK limited the capacity to process information and to mount a security operation should suspicious information come to light (Author's contacts). Secondly, officials considered it politically impractical to impose passport controls at the border with the north. As one official said: 'Can you imagine [Sinn Féin President] Gerry Adams's reaction?' Thirdly came a consideration of resources and the waste implied in monitoring within the Common Travel Area if the UK government was already doing so (Author's contacts). But the British proposals suffered a setback when in July 2009 the Borders, Citizenship and Immigration Bill was defeated in the House of Lords. Unionists' bitter opposition to the bill's imposition of passport controls on British citizens in Northern Ireland contributed to its defeat. A UK Home Office spokesman in a statement to the author confirmed the British government's intention to reintroduce legislation. The spokesman said:

> The Common Travel Area proposals are important if we are to prevent abuse of the UK and the Republic of Ireland border by third country nationals … We still intend to pursue these changes necessary to enhance the security of our borders and we will be looking to bring these proposals back to parliament at the first possible opportunity.

However, sufficient political support to make worthwhile a reintroduction of the bill could not be assumed. For now, at least, e-borders within the Common Travel Area had come unstuck. Immediately following the bill's defeat Irish officials showed no interest in expanding the remit of the State's system to compensate for the loss of the UK's capability; such a move could inflame opinion in the north and, operationally, would be prone to the journey times between the islands (Author's contacts). At the time of writing the Department of Justice had prepared tender documents to develop a pilot version of the new system and, in terms of the Common Travel Area, were content to rely on existing pathways of information exchange with their UK equivalents. At any rate, passengers were, perhaps, well prepared for the change by the 1997 modification of the Irish passport inspection regime and the decision of budget airline Ryanair, following 9/11, that photo identification was a mandatory requirement for passengers checking in to their flights (Collins and Keenan 2007).

As regards asylum seekers, the numbers began to fall sharply in 2003 when the first Immigration Act was enacted. By the end of 2006 the rate of asylum seekers coming to Ireland was expected to reach a ten-year low, falling to less than 3,800 for the year. The speed at which decisions were made on asylum seekers had increased markedly (Lally 2006b). Hence, whatever human rights concerns that might or might not arise, there was less of a chance of sleepers coming into the State or being able to stay while their applications were processed. According to the United Nations High Commission for Refugees, some one in ten asylum claims lodged in Ireland over a ten-year period up to 2006 were eventually granted the right to stay in the country. Of 63,402 claimants who attempted to seek asylum, 6,841 were sanctioned and another 381 allowed to stay on humanitarian grounds (Sweeney 2006).

Outside the sphere of immigration, the State has undertaken various legislative measures designed to deter and punish transnational terrorism since 9/11. The primary instrument enacted in response to transnational terrorism was the Criminal Justice (Terrorist Offences) Act 2005 which made provision for terrorist offences as a separate and distinct category of offence in Irish law. Pressure for the Act was driven, at least in part, by international demands to incorporate into Irish law several UN and EU Conventions on countering terrorism (Ireland, Department of Justice, Equality and Law Reform 2005). Perhaps the most significant of these is the European Union Framework Decision on

Combating Terrorism. The Act provides for the retention of communications data and makes certain amendments to the European Arrest Warrant Act 2003 (Ireland, Department of Justice, Equality and Law Reform 2005). It also gives effect to four UN conventions: those dealing with the taking of hostages, the prevention and punishment of crimes against Internationally Protected Persons, the suppression of terrorist bombings, and suppression and financing of terrorism.[8] The government attributed the three-year delay in passing the 2005 act through the Oireachtas to the need to address the concerns of human rights activists (Coulter 2004b). The Act passed into law, equipped both with its original definitions and a rider designed to prevent those engaging in protest, advocacy, dissent or industrial action from being categorised as engaging in terrorist or terrorist-related activity.

Separately, the Maritime Security Act 2004 gives effect to the 1988 UN Convention for the Suppression of Unlawful Acts against the Safety of Maritime Navigation. This act creates specific offences against actions threatening the safety of Irish ships and other ships which are in Irish territorial waters, and actions against fixed platforms on the Continental Shelf (Ireland, Department of Communications, Marine and Natural Resources 2004).

In addition to the above, Ireland is a party to various international agreements on immigration including the EU's Dublin and Dublin II accords (and the Dublin-Net intelligence system provided for in Dublin II). Asylum seekers from certain states that have been designated as safe countries must, in making their cases for asylum, reach a higher standard of validation. A separate agreement was reached with Nigeria (from which most asylum seekers were coming), to facilitate speedy deportations (Bracken 2005).

To summarise, immigration control is a central pillar of Irish national security policy. The State's membership of Frontex and the planned introduction of an electronic passenger data-gathering system are to be seen in this context. So too is the work of the Garda's national immigration bureau. The 9/11 attack reinvigorated official concern at the unprecedented influx of migrants leading, within three years of it, to the introduction of several laws restricting the rights of foreign nationals and providing for various punitive sanctions. These laws now constitute powerful weapons in the State's counter-terrorism armoury.

Critique

This section explores the balance struck between immigration control, on the one hand, and integration of immigrants in the interests of national security, on the other. The objective is to establish whether or not policy has worked to integrate new migrant communities in Ireland, so lessening their vulnerability to radicalisation. It begins with a discussion on research that links integration of immigrant communities to the origins of transnational terrorist networks. From here it introduces measures taken by the State to encourage integration.

These measures are then evaluated in the context of the study's key claims regarding political and financial pressures.

In September 2005 the Irish Central Statistics Office (CSO) published population figures showing that foreign nationals constituted around 9 per cent of Ireland's population of 4.13 million people. That was projected to increase to at least 10 per cent in the short term (Humphreys 2005). Whereas the 2002 Census showed that 19,147 Muslims lived in Ireland, by 2006 the figure was estimated to be about 40,000 (*Irish Independent* 2006b). These figures signal a rapid demographic shift to a more diverse Irish population. They make more relevant to the Irish case socio-psychology scholarship on the origins of transnational terrorist networks. Sageman is particularly instructive here (Sageman 2004, 2005). He finds to be misconceived assumptions that global *jihadi* terrorists have some form of unique psychopathology, or are poor, or have been motivated by extreme religious zeal. Instead, the strongest causal link for migrants to become radicalised is a desire to escape social isolation. In European states, this appears to be a pattern most prominent among immigrant workers and their successive generations. For example, it applied to three of the four men who bombed London in July 2005. Groups of friends existing on the margins of society discover deeper kinship in cultivating among themselves hatred of the society and the state that they have become isolated from. Far from being sleepers sent on a mission, these terrorist cells strike up organically from within countries to carry out attacks often without ever having direct contact with any transnational leadership. Sageman calls this the 'Bunch of Guys' theory.

> The global Salafi jihad has now become a fuzzy idea-based network, self-organizing from below, inspired by postings on the Internet. It will expand spontaneously from below according to international political developments, without coordination from above, except for general and blind guidance. (Sageman 2005)

Sageman and others following a broadly similar research agenda find that the policy route for governments is to combat harmful anti-state, anti-societal ideas with healthier equivalents. For national security agencies the task is to identify vulnerable close friends and those figures at the periphery that may influence them (Sageman 2004; Altran 2003). Underpinning both is the need to encourage integration from which can flow stronger police–community relations and better intelligence.

There is evidence to suggest that the Irish government has recognised the need for better integration. In 2007 Taoiseach Bertie Ahern created a junior ministry to take responsibility for integration policy.[9] The new post was aligned with the Departments of Community, Rural and Gaeltacht Affairs, Education and Science and Justice, Equality and Law Reform.[10] The first appointee was a Fianna Fáil TD, Conor Lenihan. A year earlier the minister for social affairs, Seamus Brennan, warned that Ireland would face violent civil unrest, as France had done, if new immigrants were not well integrated into Ireland. He pinpointed better access to education as well as welfare and social employment policies as key steps to avoiding future trouble. Significantly, he noted that the Irish government was only 'starting to get it right', suggesting that integration was a policy weakness beforehand (Hennessy 2006).

Government action to improve integration began a year earlier. A national action plan against racism was announced and a dialogue proposed between the various churches, faith communities and non-confessional organisations (Downes 2005b). At its first plenary session in February 2007 the Taoiseach, Bertie Ahern, denounced 'aggressive secularism … [which] would diminish our democracy' (Cooney 2007). The rules of entry into the Garda were amended to allow ethnic minorities to join the force. In parallel, human rights courses were promoted in the curriculum at the Garda College in Templemore. The minister for defence, Willie O' Dea, requested that the Defence Forces chief of staff, Lt. Gen. Dermot Earley, examine ways to encourage more foreign nationals to join the military (Lally 2007b). Hence, if integration efforts have been a policy weakness since 9/11, the analysis of whether it is a persistent problem has to acknowledge that measures are being taken to address it.

It is too early to judge the success or otherwise accruing from the decision to create a junior ministry for integration. In one of his first public comments following his appointment, Minister of State Lenihan said that 'we have approximately two to three years to get the structures right', and to fix the gaps in the system including language (O' Halloran 2007a). In this regard the minister appeared favourably inclined towards the idea of linking long-term residency and citizenship to the applicant's proficiency in the English language (Fitzgerald 2007). Shortly afterwards, in August 2007, he announced the establishment of a task force to identify the challenges facing immigrants integrating into Irish society; an admission, perhaps, of the government's sparse knowledge of the problem heretofore. He also called for the introduction of a recruitment programme for foreign nationals into the Civil Service, along the lines of that put in place in the Garda (Lenihan 2007).

However, various measures taken by government have been problematic. The inter-belief dialogue took almost two years to begin, although it was reportedly the first of its kind in the EU (Cooney 2007). As regards the broadening of Garda entry requirements, in July 2007 the minister for justice, Brian Lenihan, confirmed that the policy of encouraging foreign nationals to join the force would have to be revised. Of more than 7,000 foreign national applicants to join the Garda in the previous three years, only 200 had passed the aptitude test and of these just 11 had progressed through the interview stages and into training. This group comprised six Chinese, two Poles and one recruit each from Romania, Denmark and Canada (Lally 2007a).[11]

Separately, the London-based Metropolitan Police Sikh Association accused the Garda of racial discrimination for refusing to allow a Sikh recruit to the Garda Reserve wear a turban as part of his uniform (O' Brien 2007). An association spokesman pointed out that the uniform of the London Metropolitan Police Force was modified to allow Sikh members wear turbans coloured police blue and sporting an official police crest and chequered markings. The issue raised some awkward, albeit not insurmountable, questions: Would it be operationally feasible, for example, for female gardaí to wear a burka? More fundamentally, was there value at all in pandering to cultural and religious symbolism when the experience of the UK was that police recruitment from within migrant communities was not enough, in itself, to prevent the conditions arising for the cultivation of radical anti-state/society ideas? The Irish government's position on the issue, as articulated by Minister Conor Lenihan in somewhat colourful style, was that the acceptance of their host's cultural requirements was the norm 'when the President and ministers travel to the Middle East' and that the Irish government expected foreign nationals coming to Ireland to extend the same courtesy (O' Brien 2007).

The prospect of more foreign nationals requesting entry into the Defence Forces raised fears within the organisation and the Garda as to how background checks of each new recruit for security purposes could be effectively carried out (Author's sources). The Defence Forces had learned the value of such checks during the Troubles. In certain cases, soldiers were discovered to have close family ties to members of the IRA (Author's interviews).

On education, which Minister Brennan identified as key to avoiding future strife, a study conducted by a Dublin inner-city NGO found financial and other barriers were preventing foreign nationals from accessing learning opportunities. The report was critical of the absence of education grants for non-EU nationals. Access to social welfare was a recurring theme (Holland 2006b). Perhaps most serious of all was the outcome of research by primary school principals in areas of north-west Dublin heavily populated by immigrant families; a 'white flight' of Irish pupils was taking place from their schools. The report concluded that urgent action was needed to avoid ghettoisation and social fragmentation (Donnelly 2007).

In terms of financing integration and anti-racism measures, the budget of the Office of the Minister for Integration was cut by a quarter and State funding of the National Consultative Committee on Racism and Interculturalism (NCCRI), the advisory body on racism, was withdrawn as Ireland entered recession in 2008 (*Irish Times* 2008). The functions of the committee, which was established in the late 1990s, were incorporated within the office of the Minister for Integration. But its employees were let go, leading NCCRI chief executive Philip Watt to warn that there was 'no way you could transfer over ten years experience without transferring any staff' (McGee 2008). The NCCRI had reported on and monitored incidents of racism, conducted extensive research, promoted interculturalism and conducted anti-racism workshops.

In addition, the National Action Plan Against Racism was wound down without replacement. The Combat Poverty Agency and the Centre for Early Childhood Development and Education, which focused on children in disadvantaged areas, was abolished. The chief executive and half of the board of the Equality Authority resigned when the budget of the agency – which provided legal advice and representation to people experiencing discrimination – was cut by 43 per cent. The budget of the Human Rights Commission was also heavily reduced. According to two members of the commission, Katherine Zappone and Michael Farrell, all of these measures occurred, 'just when poverty is set to grow exponentially and racism is again a danger' (Zappone and Farrell 2009). But the pattern of expenditure prior to these cuts was also problematic. In 2007, as noted above, the Department of Justice provided spending estimates of €3.2 million on measures to encourage integration and €1 million to support the National Action Plan against Racism. In contrast, €136.5 million was to be set aside for immigration services (Ireland, Department of Justice 2006). Government agreed these relatively small amounts despite a 2005 report by an alliance of leading NGOs which concluded that State policies were segregating immigrants from the rest of society and helping to foster resentment against them as 'spongers'. The alliance stated that, 'the government not only fails to acknowledge the seriousness of racism in Ireland today, but on occasion seeks to deny its existence' (Holland 2005).

The Irish Refugee Council has called into question the government's commitment to integration:

> Integration of communities who will be long-term resident in Ireland has played a distant second fiddle to the security-driven approach dictated by the Department of Justice, Equality and Law Reform ... The lack of any adequate commitment to integration will ultimately mean that communities of immigrants, or their first or second generation descendants, will remain largely cut-off from future Irish society. (O' Mahony 2004a)

The 'security-driven approach' has resulted in immigration control outcomes being out of step with the encouragement of integration. In 2005, members of the Garda National Immigration Bureau conducted raids on schools to remove children for deportation. In another case children were hospitalised as 'social admissions' for several days after their mother was wrongfully arrested (O' Mahony 2004b). Lawyers with immigrant clients claimed that gardaí deliberately threw away faxes notifying them of court proceedings to prevent the deportation of seven Nigerians (RTÉ News 2004b). The Irish Refugee Council claimed that one applicant was refused citizenship on grounds of not being 'of good character' because of having incurred a €100 fine for a road traffic offence. Another was refused because he had been dependent on State welfare for some period immediately prior to a decision on his citizenship application (O' Mahony 2004a).

It is worth briefly considering whether a drop in the number of migrants coming to Ireland as a consequence of economic conditions, the imposition of restrictive legislation and the planned operation of electronic border controls will result in a softening of the State's approach so as to avoid the sort of problems listed here. Clearly a significant lowering in numbers to be processed has the benefit of removing strain on Garda manpower and, perhaps, a reduction in scope for human error. But the reassurance which electronic data gathering can provide to immigration enforcement personnel must be qualified: the Irish and UK systems combined, assuming the latter can be salvaged from its political defeat, are intended to secure the Common Travel Area's external borders. It flows from this that the terrorist risk from immigration decreases and the focus switches, instead, to the potential for problems within existing communities. But the effectiveness of any such technological measure depends on whether terrorists or criminals can outmanoeuvre it, as they may also the airlines' insistence on reliable forms of passenger identity. Immigration personnel may choose not to take the chance and continue with existing tactics. As it stands, in the absence of the UK's system GNIB members must rigorously monitor passengers from within Common Travel Area; this places the gardaí concerned in a difficult and potentially confrontational position. Effectively – and despite Irish policy to preserve the area – they must treat with suspicion all 'foreign-looking' passengers arriving from the UK and its surrounding islands (Author's contacts, Department of Justice). Hence retained in the immigration control process is a systematic focus on racial difference. Such a systemisation is an obstacle for integration holding open, as it does, the prospect of migrants with rights of residency in Ireland coming under routine suspicion – and perhaps interrogation – without substantive reason.

The State's approach to integration also seems at odds with that taken towards protecting the rights of employment of migrant workers. Ireland was one of just three EU member states that offered unrestricted access to workers from those countries that joined the EU on May 1 2004. Yet the State maintained twenty-one labour inspectors (or less than one per county) to ensure foreign nationals, many unfamiliar with Irish employment entitlements, were not singled out for discrimination. Three years later the Fianna Fáil/Progressive Democrats coalition (2002–07) established a new National Employment Rights Authority (NERA), employing an increased number of labour inspectors, following the discovery of multiple cases of exploitation (Brennan 2007). In the same year the Equality Tribunal reported a rise in the number of complaints made relating to racial abuse and discrimination in the workplace (*Irish Times* 2007b).[12] It remains to be seen whether NERA is effective in containing an apparently widespread issue.

There is some evidence to suggest that segregation rather than integration of immigrant and indigenous communities is already occurring. The National Consultative Committee on Racism and Interculturalism found evidence of racial discrimination against Chinese people in Ireland. In general, the Chinese community remained isolated from mainstream Irish society. Lack of access to low-cost English classes was considered to be a significant problem (Wall 2006b). A report by the Migrants Rights Centre of Ireland (MRCI), an advocacy organisation, and Dublin City Development Board found that migrant workers in Dublin were often treated as second class and this was preventing them from integrating. The report also expressed concern over migrant workers feeling a sense of isolation and having little control over decisions that affected their lives. Poor employment conditions were a key issue and many migrants were over-qualified for their jobs (MRCI 2007; *RTÉ News* 2007a). In the first Irish media poll of Muslim opinion in Ireland 77 per cent of Muslims believed that they were accepted in Irish society. But younger Muslims in Ireland were more likely to want an Islamic state. A narrow majority favoured the imposition of Sharia law. A substantial minority believed that violence for political ends was sometimes justified (*Irish Independent* 2006b).

In 2008 the EU Agency for Fundamental Rights confirmed that on the basis of police statistics for 2005/06, the number of race crimes reported in Ireland was rising faster than in 11 other member states that kept comparable statistics. The Garda recorded 174 incidents of race crime in 2006 compared to just 94 a year earlier. This reflected a continuing upward trend over the previous six years, with a 31 per cent rise reported between 2000 and 2006. The police figures for 2005/06 showed an 85 per cent rise in Ireland, a 54 per cent rise in Slovakia, a 14 per cent rise in Germany and an 11 per cent rise in Britain. The report stressed that the low absolute crime figures in Ireland meant a smaller increase in incidents could lead to a higher percentage increase but also noted that compilation of data in Ireland was mixed. (Smyth 2008)

So, in sum, the Irish government has, ostensibly, recognised the need for integration in the face of early weaknesses in policy. At the same time measures taken in the name of limiting immigration have been out of step with the goal of cultivating a cohesive bond between new communities and the State. No evidence is presented here to link the enforcement problems identified with heightened political or financial pressures on the agencies. That being said, it would stretch reason to suggest that Ireland's rigorous immigration controls were entirely removed from domestic political pressure or from pressure on governments at EU level to crack down on illegal immigration to the Union. Conceptually, the government's objective of improved integration can be understood in terms of an attempt to protect the binding idea of the state. The binding idea also helps to account for other features of policy. For example, subjecting a law such as the Criminal Justice (Terrorist Offences) Act 2005 to human rights review has a pay-off for Irish national security by reinforcing the bond between population and State.

The probability and consequence of threat

Whereas in the last section the objective was to conduct a critique of the State's response to what was perceived to be the nearest threat to Ireland, here, the focus is on how the agencies calculate the likelihood of threat. The discussion begins with an overview of some key assumptions about threat to Ireland. Unlike in the previous two analyses – specificity of threat and range of threat – here the section on manifestations is set aside. This is because the security community argues that the main manifestation of the threat assessment is Irish national security policy. Instead, matters will proceed directly to the critique, which will focus on the validity of the intelligence process underpinning Irish assessments of threat.

The dominant wisdom within the most senior ranks of the Irish national security community is that terrorists selectively choose the highest-value target possible within their limited means and resources (Author's interviews). The goal is to achieve the optimum 'economy of force'. Targets are more valuable by merit of the political and media impacts that an attack on them will generate. A high-value target may be too expensive to attain if doing so involves, for example, an untenable loss of operatives or financial resources relative to gains made. An alternative target may not offer the same degree of impact to make an attack worthwhile but it may appear more attractive if the costs of striking the higher-value target appear too high. Applying that to the Irish situation a senior military officer said a bomb attack in London, 'would be global news', whereas international attention on an attack in Dublin would pass in a much shorter period (Author's interview). In the same vein, a senior Department of Justice official said:

> I think, look, to quote a previous American diplomat, we're small potatoes in the context of international terrorism … if they want to carry out a high profile attack, one against Ireland wouldn't necessarily register in that context … Part of the 9/11 stuff was the dramatic effect it was intended to have. I would think just as a matter of common sense that in terms of terrorists wanting to have spectacular effects, that frankly they'd prefer to have the spectacular effects against America.

The same official warned, however, that the equation could rebound against Ireland if primary political and propaganda targets were so secure that attacking them was too problematic a proposition:

> If it becomes virtually impossible to carry out these attacks in their most favoured areas they are still willing to take on the Western world, as it were, and we're certainly conscious that Ireland could become a target in circumstances where such conclusions are reached. Like I say it could become a target of opportunity … (Author's interview)

Or, as another senior Justice official put it:

> I don't think that they would refrain from hitting us because we're nice and green and Irish. They might choose to make a point here because it might be more difficult to make it somewhere else. (Author's interview)

Several respondents warned that terrorists might see a reasonable gain from attacking an asset associated with one of their primary target countries but located on Irish soil (e.g. an embassy or diplomat). According to a senior G2 officer:

> If you want to blow up the American Embassy, blowing up the one in Rome is more valuable than blowing up the one in Denmark or Ireland. But remember Nairobi and Dar es Salem. (Author's interview)

Another said it was 'not to say there are not targets of opportunity; that they would not attack our commercial concerns' (Author's interview).

So the Irish agencies calculate Ireland's target value on the basis of 'economy of force' whereby terrorists must strike a balance between rewards like publicity and the achievement of aims and costs such as the number of operatives lost. But it is worth emphasising that the agencies are sensitive to exceptions. While they consider Ireland to be at low risk of attack because terrorists can achieve far higher rewards by striking the UK, intelligence personnel acknowledge that exceptions can occur and vigilance is necessary.

Critique

Clearly the reliability of a threat assessment depends on the validity of the intelligence process underpinning it. The threat assessment that emerged from the re-evaluation of policy after 9/11 relied upon the intelligence available to the agencies and how they interpreted it. Several senior officials and officers argued that the agencies had a strong capacity to access intelligence about transnational terrorist networks (Author's interview). Army officers emphasised connections built up through overseas missions and Defence Forces' participation in EU Military Staff (EUMS). Senior gardaí emphasised the force's close links with other security and intelligence agencies (Author's interviews). As regards more general intelligence a senior CSB officer said that the introduction of new institutions, such as the Office of the Director for Corporate Enforcement, enhanced intelligence reliability not least because they produced open source reports that could trigger alarms (Author's interview).

But these strengths must be offset by significant structural weaknesses. Firstly, when re-evaluating policy after 9/11 the Irish agencies had to rely heavily on the agencies of other states for foreign intelligence. In this regard the following extract of an interview with a senior Department of Justice official is revealing:

> *MM:* Our view of the global terrorist capability of terrorists was to some degree informed by what the agencies of the bigger countries were telling us?
>
> *Official:* Oh, I think it was almost exclusively informed by that. That, and as I say just making with a small 'p' political judgements. (Author's interview)

This is at odds with a canon of intelligence work – the need, as Herman puts it, for analysis to retain intellectual independence (1996, p. 112). The other agencies have set out the main intelligence interpretations; the Irish make only minor modifications. This situation continues unchallenged. Ireland has no dedicated foreign intelligence capability supplying information to counterbalance whatever rainbow of agendas, norms, values and traditions inform other countries' perspectives.

Interview evidence suggests that there are other problems. Two years after 9/11 a Defence Forces officer suggested that the Garda knew little or nothing of the extent of extremist Islamic activities in Ireland outside of certain areas of Dublin (Author's sources). A Department of Foreign Affairs official complained that it was tough to strike up intelligence share with the Garda (Author's interview). The point was echoed by a senior Garda officer on the policing side, who maintained it was difficult to get information out of CSB (Author's interview). This suggests that CSB have hoarded information on a 'need-to-know basis', a practice which is, among responsible agencies, outdated and should be abandoned, according to a leading US intelligence official (McConnell 2007). In this regard it is worth recalling earlier evidence from senior Army and Department of Foreign Affairs officers calling for an overarching national intelligence coordination agency. Their expressions of concern suggested that information share and the scope of intelligence gathering needed adjustment (Author's interview). Taken together, the evidence of all of the interviewees raises significant issues of validity for the intelligence process.

But have financial and/or political pressures contributed to these problems for policy? There is evidence that financial pressures have had a negative effect. Here it is worth recalling that the re-evaluation of Irish national security policy took place against the backdrop of a sudden slowdown in the Irish economy and public spending. When, in the wake of this slump, Defence Forces management was forced to prioritise key spending areas G2 received no additional revenue (Author's interviews). The Garda prioritised intelligence gathering against dissident republicans, gambling that investigators would also happen upon the activities of transnational terrorists (Author's interviews). A senior Air Corps officer, and former intelligence officer, said that some time before 2001 his overseers had curtailed basic intelligence-gathering activities to save money. He maintained that nothing had changed since 9/11. Financial pressures continued to cause significant gaps in intelligence.

> My big problem was getting people to accept that what I was saying was valid. What people don't realise is there are 150 or 170 airfields around Ireland. Now, some of them are only a grass field in the middle of nowhere. But I can think of one immediately, in the middle of Tipperary, which is a field down in the bottom of a valley with mountains all around it, which anybody could be bringing anything into. Now I'm not saying they are. But they could. Again, I hate to mention the filthy lucre but when we did this survey, when we pointed it out, we were told, 'Oh, you're only looking for more mileage, you're only looking to go and visit all these and stay in touch with them'. Yes, but that's because if you're going to do intelligence properly, that's what you need to have. You need to know what's going on. You don't need to know what's going on in every field. But you need to build a network of contacts. You need to know what's going on. So, nothing has changed in relation to air intelligence. (Author's interview)

In summary, a number of issues call into question the validity of the intelligence process. Irish policy relies heavily on intelligence supplied by the agencies of other states that do not obviously have Ireland's security as their key concern. Inter-agency/departmental communication and the scope of intelligence activity are points of concern. Among other things, financial pressure meant that policy was formulated on the basis of intelligence suffering significant, if avoidable, gaps.

The historical dimension of threat

Here traditionally high public support for the State's efforts to counter terrorism is discussed. The purpose is to set the stage for a critique that will consider the state of policy in the context of public cooperation with the Garda.

During the Troubles the frontline security agencies enjoyed a relatively high degree of public and media support for their activities. This endured despite such moments of crisis as the Hunger Strikes in Northern Ireland, the enactment of counter-subversion laws constraining human rights, Garda involvement in politically oriented activities (including the tapping of journalists' phones) and revelations of the 'Heavy Gang', among other matters. Various senior interview respondents argued that the public would continue to cooperate with the Garda against transnational terrorism despite recent controversies surrounding the force. A senior Department of Justice official said:

> I'm listening to people regularly saying 'they're a shower of bastards, they sit on their arse and they don't do anything'. I'm listening to it all the time ... So I mean I think there is a certain amount of disenchantment with their efficiency. That said there is an awful lot of confidence still as well. And I don't think that people that would have information about something serious going down of a terrorist nature, wouldn't go down and talk about it because the gardaí shot someone ... or because they acted the bollix in Donegal. (Author's interview)

A senior Garda said:

> I think that the people out there, for all the right reasons, would see us as a police service that they can trust – I would hope – and that information would flow from them to us. After all, what are they doing? They're actually trying to prevent something happening in their own country or maybe in their own community. (Author's interview)

Manifestations

After 9/11 CSB's Middle Eastern Desk was expanded. Changes to informer-handling procedures were introduced and a liaison system between CSB and senior personnel in the regions and divisions established as a consequence of the Morris Reports (*Communique* 2008, Lally 2006a). But fundamentally the agency carried on as the rather centralised structure it had always been with its personnel largely Dublin-based. Consequently, CSB remained very reliant on cooperation between the public and ordinary policing members around the country who could accrue intelligence on its behalf through casual and informer contacts. A senior Garda provided the following insight:

> I'm coming from the premise of having seen information coming from our uniformed people in various parts of the country in relation to the acts of certain individuals. I would say that if you have a very good police operative, whether he's in uniform or plain clothes, and he's an individual that is totally trusted in the area that he's policing and, let's say, whether it be terrorists, drug activities or whatever he will get the information. It has been proven to me several times over, even in very recent times.

The same officer said that the lesson of transnational terrorism for the Garda was that the force was highly dependent on the cooperation of the public to report suspicious activities.

> For this country, I suppose you could say, to a lesser degree, our lessons would be ensuring that we have an embracing co-operation with, particularly, employers employing people, let's say, in taking them into this country. (Author's interview)

It is worth noting Garda acknowledgement of the need to engage positively with members of the public, particularly those who may unwittingly employ or provide cover to a 'sleeper' terrorist. But this acknowledgement is predicated on the assumption of the force's ongoing capacity to gather effective intelligence from within the community and feed it back to CSB based at Garda Headquarters. It is an assumption, as we shall see, which is open to serious question.

Critique

In this critique the capacity of the Garda to gather intelligence is questioned in the context of changing demographic patterns in Irish society and the continuance of the system of centralised political control over the force. The discussion encompasses the growth in commuter-belt towns, the arrival of immigrants in unprecedented numbers and the passing into memory of the Garda's role during the Troubles.

Ireland's changing demographic profile challenges human intelligence (HUMINT) gathering from general contact with the public. Since the Celtic Tiger economic boom there has been a fast growth of commuter towns. In these towns regular interaction with the local garda to build up trust is no longer as common. The age profile of the Irish population is such that many of those Irish who have left their communities to reside in the commuter belts have little or no first-hand memory of the Troubles. Nor of the benign role which many of their elders assumed the authorities played in combating republican subversion. A similar argument can be made regarding Ireland's increasing population of foreign nationals. In addition, contemporary lifestyles may not lend themselves to the sort of Garda monitoring possible when, as during the Troubles, the framework of parish life helped expose what was conspicuous and much else besides. It is getting more difficult for local gardaí to know what is 'going on in their patch' (Author's interviews). This places a question over CSB's system of relying upon local units to gather intelligence and 'pass it up the line'. Similarly, it makes more challenging the task of spotting vulnerable groups of individuals in situations of social isolation who may become involved in a terrorist cell.

Furthermore, evidence suggests that public confidence in, and satisfaction with, the Garda have been challenged by controversies involving the force. It was against the backdrop of these controversies that Gordon Holmes of the Garda Complaints Board said in January 2004 that, in his view, public confidence in the Garda was at or near an all-time low (Lally and Hennessy 2004). Leading members of the opposition, Garda representative associations, civil liberties organisations and media commentators are among those to have expressed similar views since 2001 (Fine Gael 2004; Green Party 2005; Irish Council for Civil Liberties 2004; *Irish Times* 2006a). There are also quantitative indicators to the effect that the link between the citizens and the Garda has weakened in the post 9/11 years (Central Statistics Office 2004; Brennock 2004; Garda Síochána 2004, 2005; Fine Gael 2004).

On the plus side, some several thousand people applied for membership of the new Garda Reserve when recruitment to it was first advertised, in 2006. Various reform measures have passed into law with the implementation of the Garda Síochána Act 2005. Management structures in the force have been significantly altered. But it remains to be seen whether these legislative and structural changes succeed in the goal of instilling a new 'culture of performance management and accountability' in the force (Dáil Debates 2006b, pp. 13–18). As noted in Chapter 3, the new regime remains subject to centralised political control, the system which helped to cause the problems that made necessary the various reforms. It appears that routes remain open to government to interfere negatively and without trace in the good running of the force. It is still problematic for the government and for those holding the highest positions in the Garda to acknowledge systematic problems. Should these problems result in actions leading to a serious corrosion of Garda–community relations the task of detecting, through intelligence, extremists emerging from socially isolated circumstances may become even more difficult.

Conclusion

Expressed in the terminology of Buzan's model, after 9/11 the Irish authorities focused themselves on diffuse threats, especially problems within emergency response management. It is worth emphasising their concerns over government continuance, the State's primary institutional expression, and with mass communication reflecting the importance of maintaining the binding idea. Regarding range of threat, terrorist abuse of the State's immigration processes was judged the nearest major problem for national security not least because a feature particular to Ireland and the UK, the Common Travel Area, amplified distance perceptions. Again the State's effort to safeguard the binding idea is worth noting, with the Human Rights Commission having the opportunity to review key counter-terrorism legislation. Policymakers' anxieties at the prospect of sleeper cells targeting Ireland reflected concern with the security of both the binding idea and the State's institutions. However, Irish policy is undermined by significant intelligence gaps – a point developed by investigating from the perspective of probability and consequence and in terms of historical development. Taking this range of findings into account and making the usual warning that this is but a single enquiry, Buzan's model provides a rewarding means to explore national security responses to identified threats.

Empirically, the analyst of contemporary Irish security is faced with an official view of threat that has remained consistent since the re-evaluation that followed the 9/11 attack. This assessment, which plays down the likelihood of a direct attack on Ireland but warns of targeting for terrorist logistical purposes, is the bedrock on which policy has been justified. An important undertaking of this chapter has been to question the validity of the assessment process and, as a consequence, the usefulness of policy positions taken on the basis of it. Beginning with the overhaul of emergency response management, the State's mainstay national security response to the spread of international terrorism, the analysis reveals progress made but also ongoing problems of significant scale.

The revision of emergency planning management was done at a hurried pace and in an atmosphere of immense political pressure on government in the wake of Joe Jacob's radio interview on nuclear preparedness in late September 2001. In an atmosphere of intense political pressure fundamental mistakes were made. Despite a second chance to get things right – the major review of emergency planning management of 2006 – the problems remain. Created by the second review was a new steering group which appeared to overlap and duplicate the functions of existing management entities at national level.

On proactive national security policy the various measures so far in place have met the State's objective of reducing immigration. But Irish policy, while strong on keeping immigrants out, is weak as regards the critical objective of integrating those allowed to enter the State. It is worth re-emphasising the research indicating that integration should be a priority concern of states to prevent a transnational terrorist attack.

The assessment that the threat to Ireland is low is the outcome of guesswork by the agencies, which balances available intelligence with modelling of Ireland's target value. The agencies take a careful approach to what they do. But again, there are problems. The off-island intelligence that the Irish agencies have used to formulate the threat assessments has had to come, almost exclusively, from the security and intelligence agencies of other states. Clearly, these do not have Ireland's security as their main concern. In addition, when national security was being re-evaluated after 9/11, Garda and Defence Forces management was, simultaneously, under pressure to cut or cap budgets. In both cases intelligence budgets were constrained and, as in aviation intelligence, clear knowledge gaps left open.

More specifically in terms of on-island intelligence, Garda management argue confidently that the tradition of public support for the force's counter-terrorist activities will continue as it always has. This is to deny that shifting demographic and lifestyle patterns and, of course, successive revelations of Garda misbehaviour are impacting negatively upon the capacity of local gardaí to engage with the community to gather intelligence. It is to defend the concomitant centralisation of CSB in Dublin. Garda managers routinely cite positive public attitude surveys to support their claims but other public opinion evidence points to less favourable conclusions. Such mixed results limit the value of such data as a means to readily conclude on the state of cooperation with the force. Matters are open to doubt.

The absence of any mechanism to shield the agencies from political and financial pressures when they formulate security advice to government, in as far as may be practical, is a major lacuna. Ongoing weaknesses in policy, including but not exclusively those concerning aviation and maritime security, stand as tangible evidence of the failure to constrain the influence of these pressures. In the next chapter the objective is to further explore the various policy problems identified so far, by investigating how key security decisions were made in the 'crisis atmosphere' of mid- to late September 2001.

Notes

1   Almost half a million US military personnel, mostly en route to and from Iraq and Afghanistan, were transported through Shannon Airport between January 2002 and June 2005 (See Deegan 2005).
2   Joe Duffy was the host of an RTÉ Radio 1 live-on-air public phone-in show which was broadcast some hours after the Jacob interview went out.
3   Environment was the more active operational department on emergency planning.
4   See 'What We Do – Fire Services and Emergency Planning', www.environ.ie.
5   'What We Do – Fire Services and Emergency Planning', www.environ.ie.
6   The Irish Nationality and Citizenship (Amendment) Bill 2004 provided for some 17,000 existing residency claims placed in difficulty by the Supreme Court ruling.
7   It is debatable as to whether the Irish authorities, by 2007, were automatically bound to follow the lead of their British counterparts; the Taoiseach Mr Ahern said merely that to do so was 'sensible' (RTÉ News 2007b).
8   Provision is also made for a number of additional measures in the financial sphere, including various procedures allowing for the freezing of funds used or intended for terrorist offences or terrorist groups.
9   A junior minister is more formally referred to as a minister of state. Such ministers do not attend cabinet meetings unless they hold policy briefs considered to be of particular importance (e.g. children). These 'super-juniors' sit at cabinet meetings but are not permitted to vote. The new post of minister for integration policy was not considered to be of sufficient significance to merit the status of 'super-junior'.
10   Gaeltacht refers to an area where Irish is the primary spoken language.
11   Minister Brian Lenihan's admission came some two weeks before his brother, Minister of State Conor Lenihan, cited the Garda's new recruitment policy as something which the wider

Civil Service could emulate. This would appear to point to some incoherence within government on integration issues.

12 While the number of those who made complaints of racial harassment – at less than 150 – is small when set against a workforce of approximately two million people, the figure has also to be seen in the context of other cases not reaching tribunal adjudication. Such cases may well have been resolved informally through local procedures or not reported at all.

13 The Military Staff of the European Union is made up of military experts seconded from member states to the Council Secretariat and is the source of the EU's military expertise. The EUMS provides an early-warning capability. It plans, assesses and makes recommendations regarding the concept of crisis management and general military strategy.

6

Decision-makers under pressure

Introduction

So far, this study has examined Irish policy over a timeline stretching over the seven years after 9/11. Now, the focus narrows to the period immediately after the attack, during which Irish security policy underwent rapid review and all the main aspects of current policy were put in place (e.g. the decision to emphasise emergency planning as the primary concern). The dates in question are between September 11 and approximately October 3 2001.

On the afternoon of September 11 the Taoiseach, Bertie Ahern, and the Tánaiste, Mary Harney, convened a meeting of the 'heads of the security services of key government departments'. Shortly afterwards they reconvened the dormant National Security Committee to review existing policy and bring forward recommendations (*Irish Times* 2001a; Author's interviews). On September 25 the government, through its spokesperson, stated that Ireland was not subject to a direct threat but could fall victim to 'collateral damage' in the event of an attack close by (O' Connor and Minihan 2001). On September 26 Minister Joe Jacob gave his interview on nuclear preparedness, causing public fury (Jacob 2001). On October 3 the Taoiseach announced the establishment in the Department of Defence of an Emergency Planning Office to coordinate the response to future possible emergencies and attacks on the State (O' Connor 2001b).

This chapter questions whether heightened financial and political pressures on the agencies influenced their decisions during this period. Or in this time of crisis for national security policy worldwide did these pressures temporarily ease, leaving the agencies to consider threat on the basis of intelligence and expert prediction alone? Or perhaps pressures continued, but agency managers departed from the traditional ways of dealing with them as they endeavoured to make policy choices in quick-fire succession and in a hothouse of uncertainty.

Allison and Zelikow's model of governmental politics is used here. Among other things, it is designed to identify how competing obligations on policy managers influence their view of a problem. Applied to the Irish case it will be used first to shed further light on who played key roles in the review of national security policy after 9/11. Then it will help to investigate whether competing financial and political obligations on those carrying out the review influenced the findings they arrived at in relation to the threat of transnational terrorism. Thirdly, it will support enquiry into which players impacted most on the review of security policy after 9/11 and whether their dominance had to do with heightened financial and/or political pressures on the agencies. Finally, it will be used to find out if the 'rules' governing the scope, extent, style and pace of the review increased the influence of these pressures.

The technicalities of the model were outlined in Chapter 1. But for the purposes of clarity its organising concepts have been translated as four interrelated questions. They are:

- Who plays?
- What factors shape players' perceptions, preferences and stance on the issue?
- What determines each player's impact on results?
- What is the nature of the game?

In terms of who plays, Allison and Zelikow argue that a decision-making group, such as the Irish national security community, 'is neither a unitary agent not a conglomerate of organizations, but rather a number of individual players … Players are individuals in jobs' (p. 269). They categorise players into four distinct categories. These are Chiefs, Staffers, Indians and Ad-hoc players. Chiefs include the most senior figures within government and the security forces. Staffers are the immediate staff of each Chief. Indians work within government/security forces but operate outside the inner circle of chiefs and their staffers. Finally, Ad-hoc players include journalists and spokespersons for important interest groups. Sometimes, and depending on the issue, other Chiefs, Staffers, Indians and Ad-hoc players will become relevant. For example, Irish neutrality does not seem to exercise immigration NGOs but it is of central interest to Irish anti-war NGOs. Allison and Zelikow argue that 'the decisions and actions of government are intranational political resultants' among these various players (Allison and Zelikow 1999, p. 295). But the price of more participants is the inclusion of multiple autonomous interests which each participant holds by merit of their position, which each have an ongoing duty to fulfil and which act to colour the face of the issue that each sees (1999, p. 298). So, for example, the seemingly simple request from on high for experts' advice actually triggers a complex group action process (1999, p. 259). This suggests that the Irish national security response after 9/11 was an outcome of the diverse interests and unequal bargaining influences of the leading players and their subordinates. These decision-makers and framers carried with them a range of values, norms and historical backgrounds. Their deliberations were conducted in an environment of speed, compromise, conflict and confusion.

As regards 'what factors shape players perceptions, preferences and stance on the issue', Allison and Zelikow posit that major policy decisions are coloured by the positions of the players who determine them. The governmental politics model provides four focus points to help identify players' perceptions, preferences and stance on a policy problem. These are parochial priorities and perceptions, interests and goals, stakes and stands and, finally, deadlines and faces of the issue. Regarding parochial priorities and perceptions, Allison and Zelikow note that players representing their organisation in a decision-making process will be sensitive to their organisation's orientation (1999, p. 298). Goals among players will diverge where interests differ. Interests can be personal, domestic political or organisational in nature. Stakes and stands reflect that policy 'games' are played to determine the decision and actions. Stakes are the mix of individual interests, shaped by the issue at hand. In light of these stakes a player decides on a stand to make (1999, pp. 298–9).

When they discuss 'what determines each player's impact on results', Allison and Zelikow argue that power (i.e. the effective influence on government decisions and actions) is an 'elusive blend' of at least three elements: bargaining advantages, skill and will in using bargaining advantages, and other players perceptions of the first two ingredients (1999, p. 300). The sources of bargaining advantage include formal authority and responsibility (stemming from positions); actual control over resources necessary to carry out action; expertise and control over information that enables one to identify the problem, identify options and estimate feasibilities; the ability to affect other players' objectives in other games; and access to, and persuasiveness with, players who have bargaining advantages drawn from the above. However, Allison and Zelikow warn of the dangers around consensus opinion forming in dominant groups. They claim that out of small, cohesive groups, where members continuously have dealings with one another, the psychological drive for consensus tends to suppress both dissent and consideration of alternatives (1999, pp. 283–4). 'Small groups, for example interagency committees … tend to be consensus seeking' (pp. 279–80). Such groups become enmeshed in 'groupthink'. Interestingly, the phenomenon is claimed to be particularly acute in small groups of six to twelve decision-makers.

Finally, Allison and Zelikow argue that policy-making is a 'game' defined in terms of action channels and certain rules/laws (pp. 300–4). Action channels structure the game by pre-selecting the major players, determining their usual points of entrance into the game and distributing particular advantages and disadvantages for each game (p. 301). Rules/laws determine how the game is played in terms of how players can act, the pace they must make decisions at and so forth. One law of the game is that 'he who hesitates loses his chance to play at that point and he who is uncertain about his recommendation is overpowered by others who are sure'. The reward of the game is effectiveness, i.e. impact on outcomes as the immediate measure of performance (p. 303).

Making an impact translates into enhanced reputation, organisational well-being, and players getting adopted what they passionately believe is right as shaped, however implicitly, by the first two benefits.

The theory summarised, matters move now to the first analysis: who plays?

Who plays?

Allison and Zelikow's division of players into four distinct categories helps to identify those who played key roles in the review of Irish national security policy immediately after 9/11. Among the Chiefs were certain cabinet ministers, including the Taoiseach and the other security ministers, members of the reformed National Security Committee, other senior departmental officials and officers of the frontline agencies (i.e. the DF's three-member general staff and the Garda's assistant commissioner for crime and security). Staffers who were immediately subordinate to the Chiefs included officers of the frontline agencies who advised the agency Chiefs on such matters as intelligence and emergency planning. Indians in the Irish case included mid-ranking officials and officers of the departments and agencies who occupied roles that allowed them to influence the outcome of their seniors' deliberations. Finally, Ad-hoc players included the media and leading figures of important interest groups such as immigration or human rights NGOs.

What factors shape players' perceptions, preferences and stance on the issue?

This section will investigate whether competing obligations on the agencies carrying out the review influenced the findings they arrived at in relation to the threat of transnational terrorism. Here, it is worth recalling a theoretical point mentioned in the introduction. Allison and Zelikow posit that major policy decisions are coloured by the positions of the players who determine them. The governmental politics model provides four focus points to help identify players' perceptions, preferences and stance on a policy problem. These are parochial priorities and perceptions, interests and goals, stakes and stands and, finally, deadlines and faces of the issue (pp. 298–330). They are used here to analyse the Chiefs' decision to advise government that the major issue for Ireland after the 9/11 attack was reactive security (i.e. emergency response after an attack) and not proactive security (i.e. attack prevention).

The attack of 9/11 left certain senior position holders in the Irish national security community facing complex dilemmas. But the political pressures arising from it presented them with a deadline to act (Author's interviews). These players included high-ranking Garda officers who were among the government's lead advisors on the threat facing Ireland and on the response needed to counter it. Simultaneously, they held positions as key advisors on/managers of the security aspects of the Northern Ireland Peace Process. In both spheres they worked closely with high-level officials of the Department of Justice.

On August 10 2001, weeks before the 9/11 attack, the Northern Ireland peace process entered another crisis. The local assembly at Stormont was suspended as part of a dispute over the IRA's refusal to decommission weapons. Two days later, on August 12, three republicans were arrested in Bogota, Colombia. One had been recently named in the British parliament as a member of the IRA's General Headquarters' (GHQ) staff. Another had been shot and wounded by security forces in a 1982 undercover operation aimed at catching a bombing team in County Armagh. A third was 'Sinn Féin's man in Havana, the party's unofficial ambassador to the Fidel Castro regime' (Moloney 2002, p. 487). They were detained on suspicion of aiding the Fuerzas Armadas Revolucionarias de Colombia (FARC) guerrilla group.[1] FARC was second only to Al-Qaeda on the US government's list of terrorist enemies (Cusack 2001b). Well-known US allies and influential friends of the Sinn Féin President, Gerry Adams, including those who had organised Adams's first visit to the US in 1994, were 'angered and embarrassed' at the development (Moloney 2002, p. 489).

Within hours of the 9/11 attack pressure on republicans was ratcheted up further. President George W. Bush's advisor on Northern Ireland, Ambassador Richard Haass, held a scheduled meeting with Adams in Belfast to discuss the Colombian arrests. Journalist Ed Moloney provided the following report of that meeting:

> He [Haass] had already signalled that, as far as Ireland was concerned, the laxity and tolerance toward the IRA of the Clinton days had ended. On that September 11 afternoon, he was in no mood to mince his words. It was by all accounts a tough and direct encounter between the American diplomat and the Provisional leadership. It ended with Gerry Adams and his colleagues in no doubt about what the White House wanted to happen. The only way to dispel doubts about the IRA's bona fides … was to decommission. For the IRA, as for many others, it was time to choose sides. (Moloney 2002, p. 491)

On September 17 the *Irish Times* leader writer warned that in the space of a week 'the world has changed utterly' in its attitude to terrorism and that the IRA would do well to take note (*Irish Times* 2001b). On October 10 President Bush's director of counter-terrorism, Francis Taylor, told the US Congress that the IRA posed a threat to Americans (Cusack 2001b).

The US stance made perfect sense in the context of the priorities, interests and stakes facing the Bush administration in the wake of a major terrorist attack. But things were not so clear-cut within the Irish government. At least some of the government's most senior security advisors believed that too much pressure on the Provisionals would backfire. In this vein, a senior CSB officer said that the ceasefire of 1994–96 could have held indefinitely 'if people hadn't put on pressure and issued statements they were advised not to.' He continued:

> There was no flexibility given for time to run down the organisation. Decommissioning should never have become the issue it did. It was ridiculous.

It did untold damage, mayhem. (Author's interview)

Similarly, a senior Justice official warned that severe crackdowns on terrorism could diminish the chances of more 'enlightened' approaches:

> You won't beat effective terrorism by shooting at it and you can address it – but it's very long term and very painful – by looking at it in a more enlightened way and by drawing in and by considering what the terrorists are actually asking for. It doesn't mean that you concede it, but you come up with an enlightened mechanism. (Author's interview)

Essentially the Irish authorities, conscious of available intelligence and experienced in the complexities of the Northern Irish peace process, were discomforted at the prospect of pushing the Provisionals to 'a point they could not credibly go' without a return to violence. Notwithstanding the loss of life, a resumption of the Troubles risked a range of policy positions taken by the Irish and British governments going back at least a decade. Only a year earlier the Irish government published its White Paper on defence which reflected the new Northern Ireland dispensation. Ostensibly on G2 and CSB advice, the White Paper stated that the on-island security situation had been 'transformed' as a consequence of the peace process (Author's interviews; Ireland, Department of Defence 2000a, p. 18). The transformation was used to help justify the modernisation of the Defence Forces in a relatively inexpensive fashion. In the wider sphere of Anglo-Irish relations the degrading of UK military capabilities in Northern Ireland was under way. The cessation of violence had allowed the British government to spread the effects of a major round of defence cuts to the military forces stationed there (West 2004; *BBC News* 2004). In the following years three Royal Navy Hunt-class vessels providing anti-terrorist maritime patrolling off the Northern Ireland coast were sold off (West 2004). British Army watchtowers were removed and, most controversially, the 'home battalions' of the Royal Irish Regiment (RIR) were stood down (*BBC News* 2005). One of many pressures on the Irish government in its stewardship of the peace process was to push for demilitarisation in the North with greater speed (*BBC News* 2001). If it went well the opposition would be denied ground on which to attack the government in the 2002 General Election year (*Irish Times* 2002b). The government could instead claim credit for the perceived economic benefits arising from peace, in terms of attracting investment and job creation, which had begun to accrue north and south of the border.

So, at issue after 9/11 were high political and financial stakes. In this context the frontline agencies came at their task of identifying the level of threat to Ireland from transnational terrorism and how the State should respond to it. This study accepts that they were led in their considerations by available intelligence and experience. A finding from them that Ireland faced a substantial risk of transnational terrorist attack would have suggested a vigorous proactive security crackdown. The side effect of this would almost certainly have been added pressure on the Provisionals which, in the argument of some, could have proved to be a tipping point back to war. Instead the agencies found that the risk was low and the need for proactive measures marginal.

While arriving at their positions on the threat facing the country, the agencies' Chiefs and Staffers also had to deal with separate more parochial concerns. The small number of senior Garda officers advising the government on tackling transnational terrorism in the wake of 9/11 were simultaneously obliged to manage their organisation's responsibilities towards tackling crime and maintaining State security in a resource-efficient way. Subjected by their statutory basis to tight central political control and answerable to the cabinet for funding and senior appointments, top-level officers had to ensure that Garda activities broadly matched government priorities (Walsh 1998). No indication was apparent in the wake of 9/11 that transnational terrorism would become such an issue over a sustained period.[2] This is not to say that political considerations outmatched intelligence-led ones. But once more it points to the structure by which such an outcome could manifest in the future.

Of course if intelligence led Garda managers to refocus, in a major way, on a new area of operations they would have had to have risked organisational and personnel tumult within the force. CSB had been organised and honed around the thirty years' experience of the Troubles in Northern Ireland. It had relatively little experience or proven strength in dealing with terrorism of the transnational variety (the assumption being made here that there are several important strategic and tactical differences, e.g. suicide bombing). Change would have represented a significant management challenge at a time when, as the Morris Tribunal subsequently found, management was in a weakened state and indiscipline widespread (Tribunal of Inquiry Set up Pursuant to the Tribunal of Inquiry (Evidence) Acts 1921–2002 into Certain Gardaí in the Donegal Division 2004, 2005).

But the decision that the principal proactive security challenge was to prevent Ireland's use as a logistical base for attacks on the UK and, further, that immigration underscored the problem, suited the force's goals rather well. There was a fit between the threat of terrorist operatives who were criss-crossing jurisdictions and the Garda's experience at handling that problem, republican subversives having profitably used the Common Travel Area during the Troubles. The force had a long tradition of robust immigration control going back to the foundation of the State (O' Halpin 1999). A dedicated structure, the Garda National Immigration Bureau, was already in place when 9/11 occurred. In addition, it had been a source of some pride within the force's management that the government, in the face of growing immigration, had retained immigration services within the Garda and not, as in the UK case, outsourced them to other state or private entities (Author's interview).

The overhaul of anti-terrorism legislation and the new structures for emergency planning, which were also embarked upon, merged with the force's priorities and experience. The most significant legislative change was the passing of the Criminal Justice (Terrorist Offences) Act 2005. Its main effect was to strengthen measures that the Garda had been deploying for over sixty years since the passing of the first Offences Against the State Act, of 1939. Regarding emergency planning, the Garda had a long-standing role in reactive security with each Garda divisional commander (i.e. uniformed chief superintendent) having 'on the shelf' their own emergency response plan. The new arrangements held these in place but also provided that the commissioner and other senior officers were given leading expert roles within the new institutional apparatus put in place to better coordinate national policy in this area.

Garda leaders were not alone in advising government after 9/11. The Defence Forces concurred that there was no significant threat of attack on Ireland. It is worth considering the stakes for the Army had the decision gone the other way and proactive security had been emphasised instead. The general staff had just secured the financial stability of the Army by tying it to greater international security commitments. Agreement had brought to an end years of negotiations between the Defence Forces and the Departments of Defence and Finance which had publicly soured. The resulting document, the *White Paper on Defence 2000*, was widely perceived within the military to be nothing more than a charter for further cuts (Author's interviews). However, it provided enough financial leeway to modernise the Army along the lines whereby Irish personnel could carry out certain important roles in the new generation of militarily more robust peace enforcement missions. By September 2001 money was already being drawn down from retained funds accruing from the sale of barracks to pay for a programme of force modernisation.[3]

The Defence Forces management knew at first hand, having served during the Troubles in the 1970s, that overseas missions could be de-prioritised, scaled down or temporarily suspended in times of national emergency. They would be replaced instead by a heavier burden of national security duties. A greater overseas military commitment and the investment that came with it would fall down the government's agenda. The thinking of Army leaders on such a reversion had been clear for some time. Overseas missions were critical to the future of the Defence Forces (Author's interview). A return to the 1970s when national security dominated operations must never be allowed to happen (O' Halpin 1999, p. 343).

The finding that Ireland faced no significant on-island threat of attack but that emergency planning needed an overhaul kept the Army on track for an overseas future. It also created the need for a military equipment investment programme beyond that envisaged following the White Paper. Government agreed to procure a range of kit to deal with a nuclear, radiological, chemical or biological incident (e.g. the 9,500 protective suits and other equipment mentioned in Chapter 5). This was both an investment in national security and in the Army's capacity to carry out missions in hostile environments overseas. The decision also led to the establishment of the Office of Emergency Planning, the first joint military–civilian office within the department. In interviews senior Army officers were clearly pleased with the establishment of this office. They argued that one of the benefits of 'jointness' was that it provided a means to influence civilian decision-makers in the Department of Defence, who were suspected of harbouring allegiances first and foremost to the Department of

Finance (Author's interviews).

It is striking that the military advice to government, although intelligence-led despite these high stakes, was arrived at without the direct inputs of members of the minor services (Author's interviews). Instead, officials and Army officers held to a somewhat hazy notion about asking the British government for Royal Navy and Royal Air Force cooperation in the event of an emergency (Author's interviews). Furthermore, over an altitude of 10,000 ft the State had no high-speed air protection of its own.

The smaller services' exclusion caused them some frustration, as the comments of a senior Naval Service officer suggested:

> There is a tendency for the current architects of defence strategy to see strategy formulation as a medium to advance their own sector's interests … You should really be in a situation where the public interest comes first. (Author's interview)

Their lack of direct contact with the re-evaluation process meant that the Naval Service and Air Corps were denied ground on which to argue that Ireland's maritime and aviation interests required basic protection. A year earlier the White Paper had dashed expectations that government would increase the State's military aviation and naval capabilities. The Army was modernised while the two minor services were instructed to extend capabilities by making further efficiencies (Ireland, Department of Defence 2000a, pp. 39–40, 45). Top-ranking Army officers justified this outcome on the grounds that they had to maximise the Defence Forces' effectiveness within a tight funding envelope (Author's interviews). Between 1999 and 2004, when the money from barracks sales was reinvested in the military, the percentage of GDP for defence decreased from 0.9 per cent to 0.7 per cent. Hence, there was no room to develop alternatives or accompaniments to the light infantry model that could have better integrated the smaller services (e.g. fully equipped and trained marine commando and/or airborne force structures) (Author's interviews).

It is worthwhile pausing briefly to consider the failure to adequately resource the other services. One cost was that Irish military personnel serving on the riskier, new generation of overseas missions remained reliant on airborne and naval capabilities of other states' forces. Senior Air Corps officers warned that current arrangements could leave Irish troops trapped in a 'hot zone' in which other states' commanders might be unwilling or unauthorised to risk their own personnel to intervene. In that event, according to a senior Air Corps officer:

> The grand answer was we would hire an aeroplane to get them out. But you won't hire an aeroplane to go into a hotspot. Its insurance is null and void, in which case the minister has to carry it and if something happens, he would have been better off buying the aeroplane in the first place and letting us operate it. (Author's interview)

In the maritime sphere, Naval Service management had submitted a service development plan as part of the White Paper negotiations, which centred on a

'Post-Modern Navy' concept (Lynch and Mellett 2004; Mellett 2005). Embracing 'joined-up thinking', it set the goals and interests for the organisation around securing as many 'service level agreements' as possible with other military and civilian service providers to enhance the capabilities they could offer the State (Author's interviews). In parallel, a new fleet shape was devised in the context of three of the service's eight ships being decommissioned before 2010 and three more by 2015. This gave rise to what was known as the 'multi-role vessel' (MRV) or, colloquially, a 'blue-green ship'. The selling point of the MRV was that in exchange for a marginally higher investment, the State would gain a platform that could, with ease and efficiency, 'swing' to serve multiple blue (maritime) and green (land) requirements. It could, to cite a number of examples, provide:

a) A flexible deck area capable of carrying a variety of loads from containers to vehicles, both military and civilian;

b) a built-in medical facility that could be manned by national or NGO medical staff, who could join the ship at the scene of crisis;

c) accommodation capacity for evacuation operations or troop deployments;

d) a command control communications centre for crisis coordination; an anti-radiation citadel to enable it to function close to a crisis scene in the case of radioactive fallout arising from civilian or other radioactive discharge. (Mellett 2005, p. 11)

The MRV also addressed Naval Service concerns related to hull/crew survivability in harsh North East Atlantic conditions, where dangerous giant waves were becoming more common.

In the two years before 9/11 the Naval Service received two new small vessels to replace those that had reached their maximum service life and to maintain the controversial eight-ship cap. However, the government also equipped, among others, the Maritime Institute, the Revenue Commissioners Customs and Excise and at least one fisheries agency with their own craft. So, the State, in a demonstration of strategic incoherence, went to the expense of establishing a range of little navies of largely single-capability ships over the flexibility envisaged under the post-modern concept. The reassessment of national security in the wake of 9/11 provided an opportunity to revisit matters. In this regard it is worth recalling the State's threat assessment. It warned about Ireland's use as a logistical base for the preparation of attacks on other states (Author's interviews). Prior to the White Paper's publication, the Naval Service had intercepted off the Irish coast several major shipments of weaponry and drugs belonging to major crime gangs (but presumably missed far more). It was also widely accepted by then that despite the service's efforts and advances in electronic and other surveillance capabilities, the majority of the Provisional IRA's arms shipments during the Troubles had got through (Author's interviews; Moloney 2002, pp. 6–33).

Here it is worth remembering Allison and Zelikow's observation that at crisis decision-making moments, 'career officials are prone to believe that the health of their organization is vital' (1999, p. 298). They may not deliberately factor for it; and it is not suggested here that anyone involved in formulating the Army's priorities against transnational terrorism has deliberately distorted matters. But the stands of such decision-makers will, according to Allison and Zelikow, be affected by the multiple other responsibilities that they are professionally obliged to fulfil. Reflecting on all this from where he stood, in a navy that had been constrained from tri-service 'jointness' and integration, a senior Naval Service officer argued that Irish national security at the 'harder end' required fundamental reform.

> We have never really grappled with the 'jointness' required for the delivery of defence services, and this fatally wounded our defence planning prior to September 11 and it continues to wound it, post September 11 …
>
> Before 9/11 it was flawed, since 9/11 it's even more flawed because of the need to look at land, air, sea, space and cyberspace in terms of all these overlaps of environments. So you need to have a professional expertise that takes on those and doesn't drive it primarily, on one environment …
>
> We really need to re-examine, first of all, the way our decisions are made in terms of the Defence Forces. That possibly would flow down to a re-structuring of forces. (Author's interviews)

By way of a postscript, senior Naval Service officers maintained a persistent campaign for MRVs. They focused their arguments on what the ships could offer to the EU's Common Foreign and Security Policy and the NATO-led Partnership for Peace (thus building on external political pressures on the government) and Ireland's overseas development aid programmes (Lynch and Mellett 2004; Mellet 2005). Circumstances turned in their favour. The Irish commitment to the EU Battlegroup concept and the establishment of an Irish humanitarian disaster corps both pointed to the absence of naval transport capabilities. Furthermore, a joint Irish–Dutch operation in Liberia involving a Royal Dutch Navy Ship, HNLMS *Rotterdam*, appears to have provided the Irish Army's senior leaders with a taste for amphibious options overseas (Armstrong 2004). It was reported in May 2006 that the government would consider sanctioning two MRVs to replace the LE *Emer* and LE *Aoife* which had reached their maximum service life (Lavery 2006). The vessels would be larger than those they would replace although smaller than the 14,000-tonne *Rotterdam*. But in January 2007 another report suggested that while the government would spend some €180 million on three vessels, only one would be a 'large' ship. It would cost in the region of €90 million. The 'enhanced naval vessel' was expected to be 120m (394 ft) in length or approximately one-third larger than the existing flagship. The report pointed to worsening weather conditions and to the 'significant cargo-carrying capacity' of the new vessel. As with the original MRV concept it would transport equipment for Defence Forces' missions overseas. Estimates were that the first of the three ships (most likely to be one of the smaller ones) would be commissioned in 2009 (Author's sources; *Irish Times* 2007a). But a date beyond 2010 was suggested in a report of defence cutbacks forced by the economic recession (Brady 2009). The eight-ship cap remained.

In summary, senior Garda and Defence Forces leaders who advised government on the level of threat facing the State after 9/11 had considerable intelligence and experience at their disposal but also had to balance various competing parochial priorities. The government's order to review security presented a deadline for rapid decision-making. But government had taken stands on other policy areas that depended on a low level of threat to the State. The agencies also had interests and goals that stood to suffer in the event of such a threat (e.g. Army modernisation). The stand they took – that the issue was primarily a reactive one – while intelligence and experience-led, comfortably accommodated these disparate factors. But left untouched were fundamental weaknesses rooted in financial and political pressure, not least of which was naval and airborne preparedness.

What determines each player's impact on results?

Which players impacted most on the review of security policy after 9/11 and why were they dominant? Did their influence have to do with heightened financial and/or political pressures on the agencies? In addressing these questions we can draw on Allison and Zelikow's argument that gaining influence over government decisions is an 'elusive blend' of at least three elements: bargaining advantages, skill and will in using bargaining advantages and other players' perceptions of the first two ingredients (1999, p. 300). The sources of bargaining advantage include formal authority and responsibility (stemming from positions); actual control over resources necessary to carry out action; expertise and control over information that enables one to identify the problem, identify options, and estimate feasibilities; the ability to affect other players' objectives in other games; and access to, and persuasiveness with, players who have bargaining advantages drawn from the above.

A pronounced hierarchy is a characteristic of the Irish national security community. Formal authority and responsibility within it is clearly delineated. In the wake of 9/11 the cabinet stood at the top of that hierarchy. Ministers chose to delegate responsibility for advising them on the level of threat and the associated response to the National Security Committee. Civilian officials on the committee turned to their agency members, the Garda commissioner and Defence Forces chief of staff, to deliver an up-to-date assessment of threat and a range of potential strategies and tactics to address any perceived weaknesses.

Providing this advice to their committee colleagues required the commissioner and the chief of staff to draw into the process their various Staffers and Indians, particularly those engaged in intelligence duties. The structures in which they operated placed pressure on senior Garda officers to come at the problem in the context of the various competing obligations that they were also expected to service (e.g. budgets, immigration control and the peace process). Within the Defence Forces, the Staffer and Indian positions at Defence Forces

Headquarters were dominated by one service, the Army (Author's interviews). Naval Service or Air Corps personnel were not in circulation there to address, from their perspectives, the question of threat to Ireland and policy responses to it. Indeed, one senior Naval Service reflected that post-9/11, in 'decisions made in terms of security services, the marine environment didn't really feature' (Author's interview).

When asked how they approached their respective tasks in the immediate aftermath of 9/11, senior officials at the Departments of the Taoiseach, Justice and Defence, as well as Garda and Army officers enthused about the common views held among senior Irish national security managers. They attributed this to the smallness of the management community. As one senior Defence official said, when it came to doing business alongside senior officers from Defence Forces' Headquarters in an inter-agency setting, 'We very rarely these days would go from two opposing points of view on any issue' (Author's interview). Herman notes the benefits to intelligence analysis of close personal relations to facilitate 'persuasion' and 'marketing' of intelligence analysis (1996, p. 143). But it carries a particular and, perhaps, dangerous risk: the National Security Committee consists of six senior decision-makers; it will be recalled that Allison and Zelikow warn that the phenomenon known as groupthink is particularly acute in small groups of six to twelve decision-makers (1999, p. 283). The evidence of senior military respondents, who have developed and/or brought forward alternative defence service proposals to the small cadre of top policy managers (civilian and military) and their subordinates, is instructive here. It suggests that their proposals have been left aside despite their apparent criticality. It would seem the subordinates have run into the prevailing dynamic, which was summed up earlier by a senior Army officer as, 'We only recognise as much threat as we can afford' (Author's interview) or, as Herman notes, the conscious and unconscious selection of analysis by top decision-makers to suit their existing agendas and bias (1996, p. 142). Consistently, these respondents stated that they perceived that their efforts were viewed at the highest levels as mere 'empire building'. A senior Air Corps officer, detailing his experiences of putting forward proposals, expressed particular frustration:

> You know, forget the global. If I come back down to my own area, yes, there are major areas of vulnerability. There are major areas that people don't even understand, which is the failure that I would identify.
>
> When we were going through this process of briefing the chief [of staff] and the secretaries and so on, they again continued to look at us trying to create a situation that's advantageous to us, without even realising – and we did try to press it time and again – that it's no good spending money, it's no good giving us aircraft, unless you put in place the totality of the structure, and the decision making to go with it ... But we have this habit of vilifying, killing the messenger, without actually stopping to look at what the individual is saying ... You don't have to go as far as an invisible enemy. If 9/11 never happened our defence scenario wouldn't be any different. 9/11 actually had no real effect on what happens here. Debate in other countries is about

degree, not about the substantive issue. (Author's interview)

Evidence also suggests that those who may unwittingly or otherwise unsettle the consensus view are pre-emptively excluded. According to a senior Naval Service officer:

> We certainly haven't been brought into any major, let's say, changes in strategy or asked for any contributions in any significant manner. I've noticed some initiatives driven internationally which we've been asked to comment on. But in terms of the articulation of the Irish case or the formulation of an Irish position, it has been done on the basis of 'what do you think of this' and we write a note and then the articulation is done by somebody else. (Author's interview)

How far up the line of authority does this problem go? When national security was being reassessed after 9/11 one might have imagined that every effort would have been made to ensure such exclusions did not occur, by giving voice to as many relevant professional perspectives as possible. The almost immediate re-establishment of the National Security Committee as the government's primary advisory body was intended to achieve this very thing. The committee's small membership included a high percentage of members holding compressed positions, i.e. representing multiple perspectives. Presumably to represent these perspectives effectively to cabinet, they were to consult very closely with their relevant service/agency heads. However, Naval Service officers said that the most senior officers of the Air Corps and Naval Service – and their Staffers – were merely afforded the opportunity to submit to Defence Forces Headquarters their written opinions for consideration. Indeed, almost two years after 9/11 a Naval Service officer who held a top-level service position at the time, said:

> The security committee, I don't have very much knowledge of it. I'm just aware of the fact that the chief of staff is a member of a security committee but I'm not quite sure what they deal with, I don't know what their remit is, I don't think I've ever seen anything about what they're there for. I do know we would periodically be asked questions from some aspect of the maritime area. But it was only when they [the questions] came to light that I became aware that there was this particular group that the chief of staff was on. (Author's interview)

The significance of this can be seen by reference to a scheme of analysis familiar to most western intelligence agencies (Herman 1996, pp. 105–6). Whereas 'current-reportorial' intelligence describes current and recent events (rather like a news feed) and 'basic-descriptive' refers to fixed facts of a situation (e.g. an opponent's troop numbers in any given year), 'speculative-evaluative' is usually of greatest value to policy managers. It is the actual 'estimate of the situation' or as Herman puts it, 'the least voluminous but most important category of reports' (p. 106). It is, theoretically, the most fundamental determinant of security capabilities on land, at sea and in the air. Yet in Ireland the smaller services were apparently denied fulsome access to the speculative-evaluative process.

The exclusions carried over when the post 9/11 structures were put in place, as the following interview extract with a senior Naval Service officer makes clear:

NS Officer: There has been an emergency planning office and that is a classic office, which I would say for an island should have somebody with a professional maritime background on it.
MM: It doesn't?
NS Officer: No, it doesn't, no. In fact, in terms of Defence Forces Headquarters we have no maritime contribution in terms of policy, strategy, intelligence. There is no naval staff in Defence Forces Headquarters other than one officer who is on loan from my staff. So there are 278 appointments in our Defence Forces Headquarters. Not one of those 278 is naval or Air Corps. That is an example, in terms of jointness! (Author's interview)

Of course, it is also to be remembered from the evidence presented in Chapter 3 th at the aviation safety committee, established after 9/11 under the emergency planning structures, was bereft of any Air Corps representation. An Army colonel filled the Defence Forces' position.

Another senior Naval Service officer suggested that ultimately the cost of such a cloistered dynamic was worthless policy 'agreement':

I took the analysis that was provided at Defence Forces Headquarters. I would have certain awareness from my own assessment of the situation, but I would see no merit in actually writing that down. I simply go on the basis of one that was done for the Defence Forces as a whole. If you were to actually look at the ones for the Defence Forces as a whole, you're left asking the question 'you've produced a SWOT analysis on paper, but is that the whole picture'. (Author's interview)

It is not difficult to envisage how the Defence Forces' senior management structure contributed to the problems that these respondents claimed. The military advisor to the National Security Committee is the Defence Forces chief of staff. The chief of staff is a three-star appointment which, in the Irish case, implies the appointment holder will always be an Army officer. By rank and physical location those next best placed to influence are the two deputy Chiefs of Staff also based at Defence Forces HQ. Again, these two-star appointments are closed to the Naval Service and Air Corps; the flag and general officers commanding are both one-star rank. They and their staffs are based externally to Defence Forces Headquarters. During the post-9/11 deliberations this headquarters was located in the same building as the Department of Defence at Parkgate, Dublin, so providing easy access for Army staff officers to departmental officials. Location is an especially sore point for Naval Service senior officers who, as noted earlier, have been headquartered alongside their fleet at Haulbowline Naval Base in Cork Harbour since 1999 (Author's interviews).

The evidence suggests that the National Security Committee was unable to prevent the minor services' perspectives getting lost, either in the DF's flawed top management structure or in the intertwining obligations on committee members. In September 2001 the committee was ordered by cabinet to bring together all relevant perspectives on threat to the State and advise accordingly. But apart from the appointment of the secretary general of the 'neutral' Department of the Taoiseach to chair it, there was nothing put in place to account for how each member's obligations/interests/priorities consciously or unconsciously coloured their inputs. Nor was there any mechanism to challenge or disrupt the groupthink outcomes that might arise. It seems to have been assumed that the Taoiseach's department would have no biased security interests (Author's interviews). This was despite the department's role and Mr Ahern's deep, personal involvement in the Northern Ireland Peace Process.

The committee sought its expertise from those who had previously shown they had skill and will on the negotiating battlefield to protect their organisational concerns. Centralised political control meant that Garda senior management had to negotiate skilfully with government overseers anxious to ensure that strategy was formulated in a manner favourable to their political masters. In the late 1990s senior Defence Forces managers had shown that they could tune their bargaining positions to the struggle for organisational survival (Author's interview). Moreover, the National Security Committee was a formation which, even if it petered out as before, consisted of participants who would continue to do business in close association on multiple fronts. Hence, there was motivation to maintain good relations, implying compromises and ambiguities 'in the interests of the bigger picture' with unintended consequences for effective security policy. As Allison and Zelikow describe it,

> Established, continuing groups behave quite differently from ad-hoc groups. Most continuing groups display deference for seniority and also frequently for members' recognized domain of interest or expertise. (Allison and Zelikow 1999, p. 279)

Indeed, Irish officials – inside and outside the security committee – claimed near total acquiescence to the advice which they received from their expert cohort, suggesting that whatever interests might have coloured that advice went largely unchallenged. The remarks of a committee official captured the dynamic:

> Well, I think we would have relied very much – as we still rely very much – on the security services, the gardaí backed up by the Defence Forces and their international contacts, as, if you like, the framework through which any threat assessment would be carried out. We would have relied on them as we still do, of course, to flag any issues of concern or trends of concern … I think it's a balance between risk assessment, on the one hand in the broadest sense, and actual intelligence-based profiling, if you like, on the other. The judgement that has to be made at any particular time is towards which end of the spectrum the balance of probability is tending. And all of that, of course, is entirely a matter that we rely on the security professionals to do. In a sense, we are consumers of their net outcome of that analysis. (Author's interview)

Such consumer deference was compounded by the experts' tight control of information. The evidence points particularly at the Garda in this regard. Almost three years after 9/11, the Morris Tribunal would report that Department of Justice officials were 'utterly isolated' from Garda HQ in respect of the information that came to them and that they could pass on to the minister and his officials (Tribunal of Inquiry 2004, pp. 620–1). Accordingly, it is difficult to see how departmental officials were as well-equipped as they should have been to mount challenges to the thrust, if not the detail, of Garda analysis. Army respondents suggested that they had enjoyed good information share with the Garda after some turbulent decades (Author's interviews). But, as noted in Chapter 5, a senior Department of Foreign Affairs official and a senior garda on the policing side suggested that information flow was all one way – in the direction of CSB.

To summarise, the most influential players during the review of national security after 9/11 were the Garda commissioner, the Defence Forces chief of staff and their close subordinates who the officials of the National Security Committee depended upon. As Allison and Zelikow argue, they were dominant because they held the relevant formal positions, had considerable control of resources, expertise and information and had shown considerable negotiating skill and will (1999, p. 300). At the same time within the formation of the National Security Committee they – along with the committee's civilian officials – were vulnerable to the problems of groupthink and the associated pressures of a range of competing obligations on themselves and their organisations.

What is the game?

This section examines the characteristics of the policy-making 'game' in which the review of security policy was conducted. The purpose is to investigate whether the rules of this game exacerbated the influence of political and financial pressures on the frontline agencies. Conceptually, the evidence will draw on Allison and Zelikow's definition of the game in terms of action channels and certain rules/laws (Allison and Zelikow 1999, pp. 300–4).

The major players in the review of Irish national security after 9/11 were the cabinet, the National Security Committee and the government departments and agencies party to the committee by reason of their Chiefs' membership. Cabinet ministers took a fairly low-key role, charging the National Security Committee to examine threat and come up with policy recommendations. Hence, the committee was the central link in the decision-making chain. But the National Security Committee and its civilian members relied entirely upon their agency counterparts to set the scene and bring forward policy proposals. Yet under the de facto 'rules of the game', the agencies' most senior managers could not conduct the policy review entirely in isolation from other important priorities which they were also under pressure to service. At the time priorities ranged from the future of the Northern Irish peace process to Army modernisation. This complicated the agencies' task considerably and amplified the pressures upon them. In this environment some voices were heard and others marginalised (e.g. the Naval Service and Air Corps).

Another rule exacerbating the political pressure upon the agencies was the requirement to come up with recommendations in the shortest possible time frame. Mr Jacob's embarrassing radio interview on nuclear preparedness had caused ministers to come under acute media and public criticism. From the normally quiet sphere of national security, major problems suddenly cascaded onto ministers' agendas. The government required rapid responses to contain the political damage. This heightened the political pressures on the agencies at a critical time. Furthermore, they had to formulate a response that could be turned around quickly but which struck a balance with all existing priorities and responsibilities. It is worth recalling here Allison and Zelikow's argument that to attain reward in a rapid action process, policy players must bring forth a response that is deliverable within the pre-existing rules and interests (1999, p. 303). The agencies' recommendation to government led to action that was possible to implement rapidly and with relatively low cost. Substantially, it involved the creation of two governmental committees, moderate expenditure on equipment and exercises and the expansion of an already established Garda body (the immigration bureau), which, however, might have occurred anyway because of EU-wide immigration pressures. Certainly, the response, although led by the outcome of intelligence analysis, avoided the complications, both political and financial, of a substantial increase in national security capabilities, especially at the harder military end. It was, in numerous respects, the optimal reward achiever. The wide gaps of preparedness it has left open are another matter.

Put conceptually, the National Security Committee was the main 'action channel' for the review. But under the 'rules of the game', the agencies had to be cognisant of the impacts of proposals against the effects they might have had on other important priorities, in order to avoid consequences arising from political and/or financial pressures. The political requirement for a rapid review of policy increased the pressures further. The game was unusually fast-paced. However, the agencies managed to come up with a response to cabinet, a focus on reactive security, which was deliverable without jeopardising existing interests, priorities and goals. This is not to say that decision-makers deliberately designed policy to achieve rewards in a selfish way. It is more likely that in a fast-paced, competitive environment, professionals holding multiple responsibilities interpreted the intelligence in the best way that they could from the vantage points they occupied, and chose the outcome that seemed the most appropriate. In this short-termist environment, fraught with political and financial pressures, issues of longer-term contingency (e.g. Naval Service and Air Corps capabilities) had little chance of success.

Conclusion

Allison and Zelikow's model is a widely recognised means to support analysis of decision-making in times of crisis. All in all it has worked well here. Analysing 'what factors shape players' perceptions, preferences and stance on the issue?' helped to reveal, for example, the problems for Irish security policy arising out of disconnections between US and Irish approaches to defeating terrorism after 9/11. 'What determines each player's impact on results?' was used to show the effects of Garda and Army domination of the evaluation process. Responsibility for framing cabinet decisions was concentrated in a small number of top Garda and Army officers and departmental officials. Only these had the necessary formal authority and formal control over resources and information. The downside of their dominance was groupthink, seen in the marginalisation of naval and aviation perspectives.

Empirically, serious consequences could have arisen had the Garda declared a national security threat after 9/11. In the first instance it would have triggered a terrorist crackdown, almost certainly bringing further demands on the Provisionals. In addition, a range of Irish and British government major policy stands depended upon a reduced state of 'on-island' threat in Ireland. Furthermore, as leaders of a force under centralised political control, Garda managers were under pressure to match Garda priorities with political policy. There was no clear indication that transnational terrorism would become a major government priority in the long term, adding to the Garda dilemma. Moreover, switching the force to a new operational focus represented a substantial challenge at a time when management was experiencing widespread difficulties in imposing discipline. The advice that CSB provided to government ensured a relatively low state of alert. Although the product of intelligence analysis, it was also favourable to the various Irish and British government policy priorities, avoided any dramatic increase in pressure on the Provisional IRA, played to the force's current abilities and led to its most senior managers joining new government structures for emergency planning. Hence intelligence and politics flowed in the same direction on this occasion. But what of the dilemma that will face senior gardaí in the future should these factors collide?

The order to review policy presented an equally complex decision for the management of the Defence Forces. Major investment in the Naval Service and Air Corps was being avoided to incubate the Army's fragile recuperation for its future overseas. The declaration of a major national security threat to an island state with responsibility for aviation and naval corridors of international importance might well have reversed this arrangement. Ultimately, the recommendations that the general staff brought forward to government, while the outcome of an intelligence process, preserved the blueprint for the Army's progress. Such were the structures in which they worked that it was perspectives on land security which dominated. Aviation and naval considerations were effectively invisible. And so it remains.

Matters may have worked out differently had the National Security Committee not needed to rely entirely on a small officer cadre of the frontline agencies for advice and had its civilian members not accepted that advice so willingly. Because they did, what went before government came out of a process ripe for groupthink, where challenging pre-agreed priorities was not in the rulebook. The net result was policy bereft of any meaningful inputs from entire constituencies of key position holders.

Notes

1 The FARC was established in 1964 by the Colombian communists to defend what were then autonomous Communist-controlled rural areas. It conducts conventional attacks against Columbian military forces, as well as bombings, kidnapping, hijacking and extortion. The FARC is widely linked to the illegal drugs trade.
2 Author's conversation with a former TD, senator and opposition front bench spokesperson on defence and foreign affairs.
3 Some spending occurred before the White Paper's publication.

7
Contingency planning

On July 9 1976 President Cearbhall O' Dalaigh accepted the credentials of a new British ambassador. The ambassador, Christopher Ewart Biggs, had previously been posted in various trouble spots in the Middle East, North Africa and Europe and the Provisional IRA would later claim that he was a British Intelligence agent. On July 11 Ewart-Biggs had a meeting with Garret Fitzgerald at which they discussed the North. The following day, July 12, Ewart-Biggs met with senior gardaí to discuss his security. Ewart Biggs wasn't very impressed. The gardaí didn't seem to have worked out the various ways in which subversives might try to kidnap or kill the ambassador. 'They're not very reassuring', he wrote in his diary that night. 'They thought for some reason that an attack on the car was unlikely.' It appears from the diary that Ewart-Biggs raised the possibility of an attack on his car and got the reply, 'It hasn't happened yet.' Although Cosgrave [Taoiseach] and Cooney [minister for justice] were almost daily huffing and puffing about security, Ewart-Biggs wrote of his meeting with the gardaí, 'It seems to be the department of fingers crossed.'

Nine days later, two hundred yards from the ambassador's residence, the Provos exploded a bomb under the ambassador's car and killed Ewart-Biggs and a civil servant, Judith Cooke.

The coalition went berserk. (Dunne and Kerrigan 1984, p. 181)

The applicability of theory

This study was written on the elementary but frequently overlooked premise that the unexpected often happens. Hence its first task was to map out that which was expected; the normality to which decision-makers were socialised and within which they would seek to remain to avoid being cut off from well practised 'traffic rules' for conducting policy. Historical institutionalism and, more particularly, Bulmer and Burch's model of it, has emerged as a useful resource for the task of navigating the uncharted channels of Irish security policy. Its use underpins the conclusion that national security policy in the years after 9/11 was, fundamentally, the same as that beforehand. The most graphic demonstration yet of the potency of transnational terrorism it may have been, but 9/11 was no critical juncture for those with responsibility for the proactive aspects of Irish security.

Identifying the fundamental characteristics of the policy sphere is one thing. Exposing the manifestations of these characteristics is another. Buzan's framework for threat identification has helped capture the scale of several significant problems. Here it operates as what might be termed a mid-level tool between the longstanding issues, which were identified in the historical analysis, and moments of crisis, helping to identify the strategic and tactical issues arising from policy inconsistency.

One of the aims in concentrating on the period of weeks after 9/11 was to analyse how policy-makers performed when, ostensibly, they were cut loose from their traditional expectations. Allison and Zelikow's model, which is used often in the field, worked here to help capture a picture of the frantic efforts of policy decision-makers who, in the days and weeks after the attack, were stranded in the unfamiliar yet under pressure to deliver certainties in tune with important ongoing concerns. On the basis of this single effort, it can be concluded that the combination of these three models has much to offer the study of contemporary national security policies. Further application is merited.

The effectiveness of policy

When talking about the need to address unexpected events before they occur military strategists, but also hospital clinicians and emergency managers generally, use the term 'contingency planning' (Author's interviews; Smith 2004; Einav, Feigenberg, Weissman *et al.* 2004). It relates to both proactive and reactive security. NATO has defined contingency planning as:

> Plans which are developed for possible operations where the planning factors (e.g. scope, forces, destination, risks, area of responsibility etc.) have been identified or can be assumed. These plans are produced in as much detail as possible, including the forces needed and deployment options, as a basis for subsequent planning. (NATO 1997)

The task of drawing up a contingency plan can be a difficult one. This is not least because strategists can have a tricky time persuading government of the need to allocate scarce resources to meet a challenge which may not have happened, which might never happen and, worst of all, may not be high on the agenda of voters' concerns. An interview with a senior Air Corps officer provides a useful example. The officer was speaking of the need to take contingency measures to prevent a terrorist air attack impacting on Irish territory:

> The minister for defence can get up and has said – because it suits him politi-
> cally to say – that we can't afford big jets, we'd have to close schools and hospi-
> tals. That's going to be no good if al-Qaeda puts a 737 into a school or hospital
> in Ireland, having missed the parliament, or something … the minister could
> word it this way: 'no we could never afford that, it will cost us a fortune, it will
> cost us schools and houses'. Or, he can couch it as 'what will it cost us if we
> don't have a level of it' and, let's be honest about it, he has speech writers who
> can word it in any way they want. He could go out and say: 'look, if we are to
> defend ourselves, it will cost billions. We will need this aircraft, we may need
> that. We can't afford that. But what we do need is some level of defence, some
> level of capability. We're either a sovereign country, or we're not. We need to
> be able to defend our troops when they are overseas. We need to be able to get
> them out there. So we'll spend this amount.' (Author's interview)

For their part, when faced with a request for action, government decision-
makers must decide the opportunity cost of pursuing that course. In the Irish
case, the consistent official position has been that the opportunity cost of a
significant increase in national security contingency expenditure is too great
relative to the public's demand for investment in the health service, education
and so forth. In terms of defence, government thinking is that manifold advantages have accrued to the State by maintaining the Defence Forces within
very modest financial resources. Aside from the obvious savings made for an
economy which for most of the first seventy years of the State's existence was in
poor shape, the policy of keeping the Irish military small and largely impotent
was to the benefit of Anglo-Irish relations. Even at times of great tension, such
as during the events on the streets of Belfast and Derry in 1969, the Irish military leadership, had they wanted to, lacked any realistic capacity to prosecute
the anti-partitionist cause by force. Ironically, Irish soldiers deprived of and thus
unused to heavy weaponry and protective equipment adjusted relatively well to
being lightly armed and vulnerable peacekeepers overseas (Murphy 2002).

In respects, the decision to retain political control over the Garda in the
Garda Síochána Act 2005 can also be seen as one of contingency and opportunity cost. The system had, in the view of many, served the State well. It had
failed to prevent the various problems of poor management and indiscipline,
but the government view was that reform measures, including a revised Garda
code of discipline and the creation of the Garda Ombudsman Commission
and Inspectorate, would suffice to prevent a breakdown of discipline which,
after all, might never again occur on such a scale. Moreover, in terms of costs,
switching to an arrangement whereby the Garda was answerable to localised
committees would necessitate the establishment of a separate national security
agency (Author's sources). Ministers would lose the power to direct the remaining police force to cooperate more closely with their counterparts in Northern
Ireland in the interests of political progress (Author's interviews; O' Brien 1999).
If cabinet ceded control over appointments ministers would no longer be in a

position to ensure Garda officers would not stray from government policy.

But at what point are the advantages of maintaining an existing policy position outweighed by the disadvantages of amending that policy as a contingency measure? When, for example, might the advantages of very low military spending fall secondary to spending on precautions to prevent an attack on Ireland? In their interviews leading Irish national security managers took a straightforward view of this, saying that, in the first instance, they relied upon the official intelligence assessments to direct their thinking.

However, the deductions made are also an outcome of the analysts' organisational interests and path-following. Regarding intelligence, decision-makers rely most upon what in Herman's taxonomy of intelligence is called speculative-evaluative estimates, which imply a certain degree of informed guesswork (Herman 1996). As this study finds, such guesswork and the choices that high-level policy managers make in terms of their responses to it, take place in an environment that is unduly vulnerable to financial and political concerns. This in itself may not be problematic. In the view of many it is, surely, appropriate that in drawing up their national security recommendations the agencies must always consider the likely effects on, for example, spending for healthcare. But, against this, a question of scale is to be considered. For example, the Irish education and healthcare systems are, arguably, relatively well funded. Yet Ireland has no realistic means of defending the internationally important air and sea corridors passing through its sovereign territory. This is extraordinary in the context of an island state committed to supporting international efforts to combat transnational terrorism. The consequences may well be catastrophic not only for Ireland but, perhaps, for many other states. However, those within the Defence Organisation who warned that capabilities were inadequate long before the attack of 9/11 were, in effect, ignored by leaders who at all times acted professionally but were swayed in their thinking by the responsibility of modernising the Army on a minimal budget. The only threats that prompted comprehensive action were those that could be addressed by contingency measures coming within existing or expected budgets. Otherwise the policy was one of inaction. The narrow prioritisations of that time continue. The defence aspects of Irish national security are clearly inadequate, as is the flow of expenditure to support them.

Scale is also an issue regarding centralised political control. It cannot be reasonably concluded that political pressure unduly influenced the Garda's recommendations. Political objectives and available intelligence ran in parallel. But, as this book has argued, the re-evaluation occurred in an atmosphere highly charged with political and financial pressures. What will occur in a future time of crisis if these pressures on and the intelligence coming before the Garda – however reliable or otherwise it may be – flow in opposite directions? Is it that the safety of the country must depend entirely on the ability of senior officers to withstand such pressure despite the obvious costs to themselves of so doing? In this vein do the benefits of political control compensate for the potential cost of a system which, as it is presently formulated, appears to entitle cabinet to issue an order to the Garda and escape all accountability mechanisms if that order is listed as one to do with national security? What of the scope this provides for politicians to engage the force in less than appropriate deeds? It is not as if such behaviour is unknown.

What also of the long-term implications of centralised political control for public and judicial confidence in the Garda, both of which are critical to its capacity to fight terrorism? The corrosion of confidence has led, since 2005, to various measures of reform. But the mechanism of overall authority which, for decades, failed to stamp out a malignant culture of indiscipline within the force has been left in place. At a fundamental level, therefore, reform is incomplete and the public standing of the Garda remains at unnecessary risk.

The problems of Irish national security policy are not simply ones of getting the balance right between current and contingency concerns. More specifically, the Irish intelligence system, upon which various 'do nothing' contingency decisions have been justified, is seriously flawed. It is vulnerable to the agendas of the donor intelligence agencies from which CSB and G2 feed for information. In this context, considerable Irish reliance on the agencies of states which are engaged in a 'war on terrorism' should be emphasised. The boundaries between intelligence and propaganda may be particularly difficult to decipher in information that these agencies supply. Regarding on-island analysis, CSB's centralisation in Dublin coupled with shifting demographic and lifestyle patterns in Ireland present the potential for acute intelligence gaps.

Military and official practitioners have argued here for a new intelligence coordination body based in the Department of the Taoiseach which would be equipped with statutory powers. The fact that such arguments have been proposed indicates that even within the national security community, there is recognition that the intelligence system is not working as it should. However, the introduction of the proposed agency would, in probability, do little to ameliorate Ireland's overwhelming reliance on the agencies of other states. Establishment of stand-alone agencies which, by providing foreign intelligence gathering and SIGINT capabilities, would lessen that dependency appears highly unlikely at this point. Their introduction would involve significant financial and, probably, political costs. But if the opportunity cost of this contingency appears too great that must be set against the fact that Irish security policy stands on an intelligence system which is, as matters stand, structurally unsound.

Particularly as regards defence it is possible to see how, without major additional costs, institutional reform can be undertaken to reduce the influence of politically sensitive financial factors in calculations of policy, strategy and procurements. One need only think of the Health Service Executive (HSE), introduced because government accepted that political behaviour was skewing health policy in undesirable ways. It should be pointed out here that some interviewees had given consideration to such reform. In summary, they proposed a statutory body which would draw up baseline sets of capabilities and accompanying procurement options, all of which would reflect national security needs for land, sea and air as determined by experts. Over defined periods government would be obliged to choose from these options tri-service capabilities and purchase defined equipment accordingly. Even if government kept going for the cheapest options, capability development would be ongoing and coherent. As with the intelligence agency the emergence of such a proposal indicates the potency of financial and political considerations in the business of defence planning. However, such a mechanism, were it to be introduced, would involve complications. Firstly how would it avoid the tag of unaccountability that has dogged the HSE? Moreover the experience of the UK is to be considered. The Ministry of Defence (MoD) is both a department of state handling policy issues and the Supreme Headquarters of the Armed Forces. Thus, in theory at least, it is set up to prevent military policy falling victim to uninformed civilian analysis, the charge often made in the Irish case. The UK Defence Equipment and Support organisation (previously the Defence Procurement Agency), although within the MoD structure, is intended to act as a mechanism to ensure that equipment procurements are 'above politics' yet policy-focussed. It is headed by a serving British Army general known as the chief of defence material. Despite this, British defence planning is bitterly criticised from within; for example, in 2007 the recently retired head of the British Army, General Sir Mike Jackson, described the Defence Procurement Agency's decisions on arms purchases as 'less than impressive' and rounded on the stranglehold he claimed that civil servants had on the MoD (Jackson 2007, pp. 357–68). The UK experience underlines how the introduction of such quasi-independent arrangements in Ireland might not pay off as expected even if, as this book concludes, the influence of political and financial pressures is such that there are significant weaknesses in Irish policy. However, when the process of defence planning for an island state treats naval and aviation perspectives as marginal concerns, an urgent remedy is clearly required.

If it is to be assumed that when considering the opportunity cost of taking contingency measures for national security, Irish governments prefer to give higher value to spending on social well-being (e.g. healthcare, education), then the State's handling of immigrant integration should have more in favour of it. Integration is both a social and a national security issue. It clearly involves the welfare of potential citizens but raises the risk of terrorists infiltrating sensitive positions. From the tiny sums of State monies allocated to integration it is hard not to conclude that when calculating how much to invest, policy managers factored in the extent of voting power, or lack thereof, in Ireland's new migrant communities. With that said, a minister of state was appointed to carry forward an integration agenda. Early signs of progress were not terribly encouraging. In time, perhaps, the evidence will be more positive. Not that there is much time; Ireland is already home to second-generation and subsequent migrants, that is, those who, as Sageman's research suggests, are more vulnerable than most to violent radicalisation if left to fester on society's margins.

In general, the State agencies have handled well the interlinking tasks of immigration control and Anglo-Irish security in the Common Travel Area. A favourable legacy of the Troubles is easy cooperation between the Irish and UK security forces especially those in Northern Ireland. The task of jointly protecting the outer borders of the British Isles seems well in hand although clearly, as evidenced by the planned introduction of an electronic passenger data collection system with accompanying British–Irish information exchange, the authorities see no room for complacency. However, in their enforcement tactics, gardaí risked turning immigration control from being a tool to aid integration to one that serves to weaken it. Performance that does not meet the highest professional standards of immigration control risks fracturing the binding idea of what is a rapidly changing state. Arguably the proposed introduction of electronic passport controls lessens the justification for such hostile enforcement in the future; those entering Ireland from outside of the Common Travel Area will have come through a process of computerised security monitoring. But all such technology is only useful for as long as it takes subversives, criminal or terrorist, to outwit it. Knowing this, the agencies may not soften their approach.

What of the government's showcase policy for emergency planning? Significant progress has been made. Training, equipment, infrastructure and institutional reform have been addressed. But serious difficulties, rooted in the political panic that followed Minister Joe Jacob's unwitting revelations of the State's lack of preparedness for nuclear fallout, remain. At a time when government makes much of joined-up solutions, the management of proactive national security is split from that of reactive security. Furthermore, emergency planning is lower in the hierarchy of government departments. A measure of incoherence is that this occurred when reactive security was considered to be the greater problem. At the second time of asking, in 2006, the government provided a partial remedy. *The Framework for Major Emergency Management* has clarified command and control issues at regional and local levels. But the new national steering group overlaps with and duplicates the functions of existing management entities at national level. The review did not address the split in top-level management of national security policy nor its associated issues. So key weaknesses put in place following political pressure in 2001 remained after 2006.

This book has investigated what might be described as some of the less visible influences on Irish national security policy after 9/11. The evidence is that policy is flawed in several critical respects. Perhaps most worrying of all is that the political and financial pressures intrinsic to several of its weaknesses may well stifle whatever willingness and ability policy managers may have to develop a more effective alternative. To no small degree Ireland's vulnerability to attack comes, however accidently, from within the security apparatus itself.

Bibliography

Ahern, B. (2005) Interview on: *News at One*, RTÉ Radio 1, 8 July, 1320 hrs.

Air Corps (1998) *Airpower Strategies for the New Century*, Dublin: Air Corps.

Air Corps (1999) *Airpower Options for the New Century*, Dublin: Air Corps.

Allen, G. (1999) *The Garda Síochána: Policing Independent Ireland 1922–82*. Dublin: Gill and Macmillan.

Allison, G. and P. Zelikow (1999) *Essence of Decision: Explaining the Cuban Missile Crisis*, 2nd edn, New York: Addison Wesley Longman.

Alvesson, M. (2003) 'Methodology for Close up Studies', *Higher Education*, Vol. 46 (2), 167–93.

An Cosantóir (2005) 'The Need to Know', December, 28–30.

Altran, S. (2003) 'Genesis and Future of Suicide Terrorism', *Understanding Suicide Terrorism Discussion Site* [online] July 1, available at www.interdisciplines.org/terrorism/papers/1 [accessed 28 Oct. 2005].

Anderson, P. (2001) 'Health Minister apologises for radio statements', *Irish Times Breaking News*, 28 Sept., available at www.irishtimes.com/newspaper/breaking/2001/0928/breaking10.htm [accessed 2 Feb. 2007].

Archer, C. and N. Nugent (2002) 'Introduction: Small States and the European Union', *Current Politics and Economics of Europe*, Vol. 11 (1), 1–10.

Arksey, H. and P. Knight (1999) *Interviewing for Social Scientists: An Introductory Resource with Examples*, London, Thousand Oaks, New Delhi: Sage.

Armstrong, A. (2004) 'Operation Dutch Elm', *An Cosantóir*, May, 28–30.

Arnold, B. (1994) *Haughey: His Life and Unlucky Deeds*, paperback edn, London: Harper Collins.

BBC News [online] (2001) 'Pressure builds up over policing', 24 Feb., available at http://news.bbc.co.uk/2/hi/uk_news/northern_ireland/1187911.stm [accessed 3 Feb. 2007].

BBC News [online] (2004) '20,000 posts go in defence cuts', 21 July, available at http://news.bbc.co.uk/2/hi/uk_news/politics/3912283.stm [accessed 22 July 2004].

BBC News [online] (2005) 'Blair defends NI military moves', 4 Aug., available at http://news.bbc.co.uk/2/hi/uk_news/northern_ireland/4746059.stm [accessed 4 Aug. 2005].

Betts, R.K. (2002) 'Fixing Intelligence', *Foreign Affairs*, Jan./Feb.,Vol. 81 (1), 43–59.

Bhreathnach, A. (2002) 'Frank Aiken: European federation and the UN', *Irish Studies in International Affairs*, Vol. 13, 237–49.

Blair, T. (2006) Interview on: *Nine O' Clock News*, RTÉ 1, 10 Nov., 2100 hrs.

Booth, K. (1991) 'Security in Anarchy: Utopian Realism in Theory and Practice', *International Affairs*, 67 (3), 527–45.

Bourke, W. (2007) 'Tomorrow's Forces Today', *An Cosantóir*, Aug., 6–7.

Bowyer Bell, J. (1996) *In Dubious Battle: The Dublin and Monaghan Bombings 1972–1974*, Dublin: Poolbeg.

Boyd-Barrett, R. (2005) 'Like it or not, we are up to our neck in the Iraq war', *Irish Times* [online] 10 Aug., available at www.irishtimes.com [accessed 1 Feb. 2007].

Boyle, R. and P.C. Humphreys (2001) *A New Change Agenda for the Irish Public Service*, Dublin: Institute of Public Administration.

Boyne, S. (2006) *Gunrunners: The Covert Arms Trail to Ireland*, Dublin: The O'Brien Press.

Bracken, A. (2005) 'Asylum families kept apart', *Irish Times* [online], 24 June, available at www.irishtimes.com [accessed 2 Feb. 2007].

Brady, C. (2000) *Guardians of the Peace*, 2nd edn, London: Prendeville.

Brady, C. (2004) 'It's time to remove the political handcuffs from the Garda Síochána', *Irish Times*, 11 Jan.

Brady, T. (2002) 'Security alert sparks new fear of "soft" target attack', *Irish Independent* [online], 11 Sept., available at www.unison.ie/irish_independent [accessed 3 May 2006].

Brady, T. (2004a) 'Suspects to be monitored as security for Bush tightens', *Irish Independent* [online], 23 June, available at www.unison.ie/irish_independent [accessed 25 June 2004].

Brady, T. (2004b) 'Defence Forces to undergo terrorism drills', *Irish Independent* [online], 13 Dec., available at www.unison.ie/irish_independent [accessed 18 Dec. 2004].

Brady, T. (2004c) 'Scores of illegals deported after raids', *Irish Independent* [online], 12 Dec., available at www.unison.ie/irish_independent [accessed 12 Aug. 2005].

Brady, T. (2005a) 'Saddam's fighters here for a holiday', *Irish Independent* [online], 22 Oct., available at www.unison.ie/irish_independent [accessed 24 Oct. 2005].

Brady, T. (2005b) 'Terror threat prompts Army to build-up intelligence', *Irish Independent* [online], 1 Dec., available at www.unison.ie/irish_independent [accessed 1 Dec. 2005].

Brady, T. (2006a) 'Ireland joins EU borders agency in crime fight', *Irish Independent* [online], 22 Sept., available at www.unison.ie/irish_independent [accessed 23 Sept. 2006].

Brady, T. (2006b) 'Chemical Willie goes into crisis mode … silently', *Irish Independent* [online], 17 Nov., available at www.unison.ie/irish_independent [accessed 17 Nov. 2006].

Brady, T. (2007) 'Close watch on terror threat', *Irish Independent* [online], 16 July, available at www.independent.ie [accessed 17 July 2007].

Brady, T. (2009) 'Reservists overseas missions put on hold', *Irish Independent* [online], 3 Apr., available at www.independent.ie/national-news/reservists-overseas-missions-put-on-hold-1696804.html [accessed 6 Apr. 2009].

Brennan, C. (2007) 'Deering to head rights authority', *Irish Times* [online], 12 Jan., available at www.irishtimes.com [accessed 4 Feb. 2007].

Brennan, M. (2008) 'Priests to take on "immigration role" with foreign couples, *Irish Independent* [online], 4 Feb., available at www.indepedendent.ie [accessed 4 Feb. 2008].

Brennock, M. (2000a) 'Defence plan to be altered to reassure military', *Irish Times* [online] 1 Mar., available at www.irishtimes.com [accessed 3 Feb. 2007].

Brennock, M. (2000b) 'Minister issues "warning for the future" to Army leaders', *Irish Times* [online], 6 Mar., available at www.irishtimes.com [accessed 3 Feb. 2007].

Brennock, M. (2001) 'McCreevy forced to scale down spending plans', *Irish Times* [online], 16 Nov., available at www.irishtimes.com [accessed 20 Nov. 2006].

Brennock, M. (2004) 'Poll highlights lack of confidence in the Garda', *Irish Times* [online], 10 Feb., available at www.irishtimes.com [accessed 12 Nov. 2005].

Brown, C. (1997) *Understanding International Relations*, London: Macmillan Press.

Browne, V. (1980) 'Arms Crisis 1970: The Inside Story', *Magill*, May, 33–56.

Browne, V. (2000) 'New security Bill gives too much power to the Garda', *Irish Times* [online], 2 Sept., available at www.irishtimes.com [accessed 7 Oct. 2006].

Bulmer, S. and M. Burch (1998) 'Organizing for Europe: Whitehall, The British State and European Union', *Public Administration*, Vol. 76, 601–628.

Burchill, S. (1997) 'Liberal Internationalism', in S. Burchill, A. Linklater, R. Devetak, M. Paterson and J. True (eds), *Theories of International Relations*, Hampshire and London: Macmillan, 28–66.

Buzan, B. (1991) *People, States and Fear: An Agenda for International Security Studies in the Post-Cold War Era*, 2nd edn, Hemel Hempstead: Harvester Wheatsheaf.

Buzan, B. (2002) 'Implications of September 11 for the Study of International Relations', in B. Sundelius (ed.), *The Consequences of September 11: A Symposium on the Implications for the Study of International Relations*, Stockholm: The Swedish Institute for International Affairs, 25–41.

Buzan, B., Jones, C. and Little, R. (1993) *The Logic of Anarchy: Neorealism to Structural Realism*, New York: Columbia University Press.

Byrne, D. (2002) *Interpreting the Real and Describing the Complex: Why We Have to Measure*, London, Thousand Oaks, New Delhi: Sage.

Campbell, L. (2003) 'Britain's Changing Attitude to Irish Neutrality 1938 to 1950', *Defence Forces Review 2003*, Vol. 1, 29–34.

Carter, A.B. (2001) 'The Architecture of government in the Face of Terrorism', *International Security*, Vol. 26 (3), 5–23.

Central Statistic Office (2004), *Quarterly National Household Survey* [online], July, available at www.cso.ie/qnhs/pub_rel_qnhs.htm [accessed 30 July 2004].

Cha, V. (2000) 'Abandonment, Entrapment and Neoclassical Realism in Asia: The United States, Japan, and Korea', *International Studies Quarterly*, Vol. 44 (2), 261–91.

Chaulia S. (2003) 'September 11 in International Relations Theory', *Kashmir Herald* [online], 2 Aug., available at: www.kashmirherald.com/featuredarticle/september11ininternationalrelationstheory.html [accessed 2 Feb. 2004].

Chomsky, N. (2002) 'Who Are The Global Terrorists?', in K. Booth and T. Dunne (eds), *Worlds in Collision: Terror and the Future of Global Order*, Hampshire: Palgrave Macmillan, 128–37.

Clare Champion, 'Councillors defend US use of Shannon', 18 Nov. 2002, p. 6.

Clonan, T. (2005) 'What if Ireland were targeted by terrorists?' *Irish Times* [online], 20 Mar., available at www.irishtimes.com [accessed 20 Mar. 2005].

Clutterbuck, R. (1990) *Terrorism and Guerrilla Warfare: Forecasts and Remedies.* New York and London: Routledge.

Collins, G. (2007) 'Emergency centre "not a government bunker"', *Irish Independent* [online], 8 Mar., available at www.unison.ie [accessed 8 Mar. 2007].

Collins, S. (2007) 'Irish will need passports to visit Britain from 2009', *Irish Times*, 24 Oct., p. 1.

Collins, S. and D. Keenan (2007) 'Taoiseach confirms electronic border plan', *Irish Times* [online], 25 Oct., available at www.irishtimes.com [accessed 25 Oct. 2007].

Commission of Investigation into The Dublin and Monaghan Bombings of 1974 (2007) *Final Report March 2007* [online], available at http://193.178.1.117/attached_files/Pdf%20files/COMMISSION%20OF%20INVESTIGATION%20FINAL%20REPORT.doc [accessed 01 Sept. 2007].

Connect (2006) 'Cav Go Mowag', 11 (2), 1.

Cooney, J. (2007) 'Taoiseach denounces "illiberal secularist voices" in democracy', *Irish Independent* [online] 27 Feb., available at www.unison.ie [accessed 28 Feb. 2007].

Corbin, J. (2002) *The Base: In Search of al-Qaeda – The Terror Network that Shook the World*, London: Simon and Schuster.

Coughlan, M. (2005) Interview on: *Morning Ireland*, RTÉ Radio 1, 14 Oct., 0810 hrs.

Coulter, C. (2000) 'UNHRC to question use of the Offences Against the State Act', *Irish Times* [online], 21 June, available at www.irishtimes.com [accessed 7 Oct. 2006].

Coulter, C. (2002) 'The law falls into disrepute', *Irish Times* [online], 28 Dec., available at www.irishtimes.com [accessed 14 Jan. 2005].

Coulter, C. (2003a) 'Time to hold the Garda to account', *Irish Times* [online], 19 July, available at www.irishtimes.com [accessed 19 July 2003].

Coulter, C. (2003b) 'Anti-terrorism legislation causes concern', *Irish Times* [online], 27 Mar., available at www.irishtimes.com [accessed 12 Apr. 2005].

Coulter, C. (2004a) 'Opportunity to reform Garda Síochána must not be missed', *Irish Times* [online], 17 Jan., available at www.irishtimes.com [accessed 17 Jan. 2004].

Coulter, C. (2004b) 'Bill to deal with terrorist offences before committee', *Irish Times* [online], 4 Nov., available at www.irishtimes.com [accessed 6 Nov. 2004].

Coulter, C. (2004c) 'Government has failed to examine why immigrants are coming here', *Irish Times* [online], 17 June, available at www.irishtimes.com [accessed 18 June 2004].

Coulter, C. (2005) 'Plans to overhaul law for immigrants published', *Irish Times* [online], 13 Apr., available at www.irishtimes.com [accessed 14 Aug. 2005].

Coulter, C. (2008) 'Immigration Bill change urged', *Irish Times* [online], 3 Apr., available at www.irishtimes.com [accessed 3 Apr. 2008].

Cowen, B. (2001) 'Opening Address: Challenges to Liberal Institutionalism', *Irish*

Studies in International Affairs, Vol. 12, 1–5.

Cudmore, T. (2003) 'Will Defence lead National Security Planning for Ireland in the 21st Century?' *Defence Forces Review 2003*, Vol. 1, 55–63.

Cusack, J. (2001a) 'Army special forces is expanded for anti-terrorist operations', *Irish Times* [online], 22 Sept., available at www.irishtimes.com [accessed 22 Sept. 2002].

Cusack, J. (2001b) 'Decommissioning pace forced by IRA's Colombian links', *Irish Times* [online], 27 Oct., available at www.irishtimes.com [accessed 12 Feb. 2005].

Cusack, J. (2002a) 'Short-lived turnaround in fortunes of Defence Forces', *Irish Times* [online], July 06, available at www.irishtimes.com [accessed 4 Feb. 2004].

Cusack, J. (2002b) 'FBI turns spotlight on al-Qaeda's Dublin operations', *Irish Times* [online], 31 July, available at www.irishtimes.com [accessed 1 Aug. 2002].

Cusack, J. and M. Brennock (2002) 'Surprise as Smith cancels Sikorski helicopter deal', *Irish Times* [online] 6 July, available at www.irishtimes.com [accessed 4 Feb. 2004].

Deegan, G. (2005) 'Increase in US troop traffic at Shannon', *Irish Times* [online], 13 July, available at www.irishtimes.com [accessed 15 Apr. 2006].

Deegan, G. (2006) 'Record numbers of US troops use Shannon', *Irish Times* [online], 8 July, available at www.irishtimes.com [accessed 6 Sept. 2006].

Deegan, G. (2008) 'Nearly 67,000 US troops passed through Shannon in January–March', *Irish Times* [online], 11 Apr., available at www.irishtimes.com [accessed 12 Apr. 2008].

Defence Forces (1999) *Annual Report 1999*, Dublin: Defence Forces.

Defence Forces (2000) *Annual Report 2000*, Dublin: Defence Forces.

Defence Forces (2001a) *Annual Report 2001*, Dublin: Defence Forces.

Defence Forces (2001b) *Defence Forces Strategy Statement 2001–2004*, Dublin: Defence Forces.

Defence Forces (2001c) *Defence Forces Estimates 2001* [restricted], Dublin: Defence Forces.

Defence Forces (2002a) *Annual Report 2002*, Dublin: Defence Forces.

Defence Forces (2002b) *Defence Forces Estimates 2002* [restricted], Dublin: Defence Forces.

Defence Forces, Director of Personnel (2002) *Human Resource Management Annual Report 2002*, Dublin: Defence Forces.

Defence Forces (2003a) *Annual Report 2003*, Dublin: Defence Forces.

Defence Forces (2003b) *Defence Forces Estimates 2003* [restricted], Dublin: Defence Forces.

Defence Forces (2004a) *Annual Report 2004*, Dublin: Defence Forces.

Defence Forces (2004b) *Reserve Defence Forces Implementation Plan*, Dublin: Defence Forces.

Der Derian, J. (2002) '*In Terrorem:* Before and After 9/11', in K. Booth and T. Dunne (eds), *Worlds in Collision: Terror and the Future of Global Order*, Hampshire: Palgrave Macmillan, 101–17.

DeVault, M. L. (2002) 'Talking and Listening from Women's Standpoint: Feminist Strategies for Interviewing and Analysis', in D. Weinberg (ed.), *Qualitative Research Methods*, Maiden, MA: Blackwell.

Devetak, R. (1996) 'Critical Studies', in S. Burchill, A. Linklater, R. Devetak, M. Paterson and J. True (eds), *Theories of International Relations*, Hampshire and

London: Macmillan, 145–78.

Devetak, R. (1996) 'Postmodernism', in S. Burchill, A. Linklater, R. Devetak, M. Paterson, and J. True (eds), *Theories of International Relations*, Hampshire and London: Macmillan, 179–209.

De Vries, G. (2005) 'Opening address – The European Union's role in the fight against terrorism' *Irish Studies in International Affairs*, Vol. 16, 3–9.

Dixon, P. (2001) *Northern Ireland: The Politics of War and Peace*, London: Palgrave.

Donnelly, K. (2007) 'Schools warn of "white flight" of students', *Irish Independent* [online], 20 Oct., available at www.independent.ie [accessed 20 Oct. 2007].

Donohue, M. (2002a) 'Ministers given until Friday to find €100m more in cuts', *Irish Times* [online], 22 July, available at www.irishtimes.com [accessed 4 Feb. 2004].

Donohue, M. (2002b) 'State ponders option of leasing aircraft', *Irish Times* [online], 15 July, available at www.irishtimes.com [accessed 6 Mar. 2004].

Donohue, M. (2006a) 'State set to announce plans for dialogue with churches', *Irish Times* [online], 15 Nov., available at www.irishtimes.com [accessed 27 Dec. 2006].

Donohue, M. (2006b) '"Widespread" collusion by British forces behind atrocities', *Irish Times* [online], 30 Nov., available at www.irishtimes.com [accessed 3 Feb. 2007].

Dooley, C. (2002) 'Government criticised for abandoning gardaí promise', *Irish Times* [online], 24 Dec., available at www.irishtimes.com [accessed 20 Nov. 2006].

Downes, J. (2005a) 'Pakistani students missing from Waterford college', *Irish Times* [online], 21 Jul, available at www.irishtimes.com [accessed 23 July 2005].

Downes, J. (2005b) 'Dialogue is needed, says Irish Islamic cleric', *Irish Times* [online], 8 Aug., available at www.irishtimes.com [accessed 8 Aug. 2005].

Doyle, J. (1999) 'Governance and Citizenship in Contested States: The Northern Ireland Peace Agreement as Internationalised Governance', *Irish Studies in International Affairs*, Vol. 10, 201–19.

Duggan, J.P. (1991) *A History of the Irish Army*, Dublin: Gill and Macmillan.

Dunne, D. and G. Kerrigan (1984) *Round Up the Usual Suspects: The Cosgrave Coalition and Nicky Kelly*, Dublin: Magill.

Edwards, E. (2007a) 'Gardaí unable to apologise for errors – report', *Irish Times Breaking News* [online], 2 Aug., available at www.irishtimes.com [accessed 9 Aug. 2007].

Edwards, E. (2007b) 'Conroy rejects criticisms of Garda', *Irish Times Breaking News* [online], 2 Aug., available at www.irishtimes.com [accessed 9 Aug. 2007].

Einav, S., Z. Feigenberg, C. Weissman, D. Zaichik, G. Caspi, D. Kotler and H.R. Freund (2004) 'Evacuation priorities in mass casualty terror-related events: implications for contingency planning', *Annals of Surgery*, Vol. 239 (3), 304–10.

English, R. (2003) *Armed Struggle: A History of the IRA*, London, Basingstoke and Oxford: Macmillan.

European Union, European Council (2001) 'Conclusions and Plan of Action of the Extraordinary European Council Meeting on 21 September 2001' [online], available at http://ue.eu.int/cms3_fo/showPage.ASP?id=406&lang=en&mode =g [accessed 8 Dec. 2004].

European Union, High Representative for the Common Foreign and Security

Policy (2003) *A Secure Europe in the Better World* [online], available at http://ue.eu.int/cms3_fo/showPage.ASP?id=406&lang=en&mode=g [accessed 3 Dec. 2004].

European Union, European Council (2004a) 'Brief Note on Counter Terrorism' [online], 16 Dec., available at http://ue.eu.int/cms3_fo/showPage.ASP?id=406&lang=en&mode=g [accessed 13 Jan. 2005].

European Union, European Council (2004b) *Conceptual Framework on the European Security and Defence Policy (ESDP) Dimension of the Fight Against Terrorism* [online], available at http://ue.eu.int/cms3_fo/showPage.ASP?id=406&lang=en&mode=g [accessed 9 Dec. 2004].

European Union, European Council (2004c) 'Declaration on Combating Terrorism' [online fact sheet], 26 June, available at http://ue.eu.int/cms3_fo/showPage.ASP?id=406&lang=en&mode=g [accessed 9 Dec. 2004].

European Union, European Council (2004d) 'Adoption of Council conclusions on prevention, preparedness and response to terrorist attacks' [online], available at http://ue.eu.int/cms3_fo/showPage.ASP?id=406&lang=en&mode=g [accessed 10 Dec. 2004].

European Union, European Counter-Terrorism Coordinator (2004) *Interim Report on the Evaluation of National Anti-Terrorist Arrangements* [online], available at http://ue.eu.int/cms3_fo/showPage.ASP?id=406&lang=en&mode=g [accessed 12 Dec. 2004].

European Union, Dutch Presidency and Counter Terrorism Coordinator (2004) 'The fight against terrorism: Note by the Presidency in association with the Counter-Terrorism Co-ordinator' [online], available at http://ue.eu.int/cms3_fo/showPage.ASP?id=406&lang=en&mode=g [accessed 13 Jan. 2005].

European Union, Counter Terrorism Coordinator (2005) *Implementation of the Action Plan to Combat Terrorism* [online], available at http://ue.eu.int/cms3_fo/showPage.ASP?id=406&lang=en&mode=g [accessed 12 Apr. 2006].

European Union, UK Presidency and Counter Terrorism Coordinator (2005a) *EU emergency and crisis co-ordination arrangements* [online], available at http://ue.eu.int/cms3_fo/showPage.ASP?id=406&lang=en&mode=g [accessed 18 Apr. 2006].

European Union, UK Presidency and Counter Terrorism Coordinator (2005b) *The European Counter-Terrorism Strategy* [online], available at http://ue.eu.int/cms3_fo/showPage.ASP?id=406&lang=en&mode=g [accessed 12 Apr. 2006].

European Union, UK Presidency and Counter Terrorism Coordinator (2005c) *The European Union Strategy for Combating Radicalisation and Recruitment to Terrorism* [online], available at http://ue.eu.int/cms3_fo/showPage.ASP?id=406&lang=en&mode=g [accessed 12 Apr. 2006].

Fahy, D. and E. Donnellan (2001) 'Martin's assurance on iodine supply incorrect', *Irish Times* [online], 28 Sept., available at www.irishtimes.com [accessed 4 Feb. 2007].

Fanning, R. (1978) *The Irish Department of Finance, 1922–58*, Dublin: Institute of Public Administration.

Fanning, R. (1998) 'Small states, large neighbours: Ireland and the United Kingdom', *Irish Studies in International Affairs*, Vol. 9, 21–9.

Fanning, R. (2001) 'Playing it cool: The response of the British and Irish governments to the crisis in Northern Ireland, 1968–9', *Irish Studies in International Affairs*, Vol. 12, 57–85.

Farrell, T. (1997) '"The model army": military imitation and the enfeeblement of the army in post-revolutionary Ireland, 1922–42', *Irish Studies in International Affairs*, Vol. 8, 111–27.

Farrell, T. (2001) 'Transnational Norms and Military Development: Constructing Ireland's Professional Army', *European Journal of International Relations*, Vol. 7 (1), 63–102.

Fine Gael (2004) *One in Five Crimes Not Reported, One in Three Among Young People – Deasy*, [online press release], 27 Feb., available at www.finegael.ie/fine-gael-news.cfm [accessed 2 Nov. 2005].

Fisk, R. (1983) *In Time of War: Ireland, Ulster and the Price of Neutrality 1939–45*, Dublin: Gill and Macmillan.

Fitzgerald, G. (1998) 'The origins, development and present status of Irish "neutrality"', *Irish Studies in International Affairs*, Vol. 9, 11–19.

Fitzgerald, J. (2005) 'Extra security channel to reduce delays at airport', *Irish Times* [online], 24 June, available at www.irishtimes.com [accessed 25 June 2005].

Fitzgerald, M. (2007) 'English classes urged for migrants', *Irish Times* [online], 12 Sept., available at www.irishtimes.com [accessed 12 Sept. 2007].

Fitzgerald, T.P. (2008) 'The Morris Tribunal of Inquiry and the Garda Síochána', *Communique,* available at www.garda.ie/Documents/User/Communique%20Mar%2008.pdf [accessed 4 Apr. 2009].

Flynn, P. (2005) 'Airport in Crisis', *The Clare People*, 2 Aug., 1.

Foley, F. (2003) 'North–South Relations and the Outbreak of the Troubles in Northern Ireland, 1968–9: the Response of the *Irish Press*', *Irish Studies in International Affairs*, Vol. 14, 9–31.

Fontana, A. and J. Frey (1994) 'Interviewing: The art of science', in N. Denzin and Y. Lincoln (eds), *Handbook of Qualitative Research*, London, Thousand Oaks, New Delhi: Sage.

Foucault, M. (1980) *Power/Knowledge*, Hemel Hempstead: Harvester Wheatsheaf.

Garda Síochána (2000) *Policing Plan 2000*, Dublin: Garda Síochána.

Garda Síochána (2001) *Policing Plan 2001*, Dublin: Garda Síochána.

Garda Síochána (2002) *Policing Plan 2002*, Dublin: Garda Síochána.

Garda Síochána (2003) *Policing Plan 2003*, Dublin: Garda Síochána.

Garda Síochána (2004) *Garda Public Attitudes Survey 2004* [online], available at www.garda.ie/angarda/othdocs.html [accessed 1 Nov. 2005].

Garda Síochána (2005) *Garda Public Attitudes Survey 2005* [online], available at www.garda.ie/angarda/othdocs.html [accessed 1 Nov. 2005].

Garda Síochána (2008) *Communique*, March, 1–31.

Garda Síochána Complaints Board (1998) *Annual Report 1998*, Dublin: Garda Síochána Complaints Board.

Gearson, J. (2002) 'The Nature of Modern Terrorism', in L. Freedman (ed.), *Superterrorism: Policy Responses*, London: Blackwell, 7–24.

Gillespie, P. (1996) 'Ireland in the New World Order: Interests and Values in the Irish government's White Paper on Foreign Policy', *Irish Studies in International Affairs*, Vol. 7, 143–56.

Goldstone, K. (2000) '"Benevolent Helpfulness"? Ireland and the International Reaction to Jewish Refugees', in M. Kennedy and J.M. Skelly (eds), *Irish Foreign Policy 1919–1966: From Independence to Internationalism*, Dublin: Four Courts Press, 116–36.

Gray, C. (2002) 'World Politics as Usual after September 11', in K. Booth and

T. Dunne (eds), *Worlds in Collision: Terror and the Future of Global Order*, Hampshire: Palgrave Macmillan, 226–34.

Gray, T. (1997) *The Lost Years: The Emergency in Ireland 1939–45*, London: Warner Books.

Green Party (2005) 'Apr. 05 Garda Síochána Bill' [Dáil speech], 21 Apr., available at www.greenparty.ie/en/in_the_dail/speeches/21_apr_05_garda_s_och_na_bill [accessed 31 Jan. 2007].

Gutteridge, W. (ed.) (1986) *The New Terrorism*, London: Mansell.

Hall, P.A. and R.C.R. Taylor (1996) 'Political Science and the Three New Institutionalisms', *Political Studies*, Vol. 44, 936–57.

Harvey, D. (2001) *Peacekeepers: Irish Soldiers in the Lebanon*, Cork: Merlin.

Haughey, N. (2001a) 'Immigration officers to be part of Garda bureau', *Irish Times* [online], 5 Feb., available at www.irishtimes.com [accessed 10 Oct. 2005].

Haughey, N. (2001b) 'More staff for checks on entry to State', *Irish Times* [online], 10 May, available at www.irishtimes.com [accessed 10 Oct. 2005].

Harrison, H. (1942) *The Neutrality of Ireland: Why it was Inevitable*, London: Robert Hale Limited.

Heaslip, R.E.M. (2007) 'Ireland's First Engagement in United Nations Peacekeeping Operations: An Assessment', *Defence Forces Review*, Vol. 4, 83–93.

Heffernan, B. (2006) 'Worrying rise in abuse of migrants reported', *Irish Independent* [online], 8 May, available at www.unison.ie/irish_independent [accessed 8 May 2006].

Hennessy, M. (2001) 'Garda, prisons, courts all due for extra spending', *Irish Times* [online], 16 Nov., available at www.irishtimes.com [accessed 20 Nov. 2006].

Hennessy, M. (2003) 'Cutbacks lead to reduction in Swiss armoured vehicles order', *Irish Times* [online], 3 Jan., available at www.irishtimes.com [accessed 18 June 2005].

Hennessy, M. (2004a) 'Tribunal finds two gardaí offered "a tissue of lies"', *Irish Times* [online], 16 July, available at www.irishtimes.com [accessed 16 July 2004].

Hennessy, M. (2004b) 'Time wasted getting to the bottom of lies', *Irish Times* [online], 16 July, available at www.irishtimes.com [accessed 16 July 2004].

Hennessy, M. (2008) 'Checks between the North and rest of UK on way' *Irish Times* [online], 28 July, available at www.irishtimes.com [accessed 3 Apr. 2009].

Hennessy, M. (2006) 'Brennan warns of French-style race riots', *Irish Times* [online], 27 Dec., available at www.irishtimes.com [accessed 27 Dec. 2006].

Henry, G.T. (1998) 'Practical Sampling', in L. Bickerman and D.J. Rog (eds), *Handbook of Applied Social Research Methods*, Thousand Oaks, London, New Delhi: Sage, pp. 101–26.

Herman, M. (1996) *Intelligence Power in Peace and War*, Cambridge: Cambridge University Press.

Herman, M. (1999) 'Intelligence services and ethics in the new millennium', *Irish Studies in International Affairs*, Vol. 10, 249–65.

Herman, M. (2001) *Intelligence Services in the Information Age: Theory and Practice*, London: Frank Cass.

Hills, M. and R. Holloway (2002) 'Competing for media control in an age of asymmetric warfare', *Jane's Intelligence Review* [online], 1 May, available at www.janes.com [accessed 11 Mar. 2003].

Hogan, T. (2002) 'Thousands didn't receive anti-radiation tablets', *Irish Independent* [online], 3 Sept., available at www.unison.ie/irish_independent [accessed 18

Mar. 2003].

Hogan, T. (2004) 'Firefighters "not prepared" to deal with terror atrocity', *Irish Independent* [online], 14 Apr., available at www.unison.ie/irish_independent [accessed 17 Apr. 2004].

Hogan, T. (2006) 'Disaster response unit given green light', *Irish Independent* [online], 04 May, available at www.unison.independent.ie [accessed 4 May 2006].

Holland, K. (2005) 'government policies fuelling racism – report', *Irish Times* [online], 11 Jan., available at www.irishtimes.com [accessed 10 Oct. 2005].

Holland, K. (2006a) 'New plan to coordinate emergency services', *Irish Times* [online], 12 June, available at www.irishtimes.com [accessed 2 Feb. 2007].

Holland, K. (2006b) 'Non-EU nationals with study plan "devastated" by barriers', *Irish Times* [online], 21 Oct., available at www.irishtimes.com [accessed 21 Oct. 2006].

Horgan, J. (1999) 'Irish Foreign Policy, Northern Ireland, Neutrality and the Commonwealth: the Historical Roots of a Current Controversy', *Irish Studies in International Affairs*, Vol. 10, 135–47.

Humphreys, J. (2005) 'Immigrant level moves towards 10%', *Irish Times* [online], 15 Sept., available at www.irishtimes.com [accessed 15 Sept. 2005].

Huntington, Samuel P. (1996) *The Clash of Civilizations and the Remaking of World Order*, New York: Simon and Schuster.

Ireland, Dáil Debates (1999) [online] 9 Dec., available at www.irlgov.ie/debates-99/9dec99/sect6.htm [accessed 7 Feb. 2007].

Ireland, Dáil Debates (2001) [online] 23 May, available at www.irlgov.ie/debates-01/23may/sect3.htm [accessed 5 Feb. 2007].

Ireland, Dáil Debates (2004) Vol. 585 (3) (12 May), 554–57.

Ireland, Dáil Debates (2005a) Vol. 596 (1) (26 Jan.), 129–54.

Ireland, Dáil Debates (2005b) Vol. 599 (2) (8 Mar.), 237–46.

Ireland, Dáil Debates (2005c) Vol. 610 (2) (16 Nov.), 491–500.

Ireland, Dáil Debates (2006a) Vol. 620 (2) (24 May), 377–82.

Ireland, Dáil Debates (2006b) Vol. 628 (4) (29/30 Nov.), 13–18.

Ireland, Dáil Debates (2009) Vol. 681 (2) (29 Apr.), 31.

Ireland, Department of Communications, Marine and Natural Resources (2004) *Maritime Security Act 2004 Explanatory and Financial Memorandum*, Dublin: Department of Communications, Marine and Natural Resources.

Ireland, Department of Defence (2000a) *White Paper on Defence*, Dublin: Department of Defence.

Ireland, Department of Defence (2000b) *Annual Report*, Dublin: Department of Defence.

Ireland, Department of Defence (2001a) *Strategy Statement 2001–2004*, Dublin: Department of Defence.

Ireland, Department of Defence (2001b) 'Defence Estimates 2002' [press release], 14 Nov., available at www.defence.ie [accessed 20 Nov. 2006].

Ireland, Department of Defence (2002a) *Annual Report 2001*, Dublin: Department of Defence.

Ireland, Department of Defence (2002b) 'Defence Estimates 2003' [press release], 16 Nov., available at www.defence.ie [accessed 20 Nov. 2006].

Ireland, Department of Defence (2004) 'Minister's speech to a Select Committee on the Defence Estimates for 2004', 1 June, available at www.defence.ie/WebSite.

nsf/Document+ID/B552D65A6A16480F80256EA6004CC56E?editDocument [accessed 17 Feb. 2007].

Ireland, Department of Defence (2005) *Strategy Statement 2005–2007*, Dublin: Department of Defence.

Ireland, Department of Defence (2006a) 'Air Corps receive first AW 139 helicopter' [press release], 11 Aug., available at www.defence.ie [accessed 12 Aug. 2006].

Ireland, Department of Defence (2006b) 'Defence Estimates 2007' [press release], 19 Nov., available at www.defence.ie [accessed 20 Nov. 2006].

Ireland, Department of Environment, Heritage and Local government (2006) *A Framework for Major Emergency Management*, available at www.environ.ie [accessed 19 Dec. 2006].

Ireland, Department of Foreign Affairs (1996) *Challenges and Opportunities Abroad: White Paper on Foreign Policy*, Dublin: Department of Foreign Affairs.

Ireland, Department of Justice, Equality and Law Reform (2002) 'McDowell welcomes general public's satisfaction with An Garda Síochána', [press release], 1 Oct., available at www.justice.ie/80256E01003A02CF/vWeb/pcJUSQ67NKDU-en [accessed 18 Dec. 2004].

Ireland, Department of Justice, Equality and Law Reform (2003) *Strategy Statement 2003–2005*, Dublin: Department of Justice, Equality and Law Reform.

Ireland, Department of Justice, Equality and Law Reform (2005) *Criminal Justice (Terrorist Offences) Act 2005 Explanatory Memorandum*, Dublin: Department of Justice, Equality and Law Reform.

Ireland, Department of Justice, Equality and Law Reform (2006) 'McDowell very satisfied with outcome of Estimates Process' [press release], 19 Nov., available at: www.justice.ie.80256E01003A02CF/vWeb/pcJUSQ6VLKX4-en [accessed 20 Nov. 2006].

Ireland, Department of Public Enterprise (2001) *National Planning for Nuclear Emergencies*, Dublin: Department of Public Enterprise.

Ireland, Department of the Taoiseach (1998) *Price Waterhouse Report to the Steering Group on the Review of the Irish Naval Service and Air Corps*, Dublin: Department of the Taoiseach.

Ireland, Joint Committee of Justice, Equality, Defence and Women's Rights (2005) *Interim Report on the Report of the Independent Commission of Inquiry into the Murder of Seamus Ludlow*, Dublin: Houses of the Oireachtas.

Irish Council for Civil Liberties (2004) *Morris Tribunal – Garda reform must address frightening corruption and bad management* [online press release], 16 July, available at http://iccl.ie/DB_Data/press/MorrisTribunalGardareform_74.htm [accessed 01 Feb. 2007].

Irish Independent (2006a) '€100m vessel to boost navy strength' [online], 7 Sept., available at www.unison.ie/irish_independent [accessed 7 Sept. 2006].

Irish Independent (2006b) 'A question of inclusion', 19 Dec., 16.

Irish Refugee Council (2004) *Immigration Bill is bad law, say leading human rights and migrant organisations* [online press release], 03 Feb., available at www.irishrefugeecouncil.ie [accessed 11 Oct. 2005].

Irish Times (2001a) 'Taoiseach calls for "measured response" by US' [online], 12 Sept., available at www.irishtimes.com [accessed 20 Sept. 2001].

Irish Times (2001b) 'The Northern Dimension' [online], 17 Sept., available at www.irishtimes.com [accessed 20 Jan. 2007].

Irish Times (2002a) 'McCreevy memo points to government deficit' [online], 23

Sept., available at www.irishtimes.com [accessed 20 Nov. 2006].

Irish Times (2002b) 'Clashes over law and order and the economy dominated last night's television debate' [online], 15 May, available at www.irishtimes.com [accessed 3 Feb. 2007].

Irish Times (2004a) 'EU ministers discuss sharing of anti-terror intelligence' [online], 9 June, available at www.irishtimes.com [accessed 9 June 2004].

Irish Times (2004b) 'Army Reserve to be eligible for foreign duty' [online], 27 July, available at www.irishtimes.com [accessed 10 Oct. 2006].

Irish Times Breaking News (2004) 'Taoiseach confident that Garda will investigate complaints' [online], 9 Jan., available at www.irishtimes.com/newspaper/breaking/2004/0109/breaking4.htm [accessed 30 Nov. 2006].

Irish Times (2006a) 'Standing of the Garda' [online], 29 Mar., available at www.irishtimes.com [accessed 1 Feb. 2007].

Irish Times (2006b) 'Migrant access' [online], 19 Oct., available at www.irishtimes.com [accessed 19 Oct. 2006].

Irish Times (2007a) 'Upgrade of naval fleet to cost €180m' [online], 6 Jan., available at www.irishtimes.com [accessed 6 Jan. 2007].

Irish Times (2007b) 'Race discrimination' [online], 26 July, available at www.irishtimes.com [accessed 28 July 2007].

Irish Times (2008) 'Human Trafficking' [online], 20 Oct., available at www.irishtimes.com [accessed 22 Oct. 2008].

Ishizuka, K. (1999) 'Ireland and the Partnership for Peace', *Irish Studies in International Affairs*, Vol. 10, 185–200.

Jackson, P. (2000) *Defending Ireland: The Irish State and its Enemies Since 1922*, by Eunan O' Halpin, reviewed in *Irish Studies in International Affairs*, Vol. 11, 247–53.

Jacob, J. (2001) *Interview on: Marian Finucane Show*, RTÉ Radio 1, 26 Sept., 0900 hrs.

Jackson, M. (2007) *Soldier: The Autobiography*, London: Bantam.

Jamaica Observer (2006) 'Irish economy is a model to the world' [online], March 03, available at www.jamaicaobserver.com/magazines/Business/html/20060302T190000-0500_99765_OBS_IRISH_ECONOMY_IS_A_MODEL_TO_THE_WORLD.asp [accessed 2 Feb. 2007].

Jane's Sentinel Security Assessments: Western Europe (2002) [online], available at http://sentinel.janes.com [accessed 10 Oct. 2002].

Jeffrey, K. (1996) 'The British Army and Ireland Since 1922', in T. Bartlett and K. Jeffrey (eds), *A Military History of Ireland*, Cambridge: Cambridge University Press, 431–58.

Joyce, J. and P. Murtagh (1983) *The Boss: Charles J. Haughey in government*, Dublin: Poolbeg.

Keatinge, P. (1984) *A Singular Stance: Irish Neutrality in the 1980s*, Dublin: Institute of Public Administration.

Keatinge, P. (1995) *Towards a Safer Europe – Small State Security Policies and the European Union: Implications for Ireland, Summary of Interim Report*, Dublin: Institute of European Affairs.

Keatinge, P. (1996) *European Security: Ireland's Choices*, Dublin: Institute of European Affairs.

Keatinge, P. (1998) 'Ireland and European Security: Continuity and Change', *Irish Studies in International Affairs*, Vol. 9, 31–7.

Keatinge, P. and Tonra, B. (2002) 'The European Rapid Reaction Force' [online], available at www.iiea.com [accessed 8 Oct. 2002].

Kelly, O. (2004a) 'Gardaí say UK officials have no power here', *Irish Times* [online], 20 July, available at www.irishtimes.com [accessed 16 Feb. 2007].

Kelly, O. (2004b) 'Gardaí never admit fault, commander told', *Irish Times* [online], 30 July, available at www.irishtimes.com [accessed 30 July 2004].

Kenny, C. (2003) *Fearing Sellafield*, Dublin: Gill and Macmillan.

Keogh, D. (1998) *Jews in Twentieth Century Ireland: Refugees, Anti-Semitism and the Holocaust*, Cork: Cork University Press.

Keogh, D. (2000) 'Irish Neutrality and the First Application for Membership of the EEC', in M. Kennedy and J.M. Skelly (eds), *Irish Foreign Policy 1919–1966: From Independence to Internationalism*, Dublin: Four Courts Press, 265–85.

Keohane, D. (2001) 'Realigning Neutrality? Irish Defence Policy and the EU' [online], available at: www.weu.int/institute/occasion/occ24.html [accessed 25 Sept. 2001].

Keohane, R.O. (2002a). 'The Public Delegitimation of Terrorism and Coalitional Politics', in K. Booth and T. Dunne (eds), *Worlds in Collision: Terror and the Future of Global Order*, Hampshire: Macmillan, 141–51.

Keohane, R.O. (2002b) 'The Globalization of Informal Violence, Theories of World Politics and the "Liberation of Fear"', *International Organization*, Spring, 29–43.

Keohane, R.O. and J.S. Nye (1971) *Transnational Relations and World Politics*, Cambridge MA: Harvard University Press.

Keohane, R.O. and J.S. Nye (1977) *Power and Interdependence*, Boston: Little Brown.

Keown, G. (2000) 'Taking the World Stage: Creating an Irish Foreign Policy in the 1920s', in M. Kennedy and J.M. Skelly (eds), *Irish Foreign Policy 1919–1966: From Independence to Internationalism*, Dublin: Four Courts Press, 25–43.

Kyle, K. (2005) 'Anti-war protestors to hold rally in Shannon', *Irish Times Breaking News* [online], 21 Sept., available at www.irishtimes.com/newspaper/breaking/2005/0921/breaking36.htm [accessed 1 Feb. 2007].

Labanyi, D. (2002) 'Inquiry into alleged Garda corruption approved', *Irish Times Breaking News* [online], 12 Feb., available at www.irishtimes.com/newspaper/breaking/2002/0212/breaking52.htm [accessed 30 Nov. 2004].

Lake, A. (2000) *Six Nightmares: Real Threats in a Dangerous World and How America Can Meet Them*, Boston, New York, London: Little Brown.

Lally, C. (2003a) 'Bin Laden "financier" lives here, says EC', *Irish Times* [online], 11 June, available at www.irishtimes.com [accessed 14 June 2003].

Lally, C. (2003b) 'Defence Forces defer industrial action decision', *Irish Times* [online], 9 Oct., available at www.irishtimes.com [accessed 12 Oct. 2003].

Lally, C. (2005) 'Call for increase in Army's Rangers', *Irish Times* [online], 6 Sept., available at www.irishtimes.com [accessed 22 Nov. 2005].

Lally, C. (2006a) 'Shake-up of Garda informer system', *Irish Times* [online], 25 Apr., available at www.irishtimes.com [accessed 26 Apr. 2006].

Lally, C. (2006b) 'Asylum seeker numbers set to hit 10-year low', *Irish Times* [online], 7 Sep, available at www.irishtimes.com [accessed 7 Sept. 2006].

Lally, C. and M. Hennessy (2004) 'Commissioner concerned at retired judge's allegations', *Irish Times* [online], 09 Jan., available at www.irishtimes.com [accessed 12 Jan. 2004].

Lally, C. (2007a) 'Garda may alter foreign recruitment rules', *Irish Times* [online], 27 July, available at www.irishtimes.com [accessed 28 July 2007].

Lally, C. (2007b) 'Civilian role urged in running of Garda, *Irish Times*, 14 Sept., 1.

Lally, C. and R. Mac Cormaic (2006) 'Two terror suspects have Irish links', *Irish Times* [online], 22 Aug., available at www.irishtimes.com [accessed 20 Dec. 2006].

Lavery, D. (2006) 'Navy chiefs set their sights on two new ships', *Irish Independent* [online], 2 May, available at www.unison.ie/irish_independent [accessed 2 May 2006].

Laqueur, W. (2002) *The New Terrorism: Fanaticism and the Arms of Mass Destruction*, London: Phoenix.

Lee, J.J. (1989) *Ireland 1912–1985: Politics and Society*, Cambridge: Cambridge University Press.

Lenihan, C. (2007) Interview on: *9 O'Clock News*, RTÉ 1, 12 Aug., 2110 hrs.

Linklater, A. (1996a) 'Marxism', in S. Burchill, A. Linklater, R. Devetak, M. Paterson and J. True (eds), *Theories of International* Relations, Hampshire and London: Macmillan, 119–44.

Linklater, A. (1996b) 'Realism', in S. Burchill, A. Linklater, R. Devetak, M. Paterson and J. True (eds), *Theories of International* Relations, Hampshire and London: Macmillan, 67–92.

Little, R. and M. Smith (eds) (1991) *Perspectives in World Politics*, (2nd edn) London and New York: Routledge.

Lynch, F. and M. Mellett (2004) 'Countering Asymmetric Threats at Sea – The Role of Post Modern Naval Forces', *Defence Forces Review*, Vol. 2, 65–79.

Lynch, T.J. (2003) 'Gerry Adams Visa in Anglo-American Relations', *Irish Studies in International Affairs*, Vol. 14, 33–44.

Lyons, F.S.L. (1973) *Ireland Since the Famine*, paperback edn, London: Fontana.

Mac Ginty, R. (1999), 'Decommissioning in the Transition from War to Peace in Northern Ireland', *Irish Studies in International Affairs*, Vol. 10, 237–47.

McCaffrey, M. (2005) 'Islamic cleric says Ireland's a "legitimate target"', *Belfast Telegraph* [online], 17 Aug., available at www.belfasttelegraph.co.uk [accessed 20 Aug. 2005].

McConnell, M. (2007) 'Overhauling intelligence', *Foreign Affairs* [online], July/Aug., available at www.foreignaffairs.org [accessed 10 Aug. 2007].

McDonagh, M. (2005) 'Fire chiefs turn up heat on government', *Irish Independent* [online], 5 May, available at www.unison.ie/irish_independent [accessed 6 May 2005].

McDonald, O.A.K. (1998) 'Recent Developments in Peacekeeping – The Irish Experience', in E. Moxon-Browne (ed.), *A Future for Peacekeeping?* Hampshire: Macmillan, 40–57.

Mc Evoy, S. (2000) 'Communities and Peace: Catholic Youth in Northern Ireland', *Journal of Peace Research*, Vol. 37 (1), 85–103.

McGladdery, G. (2002) 'Perceptions of "Siege Mentality": Northern Irish Protestants and White South Africans in the New Political Dispensation', *Irish Studies in International Affairs*, Vol. 13, 87–103.

McMahon, G. (2000) 'Battlefield from Defence White Paper is left strewn with victims', *Irish Times* [online], 1 Mar., available at www.irishtimes.com [accessed 10 Feb. 2003].

McNiffe, L. (1997) *A History of the Garda Síochána: A Social History of the Force*

1922–52 with an Overview for the Years 1952–97, Dublin: Wolfhound.

McSweeney, B. (1985) 'Postscript: The case for active Irish neutrality', in B. McSweeney (ed.), *Ireland and the Threat of Nuclear War*, Dublin: Dominican Publications.

McSweeney, B. (1998) 'Identity, Interest and the Good Friday Agreement', *Irish Studies in International Affairs*, Vol. 9, 93–102.

McSweeney, B. (1999) *Security, Identity and Interests: A Sociology of International Relations*, Cambridge, New York and Melbourne: Cambridge University Press.

Maguire, J. (2002) *Defending Peace: Ireland's Role in a Changing Europe*, Cork: Cork University Press.

Manning, M. (2004) 'A reformed Garda could be among the best in the world', *Irish Times* [online], 24 July, available at www.irishtimes.com [accessed 24 July 2004].

Manning, M. (2007) 'Speech of Dr Maurice Manning, President, Irish Human Rights Commission at the launch of the IHRC Annual Report 2006' [online], 11 Sept. 2007, available at www.ihrc.ie/_fileupload/banners/SpeechMauriceAn nualReport2006.doc [accessed 12 Sept. 2007].

March, J.G. and J.P. Olsen (1996) 'Institutional Perspectives on Political Institutions', *Governance: An International Journal of Policy and Administration*, Vol. 9 (3), 247–64.

Mason, J. (2002) *Qualitative Researching*, London, Thousand Oaks, New Delhi: Sage.

Matthew, B., A. Miles and B. Huberman (1994) *Qualitative Data Analysis*, 2nd edn, Thousand Oaks, London, New Delhi: Sage.

Maxwell, J.A. (1998) 'Designing a Qualitative Study', in L. Bickerman and D.J. Rog (eds), *Handbook of Applied Social Research Methods*, Thousand Oaks, London, New Delhi: Sage.

Meehan, E. (2000a) 'Free movement between Ireland and the UK: from the "common travel area" to The Common Travel Area', Dublin: The Policy Institute in association with the Department of Justice, Equality and Law Reform.

Meehan, E. (2000b) 'Britain's Irish question or Britain's European question? British-Irish relations in the context of the European Union and the Belfast Agreement', *Review of International Studies*, Vol. 26 (3), 83–97.

Meehan, E (2000c) 'Bringing in Europe: the Peace Process and the Europeanisation of the Irish Question, *Irish Studies in International Affairs*, Vol. 11, 179–91.

Mellett, M. (2005) 'The "Blue-Green" Ship – Yes or No', *An Cosantóir*, December, 7–11.

Migrants Rights Centre and Dublin City Development Board (2007) *Realising Integration: Migrant Workers Undertaking Essential Low Paid Work in Dublin City*, Dublin: MRCI/Dublin City Development Board.

Millar, F. '"Gaping hole" in UK e-border defences', *Irish Times* [online], 09 Feb., available at www.irishtimes.com [accessed 10 Apr. 2009].

Millar, F. (2008) 'Travellers to Britain must carry photo ID under new legislation', *Irish Times* [online], 18 July, available at www.irishtimes.com [accessed 18 July 2008].

Miller, R. (2005) 'From 11 September to the war in Iraq: Irish responses to the global 'war on terrorism', *Irish Studies in International Affairs*, Vol. 16, 155–74.

Moloney, E. (2002) *A Secret History of the IRA*, London: Allen Lane.

Molony, S. (2006) 'Identity cards plan in UK to bring decision closer here', *Irish Independent* [online], 23 Jan., available at www.unison.ie/irish_independent [accessed 23 Jan. 2006].

Mooney J. and M. O' Toole (2003) *Black Operations: The Secret War Against the Real IRA*, Meath: Maverick House.

Moran, P.J. (1998) 'Training and Education in the Garda Síochána', *Communique*, June, 3–7.

Morse, J.M. (1994) *Qualitative Research Methods*, California, London and New Delhi: Sage.

Mouritzen, H. (1997) 'Kenneth Waltz: A critical rationalist between international politics and foreign policy', in I.B. Neumann and O. Wæver (eds), *The Future of International Relations: Masters in the Making?* London and New York: Routledge, 66–89.

Moxon-Browne, E. (1998) 'A Future for Peacekeeping', in E. Moxon-Browne (ed.), *A Future for Peacekeeping?* Hampshire: Macmillan, 192–201.

Mullan, D. (2000) *The Dublin and Monaghan Bombings*, Dublin: Wolfhound.

Mulqueen, M. (2003) 'The Paradigms of Security on the Sidelines: International Relations Theory and Small States in the Post-September 11 Risk Environment', paper presented to the Annual Conference of the British International Studies Association, Birmingham, 17 Dec. 2003.

Mulqueen, M. (2005) 'United We Stand? EU Counter Terrorism Initiatives Meet a Small Member State's Security Community', paper presented to the 46th Annual Convention of the International Studies Association, Hawaii, USA, 5 Mar. 2005.

Mulqueen, M. (2006) 'Under-siege officers just resort to circling the wagons again', *Irish Independent* [online], 21 July, available at www.unison.ie [accessed 3 Feb. 2007].

Mulqueen, M. (2007) 'A Weak Link? Irish National Security Policy on International Terrorism', *Contemporary Security Policy*, Vol. 28 (2), 330–56.

Murphy, J.A. (2000) 'Irish neutrality in historical perspective', in B. Girvin and G. Roberts (eds), *Ireland and the Second World War: Politics, Society and Remembrance*, Dublin: Four Court Press, 9–23.

Murphy, R. (2002) 'Ireland, Peacekeeping and Defence Policy', in B. Tonra and E. Ward (eds), *Ireland in International Affairs: Interests, Institutions and Identities*, Dublin: Institute of Public Administration, 13–45.

Murphy, R. (2007) *UN Peacekeeping in Lebanon, Somalia and Kosovo: Operational and Legal Issues in Practice*, Cambridge: Cambridge University Press.

Murray, N. (2000) 'Smith stresses importance of military's security duties', *Irish Examiner* [online] 8 Sept., available at http://archives.tcm.ie/irishexaminer/2000/09/08/current/i_text.htm [accessed 3 Feb. 2007].

National Forum on Europe (2002) *Report of Proceedings, 13: EU Common Foreign and Security Policy*, Dublin: The Stationary Office.

Naval Service (1999) *Naval Service, New Organisation VFM Implementation Plan*, Cork: Naval Service.

North Atlantic Treaty Organisation [NATO] (1997) *NATO Logistics Handbook* [online], available at www.nato.int/docu/logi-en/1997/defini.htm [accessed 28 Sept. 2007].

North Atlantic Treaty Organisation [NATO] (2001) *NATO Handbook*, Brussels: NATO Office of Information and Press.

Neff, S.C. (2000) *The Rights and Duties of Neutrals: A General History*, Manchester: Manchester University Press.

Newman, C. (2006) 'Defence funding set to rise above €1bn for first time', *Irish Times* [online], 17 Nov., available at www.irishtimes.com [accessed 20 Nov. 2006].

Nye, J.S. (2002) *The Paradox of American Power: Why the World's Only Superpower Can't go it Alone*, New York: Oxford University Press.

O' Boyce, M. (2006) 'From the top', *Garda Review*, September, 14–15.

O' Brien, B. (1999) *The Long War: The IRA and Sinn Féin*, 2nd edn, Dublin: O' Brien Press.

O' Brien, C. (2007) 'UK Sikh policy body criticised Garda rule', *Irish Times*, 21 August, 5.

O' Brien, T. (2004) 'State may take back iodine tablets issued to homes', *Irish Times* [online], 27 Mar., available at www.irishtimes.com [accessed 30 Mar. 2004].

O' Brien, T. (2006) 'New emergency unit planned to tackle crisis', *Irish Times* [online], 04 May, available at www.irishtimes.com [accessed 4 May 2006].

O' Connor, A. (2001a) 'Emergency plans for nuclear attack updated', *Irish Times* [online], 27 Sept., available at www.irishtimes.com [accessed 27 Sept. 2001].

O' Connor, A. (2001b) 'New office to co-ordinate response to any future attacks', *Irish Times* [online], 04 Oct., available at www.irishtimes.com [02 Feb. 2007]. O' Connor, A. and M. Minihan (2001) 'Fears of possible attack discounted', *Irish Times* [online], 26 Sept., available at www.irishtimes.com [accessed 26 Sept. 2001].

O' Halloran, M. (2004a) 'Bill would create "a nation of spies", says Fine Gael', *Irish Times* [online], 5 Feb., available at www.irishtimes.com [accessed 5 Feb. 2004].

O' Halloran, M. (2004b) 'Shannon stopover "not a threat"', *Irish Times* [online], 24 Nov., available at www.irishtimes.com [accessed 28 Nov. 2004].

O' Halloran, M. (2007a) 'Lenihan says all races must feel welcome', *Irish Times* [online], 20 July, available at www.irishtimes.com [accessed 23 July 2007].

O' Halloran, M. (2007b) 'Extending welfare warning', *Irish Times* [online], 19 Oct., available at www.irishtimes.com [accessed 19 Oct. 2007].

O' Halpin, E. (1995) 'According to the Irish minister in Rome …': British decrypts and Irish diplomacy in the Second World War, *Irish Studies in International Affairs*, Vol. 6, 95–105.

O' Halpin, E. (1996) 'The army in independent Ireland', in T. Bartlett and K. Jeffrey (eds), *A Military History of Ireland*, Cambridge: Cambridge University Press, 407–30.

O' Halpin, E. (1999) *Defending Ireland: The Irish State and its Enemies Since 1922*, Oxford: Oxford University Press.

O' Halpin, E. (2000a) 'Irish-Allied security relations and the "American Note" crisis: new evidence from British records', *Irish Studies in International Affairs*, Vol. 11, 71–83.

O' Halpin, E. (2000b) 'MI5's Irish Memories: Fresh Light on the Origins and Rationale of Anglo-Irish Security Liaison in the Second World War', in B. Girvin and G. Roberts (eds), *Ireland and the Second World War: Politics, Society and Remembrance*, Dublin: Four Courts Press.

O' Halpin, E. (2001) 'Northern Ireland: the Troubled Peace Process', (review article), *Irish Studies in International Affairs*, Vol. 12, 243–7.

O' Halpin, E. (2002) 'Ireland and EU Intelligence Assessment: The Politics of an Undeclared Petersberg Task', *Irish Political Studies*, Vol. 17 (1), 35–58.

O' Halpin, E. (2003a) *MI5 and Ireland, 1939–1945: The Official History*, Dublin: Irish Academic Press.

O' Halpin, E. (2003b) 'Long Fellow, Long Story: MI5 and de Valera', *Irish Studies in International Affairs*, Vol. 14, 185–203.

O' Halpin, E. (2008) *Spying on Ireland: British Intelligence and Irish Neutrality During the Second World War*, Oxford: Oxford University Press.

Olson, W.C. and A.J.R. Groom (1991) *International Relations Then and Now: Origins and Trends in Interpretation*, London: Harper Collins Academic.

O' Mahony, P. (2004a) *Reflections by the Irish Refugee Council on World Refugee Day* [online press release], 20 June, available at www.irishrefugeecouncil.ie [accessed 1 Aug. 2005].

O' Mahony, P. (2004b) *Open letter to Mr. Michael McDowell, Minister for Justice, Equality and Law Reform* [press release], 19 July, available at www.irishrefugee-council.ie [accessed 3 Aug. 2005].

O' Neill, J.T. and N. Rees (2005) *United Nations Peacekeeping in the Post Cold War Era*, New York: Routledge.

O' Regan, E. and B. Heffernan (2008) 'Public can dump anti-nuke pills', *Irish Independent* [online], 4 Apr., available at www.independent.ie [accessed 6 Apr. 2008].

O' Regan, M. (2005) 'Minister does not recall reading Elukanlo file', *Irish Times* [online], 13 Apr., available at www.irishtimes.com [accessed 16 Aug. 2005].

O' Riordan, P.A. (1992) *Emergency Planning in Ireland*, Dublin: Institute of Public Administration.

O' Shea, B. (ed.) (2001) *In the Service of Peace: Memories of Lebanon*, Dublin: Mercier.

O' Sullivan, M. (1994) *Sean Lemass: A Biography*, Dublin: Blackwater.

O' Toole, M. (2004) 'Iraq rebels recruit Irish fighters', *The Irish Daily Star*, 9 June, 1.

Parekh, B. (2002) 'Terrorism or Intercultural Dialogue', in K. Booth and T. Dunne (eds), *Worlds in Collision: Terror and the Future of Global Order*, Hampshire: Palgrave Macmillan, 270–83.

Parker, C.F. and E.K. Stern (2002) 'Strategic Surprise? Learning from September 11', in Bengt Sundelius (ed.), *The Consequences of September 11: A Symposium on the Implications for the Study of International Relations*, Stockholm: The Swedish Institute of International Affairs, 67–89.

Permanent Defence Forces Other Ranks Representative Association [PDFORRA] (1996) *Submission Document to Select Oireachtas Committee on Legislation and Security*, Dublin: PDFORRA.

Peterson, V.S. (1997) 'Seeking World Order Beyond the Gendered Order of Global Hierarchies', in R.W. Cox (ed.), *The New Realism: Perspectives on Multilateralism and World Order*, Tokyo, New York: United Nations University Press, 38–56.

Pierson, P. and T. Skocpol (2003), 'Historical Institutionalism in Contemporary Political Science', in I. Katznelson and H.V. Milner (eds), *Political Science: The State of the Discipline*, Washington, New York, London: American Political Association and W.W. Norton, 693–721.

Porter, S. (2002) 'Critical Realist Ethnography', in T. May (ed.), *Qualitative Research in Action*, London: Sage.

Rees, N. (2000) 'The Kosovo Crisis, the International Response and Ireland', *Irish*

Studies in International Affairs, Vol. 11, 55–70.

Regan, J.M. (1999) *The Irish Counter-Revolution 1921–1936*, Dublin: Gill and Macmillan.

Reid, L. (2005a) 'Senator critical of Garda reforms Bill', *Irish Times* [online], available at www.irishtimes.com [accessed 20 July 2005].

Reid, L. (2005b) 'State watches about 24 Islamic suspects', *Irish Times* [online], 14 July, available at www.irishtimes.com [accessed 2 Feb. 2007].

Reid, M. (1998) 'A History of the Detective Branch in Ireland 1843–1998 – An Overview', *Communique*, September, 3–10.

Representative Association of Commissioned Officers [RACO] (1996) *Review of the Air Corps: Submission to Price Waterhouse Consultants*, Dublin: RACO.

Representative Association of Commissioned Officers [RACO] (1998) *Defending the Future: Defence White Paper Submission*, Dublin: RACO.

Reuters (2004) 'UN Anti-Terror Head Wants More Intelligence Sharing' [online], 20 Oct., available at www.reuters.com/printerFriendlyPopup.jtml?type=world News&storyID=6557257 [accessed 21 Oct. 2004].

Rogers, P. (2003) '"The War on Terror": Current status and possible development', paper presented to the Annual Conference of the British International Studies Association (BISA), Birmingham, 17 Dec. 2003.

RTÉ News [online] (2004a) '1,000 US troops pass through Shannon daily', 18 Oct., available at www.rte.ie/news/2004/1018/shannon.html [accessed 15 Feb. 2005].

RTÉ News [online] (2004b) 'Court bid to jail Conroy over deportations', 16 Aug., available at www.rte.ie./news/2004/0816/deportation.html [accessed 17 Aug. 2004].

RTÉ News [television text] (2006) 'Air Corps to get new helicopters', 23 Dec., 1144 hrs.

RTÉ News [online] (2007a) 'Report highlights migrant issues in Dublin', 27 Sept., available at www.rte.ie/news/2007/0927/integration.html [accessed 28 Sept. 2007].

RTÉ News [online PDA edition] (2007b) 'Passports may be needed to travel to Britain', 24 Oct., available at www.rte.ie

Ryder, C. (2000) *The RUC 1922–2000: A Force Under Fire*, 5th edn, London: Arrow.

Sageman, M. (2004) *Understanding Terror Networks*, Pennsylvania: University of Pennsylvania Press.

Sageman, M. (2005) 'Understanding Jihadi Networks', *Strategic Insights* [online], Vol. IV (4), available at www.ccc.nps.navy.mil/si/2005/apr/sagemanApr05.asp [accessed 10 Mar. 2006].

Sageman, M. (2008) *Leaderless Jihad: Terror Networks in the Twenty-First Century*, Philadelphia: University of Pennsylvania Press.

Salmon, T. (1989) *Unneutral Ireland, an Ambivalent and Unique Security Policy*, Oxford: Clarendon Press.

Sandler, T. and W. Enders (2004) 'An Economic Perspective on Transnational Terrorism', *European Journal of Political Economy*, Vol. 20 (2), 301–16.

Sheahan, F. (2006) 'Passports go hi-tech … but no fingerprints', *Irish Independent* [online], 17 Oct., available at www.unison.ie/irish_independent [accessed 17 Oct. 2006].

Simpson, A.W. (2003) 'European Micro-states and International Politics; in Theory and in Practice', paper presented at the British International Studies Association (BISA) Conference 2003, University of Birmingham, 16 Dec. 2003.

Skelly, J.M. (1996) *Irish Diplomacy at the United Nations 1945–1965: National Interests and the International Order*, Dublin: Irish Academic Press.

Skelly, J.M. (2000) 'National Interests and International Mediation: Ireland's South Tyrol Initiative at the United Nations, 1960–1', in M. Kennedy and J.M. Skelly (eds), *Irish Foreign Policy 1919–1966: From Independence to Internationalism*, Dublin: Four Courts Press, 286–307.

Smith, D. (1990) 'Beyond contingency planning: towards a model of crisis management', *Organization and Environment*, Vol. 4(4), 263–75.

Smith, J.A. (1995) 'Semi-structured interviewing and qualitative analysis', in J.A. Smith, R. Harré and L. Van Langenhove (eds), *Rethinking Methods in Psychology*, London, Thousand Oaks, New Delhi: Sage.

Smith, M. (2004) *Interview on: Today with Pat Kenny*, RTÉ Radio 1, 31 Mar., 1000 hrs.

Smith, M.L.R. (1998), 'Peace in Ulster? A Warning from History', *Jane's Intelligence Review* [online], 1 July, available at http://jir.janes.com [accessed 28 Nov. 2004).

Smith, M.L.R. and M. von Tangen Page (2001) 'Lessons from long Good Friday', *Jane's Intelligence Review* [online] 01 Apr., available at http://jir.janes.com [accessed 28 Nov. 2004].

Smith, R. (1980) *Under the Blue Flag*, Dublin: Aherlow.

Smyth, J. (2008) 'EU body finds race crime on the increase', *Irish Times* [online], 25 June, available at www.irishtimes.com [accessed 25 June 2008].

Sreenan, J. (2005) 'Address by Lt Gen J. Sreenan, chief of staff, to the RACO Biennial Delegate Conference, Cavan Crystal Hotel, 30 Nov.' [online], available at www.military.ie [accessed 10 Dec. 2005].

Strasser, S. (1985) *Understanding and Explanation: Basic Ideas Concerning the Humanity of the Human Sciences*, Pittsburgh: Duquesne University Press.

Sweeney, C. (2006) 'Only one in 10 of asylum claims are granted', *Irish Independent* [online], 20 Apr., available at www.unison.ie/irish_independent [accessed 21 Apr. 2006].

Taylor, C. (2003) 'Ireland ranked as the most globalised of 62 states due to exports', *Irish Times* [online], 8 Jan., available at www.irishtimes.com [accessed 5 Sept. 2006].

Thelen, K. (2002) 'The Explanatory Power of Historical Institutionalism', in R. Mayntz (ed.), *Akteure – Mechanismen – Modelle: Zur Theoriefähigkeit makro-sozialer Analysen*, Frankfurt, New York: Campus Verlag.

Tonge, J. (1998) *Northern Ireland: Conflict and Change*, 2nd edn, Essex: Pearson Longman.

Tonra, B. (2000) *The Europeanisation of National Foreign Policy: Dutch, Danish and Irish Foreign Policy in the European Union*, Hampshire: Ashgate.

Tonra, B. (2002) 'Irish Foreign Policy', in W. Crotty and D.E. Schmitt (eds), *Ireland on the World Stage*, Essex: Pearson Education.

Tribunal of Inquiry Set up Pursuant to the Tribunal of Inquiry (Evidence) Acts 1921–2002 into Certain Gardaí in the Donegal Division (2004) *Report on Explosives 'Finds' in Donegal*, Dublin: Government Publications.

Tribunal of Inquiry Set up Pursuant to the Tribunal of Inquiry (Evidence) Acts 1921–2002 into Certain Gardaí in the Donegal Division (2005) *Report on the investigation into the death of Richard Barron and the extortion calls to Michael and Charlotte Peoples*, Dublin: government Publications.

Tribunal of Inquiry Set up Pursuant to the Tribunal of Inquiry (Evidence) Acts 1921–2002 into Certain Gardaí in the Donegal Division (2006a) *Report on the circumstances surrounding the arrest and detention of Mark McConnell on October 1 1998 and Michael Peoples on May 6 1999*, Dublin: Government Publications.

Tribunal of Inquiry Set up Pursuant to the Tribunal of Inquiry (Evidence) Acts 1921–2002 into Certain Gardaí in the Donegal Division (2006b) *Report into allegations relating to the Garda investigation of an arson attack on property situated on the site of the telecommunications mast at Ardara, County Donegal in November 1996*, Dublin: government Publications.

Tribunal of Inquiry Set up Pursuant to the Tribunal of Inquiry (Evidence) Acts 1921–2002 into Certain Gardaí in the Donegal Division (2006c) *Report on the arrest and detention of 7 persons at Burnfoot, County Donegal on May 23 1998 and the investigation relating to same*, Dublin: government Publications.

Tribunal of Inquiry Set up Pursuant to the Tribunal of Inquiry (Evidence Acts) 1921–2002 (2006d) *Report of the Tribunal of Inquiry into the facts and circumstances surrounding the fatal shooting of John Carthy at Abbeylara, Co. Longford on 20th April, 2000*, Dublin: government Publications.

Tseëlon, E. (2001) 'Ontological, Epistemological and Methodological Clarifications in Fashion Research: From Critique to Empirical Suggestions', in A. Guy, E. Green and M. Banim (eds), *Through the Wardrobe: Women's Relationships with Their Clothes*, London and New York: Berg.

United Kingdom, Cabinet Office (2003) *Draft Civil Contingencies Bill Consultation Document – June 2003*, London, Cabinet Office.

United Kingdom, Committee of Privy Counsellors (2004) *Review of Intelligence on Weapons of Mass Destruction*, London: House of Commons.

United Kingdom, Ministry of Defence (2006) *Operation Banner: An Analysis of Military Operations in Northern Ireland* [online], available at www.patfinu-canecentre.org/misc/opbanner.pdf [accessed 1 Sept. 2007].

United States, Senate Select Committee on Intelligence and House Permanent Select Committee on Intelligence (2002) *Joint Inquiry into Intelligence Community Activities Before and After the Terrorist Attacks of September 11, 2001*, Washington: Senate Select Committee on Intelligence and House Permanent Select Committee on Intelligence.

Von Hippel, K. (2002) 'The Roots of Terrorism: Probing the Myths', in L. Freedman (ed.), *Superterrorism: Policy Responses*, Massachusetts, Oxford, Victoria and Berlin: Blackwell Publishing, 25–39.

Walker, R.B.J. (1993) *Inside/Outside: International Relations as Political Theory*, Cambridge: Cambridge University Press.

Wall, M. (2005) 'Secret Service fund open to all ministers, PAC told', *Irish Times* [online], 11 Feb., available at www.irishtimes.com [accessed 18 Feb. 2005].

Wall, M. (2006a) 'Tánaiste advised to continue supply of iodine pills', *Irish Times* [online], 21 Apr., available at www.irishtimes.com [accessed 23 Apr. 2006].

Wall, M. (2006b) 'Chinese isolated in Ireland, says study', *Irish Times* [online], 30 Nov., available at www.irishtimes.com [accessed 30 Nov. 2006].

Walsh, D.P.J. (1998) *The Irish Police: A Legal and Constitutional Perspective*, Dublin: Round Hall Sweet and Maxwell.

Waltz, K.N. (1959) *Man, the State and War*, New York: Colombia University Press.

Waltz, K.N. (1979) *Theory of International Politics*, Reading: Addison-Wesley.

Waltz, K.N. (2002) 'The Continuity of International Politics', in K. Booth and T. Dunne (eds), *Worlds in Collision: Terror and the Future of Global Order*, Hampshire: Palgrave Macmillan, 348–53.

Ward, A.J. (1994) *The Irish Constitutional Tradition: Responsible government and Modern Ireland 1782–1992*, Washington DC: The Catholic University of America Press.

Ward, N. (2006a) 'Morris conclusions claim to go far beyond Donegal boundary', *Garda Review*, September, 4–5.

Ward, N. (2006b) 'The Commissioner in conversation', *Garda Review*, September, 6–8.

West, A. (2004) 'Personal Message From the Chief Of The Naval Staff, Admiral Sir Alan West, To The Royal Navy, 21-July-2004' [online], available at www.royal-navy.mod.uk/rn/news [accessed 10 Nov. 2005].

Whelan, R. (2006) 'Bakri's threat a wake-up call for Ireland', *Irish Times* [online], 21 Nov., available at www.irishtimes.com [accessed 22 Nov. 2006].

Wylie, P. (2000) '"The Virtual Minimum": Ireland's Decision for *De Facto* Recognition of Israel, 1947–9', in M. Kennedy and J.M. Skelly (eds), *Irish Foreign Policy 1919–1966: From Independence to Internationalism*, Dublin: Four Courts Press, 137–54.

Zappone, K. and Farrell, M. (2009) 'Cutbacks in the area of human rights are excessive and unfair', *Irish Times* [online], available at www.irishtimes.com [accessed 7 Apr. 2009].

Articles of the 1937 Constitution

Article 2
Article 13

Acts of the Oireachtas

Criminal Justice (Terrorist Offences) Act 2005
Criminal Justice Acts (various)
Defence Act 1954
Defence (Amendment) Act 1993
Garda Síochána Act 1924
Garda Síochána Act 2005
The Illegal Immigrants (Trafficking) Act 2000
Immigration Act 2003
Immigration Act 2004
Irish Nationality and Citizenship Act 2004
Ministers and Secretaries Act 1924
Offences Against the State Acts 1939– 89
Police Forces Amalgamation Act 1925
Public Order Act 1924
Public Service Management Act 1997
Refugee Act 1996

Web sites of the Irish, Danish, Norwegian, Finnish, and Swedish agencies

Ireland

Garda Síochana   www.garda.ie
Defence Forces   www.military.ie

Norway

PST   www.pst.politiet.no
FE   www.mil.no/etjenesten/english/start/

Sweden

SAPO   www.sakerhetspolisen.se
MUST   www.hkv.mil.se

Denmark

PET www.pet.dk
DDIS   forsvaret.dk/FE/eng/

Finland

SUPO   www.poliisi.fi/poliisi/supo/home.nsf
GSID   www.mil.fi

Index